Teaching and Learning
with
Infants and Toddlers

Teaching and Learning
with
Infants and Toddlers
Where Meaning-Making Begins

MARY JANE MAGUIRE-FONG

Contributions by

J. Ronald Lally   FOREWORD

T. Berry Brazelton   PROLOGUE

Ed Tronick   AFTERWORD

WestEd.org

WestEd
San Francisco, CA

TEACHERS COLLEGE PRESS
TEACHERS COLLEGE | COLUMBIA UNIVERSITY
NEW YORK AND LONDON

Published simultaneously by Teachers College Press, 1234 Amsterdam Avenue, New York, NY 10027 and and WestEd, 730 Harrison Street, San Francisco, CA 94107-1242

Library of Congress Cataloging-in-Publication Data can be obtained at www.loc.gov

ISBN 978-0-8077-5619-5 (paperback)
ISBN 978-0-8077-7352-9 (ebook)

Printed on acid-free paper
Manufactured in the United States of America

22 21 20 19 18 17 16 15   8 7 6 5 4 3 2

Teaching and learning begin with listening.
To three teachers—my mother, father, and grandmother—
patient, kind, and wise traveling companions in my search for meaning.

Contents

Foreword

I AM THRILLED TO have been asked to write a foreword to this valuable new addition to the infant care field. Selfishly, I see this book as making my work easier, because its content fits so perfectly with the philosophy of the Program for Infant/Toddler Care that I have helped to create and run for many years. From its clear explanation of the developing brain of a baby to its enlightened presentation on the art of reflective child care, I see how many times I will use this work as a resource.

This book is an invitation to those who care for babies and those who work with babies, whether in the family home or in group-care settings, to consider their practice. Drawing on the inspiring work of teachers in the early childhood programs of Reggio Emilia, Italy, Maguire-Fong invites the reader to view infant care as a system of relationships, in which each participant—infant, family member, teacher—cares for and cares about the other; is willing to be surprised; and trusts that he or she will learn from the other.

What is happening in infant care today is a revolution in curriculum, with the most critical curriculum components no longer lessons and lesson plans, but rather the planning of settings and experiences that allow learning to take place. This book sheds light on what learning looks like from infants' point of view and empowers teachers working with infants to answer critical questions, such as, "What does teaching look like with infants and toddlers? How do we know they are learning?"

As Reggio Emilia's Carlina Rinaldi (2006a) suggests, if we listen to infants and young children, they will reveal to us their thinking. Using examples from infant-care settings, Maguire-Fong illustrates how teachers and families mindfully observe infants, listen to them, document what they see and hear, and engage in reflective dialogue about what to offer next to support their learning. This book inspires curriculum that invites infants to participate in the daily routines; that offers engaging play environments; and that prompts meaningful conversations and interac-

tions. It lays out a framework for using documentation in multiple ways—to plan curriculum, to assess children's learning, to engage families, and to make visible infants' learning to those in the broader community.

I am particularly pleased that this book contains such a strong sense of respect for the importance of the experiences of infants. I see it adding to the arguments of WestEd's "For Our Babies Campaign." For advocates fighting for better treatment for babies, it provides a reservoir of resources. As a reference for policymakers it gives many specific examples of how to provide better care to America's infants. This book is also a resource for those who are trying to interpret such thorny constructs as universal standards for babies. It has the potential to help standards developers thoughtfully create standards, by showing them the uniqueness of the infancy period, and maybe keep them from throwing the baby out with the bath water.

Building on key research from infant development, psychology, and neuroscience, Maguire-Fong invites reflection on what it means to teach and to learn when working with infants and toddlers. Along the way she redefines curriculum as a dynamic process of creating contexts for learning for infants, families, their teachers, and, when done well, for the community at large. This book, if heeded, will change for the better the provision of infant and toddler child care.

—J. Ronald Lally, EdD,
Codirector, WestEd,
Center for Child & Family Studies and
Program for Infant/Toddler Care

Prologue

In the 1950s, I began studying newborns. I was among a few other researchers who believed that babies were not just lumps of clay. We had much to learn from newborns, and, as it turned out, newborns had much to teach us. Through their activity, reflexes, skin color, and sensory and social responses, infants revealed to us how prepared they were at birth to communicate what they were experiencing and to guide us in knowing how to support their development. This work shed light on the delicate interactions between infant and caregiver – caregivers influence in many ways the experience of the baby, but babies in turn shape the behavior of the caregiver. In fact, the newborn's response to his mother's and father's voices – as the baby turns to them – gives them the feeling that the baby knows him or her already, and they have the courage it is necessary to have to become a parent to the infant from this first moment. It is this back and forth exchange that informs the experience of the parent and the experience of the baby, and each of them becomes able to learn so much from the other. This exchange begins prior to birth, for we now know that even fetuses are listening and learning from the stimuli they hear in utero.

As increasing numbers of women with young children enter the workforce, relationships must expand beyond the walls of the family home, to include teachers and family support professionals. To explore how teachers and family support professionals can join with parents in learning about their babies, Maguire-Fong draws from Touchpoints, a program I initiated in 1991, with publication of the first book in my Touchpoints series on children's development. She describes infants, their families, and those who work with them as forming a dynamic system, a triangle of relationships and explores the question, "What does it mean to teach and to learn when working with babies?"

My hope is that in reading this book you will come to appreciate how competent babies are and will enjoy exploring the reciprocal relationship that exists between teaching and learning when working with babies. Babies learn from us, but at the same time, we have much to learn from babies. You will also learn many ways of helping infants and their parents alleviate the stress they may experience at certain times of disregulation, as well as ways to help them achieve balance and feel proud of their achievement.

T. Berry Brazelton, MD
Professor Emeritus Harvard Medical School
Founder, Brazelton Touchpoints Center, Boston
Children's Hospital

Preface

INFANTS ARE LEARNING from the moment of birth, and, in the words of scientists Ed Tronick and Jerome Bruner, they are "making meaning." How infants make meaning and how we can support them in doing so is the subject of this book. Carlina Rinaldi (2006a) explains that children's "search for meaning begins from the moment of birth . . . and continues all through life. . . . We are asked to be the child's traveling companion in this search for meaning" (p. 21). This book serves as a guide for those who accept this invitation. It tells the story of how infants learn, what they learn, and how to support them in learning.

Presented in three parts, the first part explores the question, "How do infants learn?" Blending findings from developmental psychology and neuroscience, and integrating practices from education and mental health, Part I invites the reader to explore research related to how infants make meaning. Chapter 1 introduces infant care as a dynamic system of relationships, building on the work of Jerome Bruner, T. Berry Brazelton, Peter Fonagy, and Ed Tronick. Chapter 2 explores how the infant brain develops within the context of relationships. This chapter uses a framework developed by Bruce Perry as well as concepts from the work of Daniel Siegel. Chapter 3 explores knowledge from the infant's point of view, including how infants learn through the lens of culture, and provides the reader with a vocabulary for "naming" infants' learning. The ideas of Barbara Rogoff inform this chapter, as do the insights of Louise Derman-Sparks and Janet Gonzalez-Mena. Chapter 4 outlines a reflective planning cycle, inspired by the work of teachers in Reggio Emilia, Italy.

Part II builds on this foundation to explore the question, "What do infants learn?" and introduces infancy research in the areas of social, emotional, cognitive, motor, and language development, with work from T. Berry Brazelton, Ed Tronick, Emmi Pikler, Alison Gopnik, Karen Wynn, and Patricia Kuhl. Each of Chapters 5 through 9 addresses a specific domain of development, yet each chapter retains a focus on the central pursuit, infants' ways of making meaning.

Part III looks at how to apply this understanding to design quality programs for infants and families. Chapter 10 gives an overview of three practices deemed essential when caring for infants in groups, drawing inspiration from Jeree Pawl, J. Ronald Lally, and Peter Mangione. Chapter 11 describes how to plan play spaces as environments for learning, incorporating ideas from Elizabeth Jones, Louis Torelli, and Bev Bos. Chapter 12 describes how to design respectful care routines that invite infants as active participants, building on the ideas of Magda Gerber, Emmi Pikler, and Ellyn Satter. Chapter 13 explores how to use respectful conversation to help infants negotiate conflicts and experience the joy of making friends and keeping friends. This chapter concludes with a special section devoted to supporting infants who are victims of trauma. To raise awareness of infancy as an important time for learning, the book concludes with an invitation to share the story of infants' learning using visual narrative, a concept adapted from the work of teachers in Reggio Emilia, Italy.

Many teachers and colleagues have been a source of inspiration for this book, and it is my hope that it bears witness to their wisdom and kindness. The first to open my eyes to observing children as a means to negotiate the curriculum was Elizabeth Jones. Emmy Werner helped me value the cultural context in which children learn. J. Ronald Lally and Peter Mangione helped me frame a broad interpretation of infant curriculum and a reflective approach to teaching. T. Berry Brazelton and Ed Tronick added complexity and coherence to my understanding of infants' meaning-making. Kristie Brandt and Maureen St. John provided a forum for my learning within the infant/parent mental health community. Bev Bos showed me and my children the deep reaches of play as a context for learning. Many colleagues contributed to the ideas in this book, among them Merrill Featherstone, Mariana Pilario, Julia Palacios, Anne Kress, Diane Cromwell, Joette Lee, Margie Perez Sesser, Marsha Peralta, Donis

Eichhorn, Lorraine Chow, Marie Jones, Betty Blaize, Marcela Clarke, Janis Keyser, and Annie White. To Edward Fong, Mariah Maguire-Fong, Ryan Maguire-Fong, Kathy and Keith Nelson, Robert Soohoo, Kristin Nelson Sletten, and my deeply comitted editor, Marie Ellen Larcada, who so generously read and advised on drafts of this book, I give my deep gratitude. What gives life to this book are the stories, generously shared by infants, families, teachers, and support staff at the American River College Children's Center and the Dixon, Madison, Davis, and King City Migrant Infant Centers, to whom I will be forever grateful.

HOW INFANTS LEARN

THIS BOOK HAS three parts, with Part I focused on exploring how infants learn. Chapter 1 introduces infants as active meaning-makers, who investigate the world around them. Chapter 2 describes how the brain develops during infancy, within the context of relationships. Chapter 3 explores what knowledge looks like from the infant's point of view. Chapter 4 offers an approach to curriculum that meshes with infants' ways of learning. It describes a reflective approach to teaching, using ideas inspired by the schools in Reggio Emilia, Italy.

CHAPTER 1

Infants as Active Meaning-Makers

What we see in the crib is the greatest mind that has ever existed, the most powerful learning machine in the universe.
(Gopnik, Meltzoff, & Kuhl, 1999, p. 1)

BABIES ARE BORN LEARNING. They arrive at birth with a wide array of skills uniquely suited to investigating the world around them. This biological capacity to voraciously explore and learn shatters the long-held image of infants as having little capacity to think, to hear, to see, or to feel. For centuries, scientists and philosophers have described infants as being helplessly bombarded by a meaningless and confusing array of stimuli. At various points in history, infants have been described as passive recipients of knowledge; as the product of maturation, like a tomato ripening on the vine; or as a lump of clay passively shaped by experience. New ways of studying infants, coupled with new technology to do so, reveal a distinctly different image of infants as actively perceiving, looking, and listening to make meaning of the environment they encounter.

Many may not realize that a healthy newborn, although not yet capable of full visual acuity, is very good at discriminating the difference between her mother's face and that of a stranger (Pascalis, de Schonen, Morton, Deruelle, & Fabre-Grenet, 1995). Research shows that newborns prefer to look at faces, as opposed to inanimate objects (Farroni, Johnson, Menon, Zulian, Faraguna, & Csibra, 2005). They are sensitive to subtle differences of facial expression. They will look significantly longer at a face with a direct gaze than at a face with an averted gaze (Farroni, Massaccesi, Pividori, & Johnson, 2004). They notice the differences between happy, sad, and surprised facial expressions (Field, Woodson, Greenberg, & Cohen, 1982) and prefer to look at a happy face, as opposed to a neutral or fearful face (Rigato, Menon, Johnson, Faraguna, & Farroni, 2011). They can even be coaxed to imitate a facial expression, like pursing the lips or sticking out the tongue (Meltzoff & Moore, 1983).

Newborns can detect phrasing and pitch that differentiate one voice from another (Nazzi, Floccia, & Bertoncini, 1998). They prefer a higher rather than a lower pitched voice (Nugent, Keefer, Minear, Johnson, & Blanchard, 2007). Their skill in detecting language is so good that they can distinguish the minuscule difference between two almost identical speech sounds, /ba/ and /pa/ (Eimas, Siqueland, Jusczk, & Vigorito, 1971). Their sense of smell is no less acute, with studies detailing how newborns can distinguish between their mother's smell and that of a stranger (Porter & Winberg, 1999). In short, newborns are wired at birth with a robust capacity to detect and distinguish a vast array of sensory information about people.

INFANTS ARE BORN RESEARCHERS

Studies show that infants actively investigate and make meaning from the world they encounter (Committee on Integrating the Science of Early Childhood Development, Board on Children, Youth, and Families, National Research Council, 2000; Gopnik, 2009; Nugent et al., 2007; Rochat, 2009). Their sensory systems are primed to seek novel, intriguing, information-rich events. Researcher Alison Gopnik (2009) compares infants' thinking with that of adults and explains that infants' consciousness is different from that of adults. Infants have a unique capacity. They have the capacity to gather immense amounts of information in a single moment of time and in a short span of time. This capacity means that infants are not restricted to focusing on just one thing at a time, which characterizes adult consciousness. Instead, infants dedicate themselves to researching the world they encounter, interacting with people and objects, gathering a broad swath of information, organizing it, and giving it meaning.

Infants notice and actively gather information, but they also actively transmit, that is, communicate,

Research Highlight:
Infants' Amazing Capacity to Gather Information

Infants construct a vast amount of knowledge in the short span of 3 years. How is this possible? Scientist Alison Gopnik (2009) suggests that babies are uniquely conscious of all that goes on around them. She explains that babies have the capacity to gather a broad sweep of information from a wide array of sources in a single moment of time. This capacity has been lost in adults, for whom it is more adaptive to focus on specific parts of the surroundings in order to execute a plan. Babies have adults to execute plans for them, so they have no need to narrow the focus of their awareness. Instead, babies are aware of a broad array of information, gathering it, assessing it for meaning, and organizing it, a pattern of consciousness that differs from that of adults. Gopnik explains this difference by comparing infants to lanterns and adults to spotlights. A lantern projects light in a wide arc of surrounding space, while a spotlight focuses light more narrowly. It is this capacity to focus on a broad swath of information in any one moment in time that makes it possible for infants to notice and decipher many small details in their surroundings and to acquire an immense amount of knowledge in a relatively short period of time.

Figure 1.1. Making-Meaning: A Meal for Maria

A teacher hears a cry from 3-month-old Maria in a nearby crib. She looks at her watch, nods, and says to the baby, "Yes, it's about that time. I thought you might be waking soon. I'll bet you're hungry." She walks toward Maria's crib. Maria feels gentle hands lifting her into encircling arms. Even though hungry, she slows her cry and calms. She sees an object approach and smells something sweet. This smell floods her with anticipation of something good. Prompted by a soft touch on her lower lip, she opens her mouth. Her lips find the nipple and she begins to suck. She pauses between bursts of sucking, looking into the smiling face above her. She looks at the teacher, who looks at her, and she hears, "Hi, Maria, you were hungry, weren't you? Would you like more? I'm glad to see you looking at me. What do you see?" Minutes pass. She starts to drowse, lulled by the rhythm of sucking and the fullness in her stomach. Her teacher carries her to her crib, covers her, and says softly, "Off to sleep, little one."

Figure 1.2. Making-Meaning: A Meal for Mario

Three-month-old Mario cries from his crib. A teacher nearby looks at her watch and says, "Oh, no, so soon? Only an hour and he's awake. I can't get anything done if he doesn't sleep." She glances at her co-worker and says, "I'm not picking him up. He's just going to have to cry." Mario's cry gets louder. "You better deal with that baby," warns her co-worker, handing her a warmed bottle, "He's going to wake everybody up, and then we'll really have trouble." Glancing at the clock, the teacher walks to the crying baby's crib, saying, "So much for my break. OK, I'm coming. Quiet down." As she lifts Mario, his cry subsides. "Already think you can cry to get what you want, don't you? That won't last long." She pokes the nipple in his mouth, his body angled away from her, and resumes talking with her co-worker. Mario begins to suck. He glances at his teacher, but her face is turned away. He stares at the wall, and in a few moments, he loses hold of the nipple. The teacher pokes it back in, but he squirms, arches his back, and spits it out. "You don't want to eat? Fine, don't eat," he hears. He starts to cry. She puts him back in his crib, saying, "You better learn that you can't always have it your way."

information. Examine the photographs in the "Reading Babies" reflection. What message is delivered when the eyebrows are lifted; when the eyes widen; or when the brow is furrowed? How do the lips relay feeling or intent? What does a direct gaze mean, as opposed to an averted gaze? How does a gesture of the arm or the hand send a signal to back away or to come close? What message do brightened eyes convey? Long before they are able to speak, infants use their bodies to communicate through

- Body position
- Gesture
- Facial expression
- Timing of response
- Eye contact, that is, gaze aversion or gaze maintenance
- Vocalizations

In a reciprocal exchange of information with those who provide their care, infants, from the moment of birth, are actively communicating.

Consider what happens when a baby smiles at you.

You can't help but smile back, which then prompts the baby to smile more, which in turn prompts a response from you. Or perhaps the baby's smile turns into a quizzical look. Most likely, in turn, you furrow your brow in a look that matches the baby's. Whether adult or infant, each reads, responds, and adjusts his or her behavior, moment by moment, as a function of the behavior and expression of the other. This reciprocal relationship influences what infants learn and how they learn it, as the actions and feelings of one influence and change the actions and feelings of the other (Tronick, 2007).

Infants not only relay information to others, but they also receive abundant information, as they watch those around them. They use their eyes, ears, mouth, skin, and nose to take in information about others. They detect nuanced aspects of behavior, like inflection or intensity of voice, gesture, and direction of gaze. Over time, their reading of what others do forms a pattern of expectation. They learn to anticipate recurring actions, events, and attitudes. This image of infants—as active seekers of new information, as organizers of information, as researchers who construct knowledge about the world they encounter—transforms how we think about infants and how we think about their care.

There is considerable variation in what babies experience within moments of care and, consequently, considerable variation in what they learn:

- One baby learns gentleness; another learns that touch hurts, feels rough, and distresses.
- One baby's cries get answered, sending the message, "I'm good at getting help when I need it," while another baby's cries get ignored or trigger sharp, angry voices, sending the message, "I'm not very good at getting my needs met."
- One baby learns, "I'm a good communicator, and others listen to me and respond, so I will do more of it," while another baby learns,

"I'm not a good communicator, so I will do less of it."

- One baby learns that meals are harmonious, while another baby learns that meals are tense, abrupt, and not satisfying.

Babies are actively engaged in learning about the behaviors and attitudes of people who provide their care. They take in information about the way people look at them, touch them, and talk with them. These experiences, repeated over time, form a pattern of expectation and influence how they know themselves in relation to others. Infants use such experiences to construct foundational maps of the world (Gopnik, 2009). They use these foundational maps to navigate all experiences that follow. In this way, infants actively organize themselves in relation to the experiences they have with others within moment-by-moment, everyday care. Those who care for infants have a profound influence on how infants come to know the world.

INFANT LEARNING: A DYNAMIC SYSTEM

The way in which infants learn can be described as a dynamic system. As an illustration, compare the etching of behaviors and attitudes in the minds of very young children to the action of raindrops that fall, one by one, in the same spot on a flat patch of dry sand (Thelen & Smith, 2006; Tronick, 2007). An impression begins to form in the spot in the sand where the first drops fall. Soon the impression grows into a channel. The channel deepens, as more drops hit the same spot. Drops that hit nearby begin to flow into the channel as well, and it deepens. Over time, a small impression becomes a deep channel that directs a torrent of water.

A simple drop of rain, when repeated over time, transforms a flat, undifferentiated landscape into a complex, rippled series of hills and valleys. As more water passes through, the valleys deepen and the hills grow higher and in time the landscape stabilizes. The landscape continues to change, but slowly, and patterns formed early are resistant to change.

This example illustrates a core aspect of dynamic systems theory. When applied to human development, this theory suggests that a child develops through a dynamic process of change, one in which everyday experiences influence how the child organizes body and mind.

Infants Are Subjects Not Objects

In this dynamic system, infants are active protagonists in their own development. This means that they are active *subjects*, who gather information and relay messages to others, with the consequences of all their interactions influencing their development. They are not passive objects, simply responding to the actions of others. They actively participate, through engaged interaction with those who provide their care. Among the foremost champions of infants' right to be treated as subjects are infant specialist Magda Gerber (2002), founder of the internationally recognized organization Resources for Infant Educarers (RIE), and her mentor, Dr. Emmi Pikler, founder of the well-known orphanage in Budapest, Hungary, known as the Pikler Institute. The following quote from Dr. Pikler (1994) captures their philosophy of respectful care: "We should never handle a child mechanically, never handle her like an inanimate object, no matter how small she may be" (p. 20). They urge us to pay close attention to the way infants respond and play, to read infants' subtle expressions as communication, to avoid interrupting infants' play, and to provide ample time and space for infants to explore freely, giving value to play and exploration as key elements in infants' healthy development.

Reflection: Your Image of Infancy

What is your image of infancy? How do you tend to view infants?

- Active learner? Or passive learner?
- Capable? Or incapable?
- Rich in resources for learning? Or lacking resources for learning?

How does this image influence the relationships you build with infants?

How we measure the quality of care for infants is directly related to the image we hold of infants. If infants are seen solely as objects in need of care, we gauge quality through measures of efficiency, expediency, and cost-effectiveness. For example, we track the schedule of diapers changed, meals served, naps taken, number of toys on the shelf, or ratio of staff to children. What gets lost in a reading of these measures is the baby's subjective experience, that is, what the baby feels, thinks, and learns. When tasks and schedules are the measure of the work, how the baby experiences being diapered, whether the baby enjoys a meal, or how a baby is comforted when sad get overlooked as indicators of quality care. How the baby as a subject experiences the group care should be a primary consideration when we think about the quality of infant care.

Infants are cared for in a variety of settings. Many families care for their infants at home, while others who work outside the home seek someone to care for their infants during the hours they work, often in group settings. Some infants and young children are cared for in small groups in home settings, known as family child care. Others are cared for in programs outside of homes, called children's centers, child-care centers, early childhood schools, or, when the care is exclusive to infants, infant-care centers.

The Triangle of Relationships

No matter what the setting, an infant program that serves families comprises three participants—infant, family, and those who provide the care. The definition of infancy used in this book is birth to 3 years of age, consistent with the definition used by the National Association for the Education of Young Children (Copple & Bredekamp, 2009). Throughout this book, I use the term *infant* to refer to both infants

Figure 1.3. Triangle of Relationships

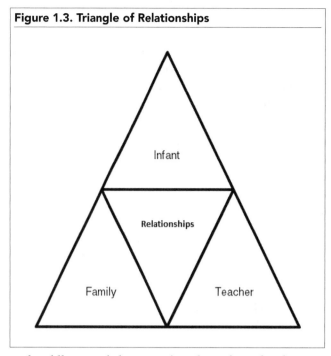

and toddlers, and the term *family* to describe those in the infant's home who assume primary care of the infant. This includes birth, adoptive, and foster parents as well as grandparents, aunts, uncles, or siblings who are primarily responsible for an infant's care.

The term *teacher* is used to refer to an adult responsible for the care and well-being of a group of children. This reference is consistent with the description of teacher used by the National Association for the Education of Young Children (Copple & Bredekamp, 2009). There are many terms used to describe those who care professionally for infants, among them caregiver, educarer (Gerber, 2002), teacher, infant specialist, family support specialist, or care provider. As used in this book, the term *teacher* is inclusive of all such terms. When describing strategies that may be applied both by the family and by those working professionally with infants, I use the term *caregiver*.

Those who come together in the context of group care form a dynamic system of relationships (Thelen & Smith, 2006). A system is defined as a complex whole comprising related parts. In infant care, the system comprises infants, their families, and those who care for infants (Malaguzzi, 2012; Rinaldi, 2006b). Each participant connects with the others and each builds a relationship with the others.

As illustrated in Figure 1.3, infants, families, and teachers influence and are influenced by (Tronick, 2007) the well-being of the others in a triangle of relationships. For the triangle of relationships to be strong, each participant trusts and learns from the others (Allen, Fonagy, & Bateman, 2008). This trust occurs when each subject in the relationship—infant, family, and teacher—is seen and valued by the others. Three features characterize a strong triangle of relationships within infant care (Rinaldi, 2006b). Each participant, infant, family, and teacher:

- Cares about the others.
- Is open to a sense of wonder.
- Trusts that he or she will learn from the others.

In this triangle of relationships, caring about the others is more than simply the act of taking care of or being taken care of. It means caring about the other and in turn feeling cared for. It also means being willing to step outside of what we know to consider what we do not know, a willingness to be surprised and to trust that we will learn from one another.

FROM RESEARCH TO PRACTICE: WHO CARES FOR BABIES?

This triangle of relationships is subject to changes in the economy. When the economy of a nation grows and prospers, more women with young children enter the workforce and require care for their infants and young children during the hours they work outside the home. This care can be costly for a family, with the costs higher for infants and toddlers than for preschool-age children. The younger the child, the higher the cost, largely due to higher staffing ratios. Staffing ratios vary depending on how the programs are regulated, but in general, with adult to child ratio used as a measure of cost, infant care is more expensive than care for older children.

Infants: A Wise Investment

Leading economists point to the folly of failing to fund programs that serve infants and their families. Nobel laureate economist James Heckman (Heckman & Masterov, 2007) presents evidence of the economic benefit of investing early in childhood. This evidence shows that when a society fails to invest in the education and care of infants and young children, the overall cost to society goes up rather than down. A society that fails to invest in the earliest years of childhood pays more in the long run to keep citizens healthy, employed, and contributing to the economic well-being of the community. Data from multiple studies show that investing $1 during early childhood results in a savings to society of between $7 and $16.

Economists (Heckman & Masterov, 2007) explain this cost savings simply: "Skill begets skill; learning begets learning. Early disadvantage, if left untreated, leads to academic and social difficulties in later years. Advantages accumulate; so do disadvantages" (p. 447). The stronger we build children's foundation for learning, the better those children will do later in school; the more productive and responsible they will be in the workforce and as citizens; and the fewer remedial services they will require later in life. Early childhood services accrue savings over time, as fewer children grow up to need costly remedial services provided by schools or by the social welfare, health-care, or criminal justice systems. A child whose early years are stable and secure is at lower risk of dropping out of school, receiving cash assistance, or being incarcerated or unemployed.

The Inextricable Nature of Education and Care

Infants and young children are part of the education continuum. As a consequence, public policies must braid care with education, to support optimal well-being and learning for all children. A report of the Committee for Economic Development (2002), a nonpartisan, nonprofit, policy organization, suggests a new definition for education, as "a process that begins at birth and encompasses all aspects of children's early development, including their physical, social, emotional, and cognitive growth" (p. 2). This report concludes, "Our democratic values are . . . betrayed when we fail to live up to our ethical and moral obligation to safeguard the health and well-being of all young children" (p. 1). A review of the research (Committee on Early Childhood Pedagogy, Commission on Behavioral and Social Sciences and Education, National Research Council, 2000) shows a developing consensus that "out-of-home care for young children should attend to their education, including school readiness, as well as providing protection and a facilitating environment for secure emotional development and sound relationships with other children and adults" (p. 25).

An equally compelling argument for investing in the early years comes from neuroscience. At birth, the brain is not yet fully formed. The architecture of the brain that will support a lifetime of learning is built during infancy. Neuroscientist and psychiatrist Bruce Perry (2014b) explains this as follows:

Childhood experiences . . . create the person. These organizing childhood experiences can . . . [result] in flexible, responsible, empathic and creative adults . . . [or] impulsive, aggressive, remorseless and anti-social individuals. . . . We must recognize that early childhood is not a passive time. It is, in fact, the most crucial time in the life of an individual— and, thereby, in the life of a society.

What infants learn, how learning is influenced by early experience, and whether a brain is built to be strong or weak—each is dependent on how infants are cared for. This raises critical questions:

- Who cares for infants, where, when, and with what qualifications and compensation?
- What is the true cost of caring for infants in a manner that ensures optimal learning?
- How does a society cover the true cost of infant care, including access to affordable, quality care during hours that parents work?

With increasing numbers of infants and young children cared for outside the family home, the stakes are high. It will take deliberate debate and thoughtful discussion to find answers to these questions (Lombardi, 2003). In the United States, 61% of children under 3 years of age have mothers who are employed, so these children most likely spend their days in out-of-home care. For infants under 1 year of age, this figure is 57% (U.S. Department of Labor, 2014).

In much of the developed world, including the United States, those caring for infants and young children are poorly compensated and offered little with respect to appropriate workplace supports (Lombardi, 2003; Whitebrook & Sakai, 2004). Low wages keep the cost of service low, easing access to infant care, yet low wages also risk lower standards of care (Helburn, Culkin, Morris, & Clifford, 1995). Three related issues weave through the discussion of who cares for whom and with what preparation:

- Quality—optimal care that supports optimal learning
- Compensation—appropriate teacher qualifications tied to fair compensation
- Affordability—reasonable cost for families

An illustration of how these issues impact services for infants and families is found in a comparison between two countries, Italy and the United States, in

the years following World War II. Both countries experienced rapid economic expansion after the war, and as the need for an expanded workforce grew, increasing numbers of women with young children went to work. However, policymakers in each country took decisively different turns (Lally, 2001).

In the United States, those who swayed public policy saw the cost of child care to be strictly the responsibility of the family. The national policy adopted was that government funding for education was for children 5 to 6 years of age and up. However, as the U.S. economy grew and increasing numbers of women with young children joined the workforce, many called for federal funding to help subsidize the cost of child care for low-wage families with young children. After a series of presidential vetoes, a law was eventually passed that allocated funds to help low-wage parents pay for child care and to help unemployed parents receiving cash aid to move off cash aid and into the workforce.

This funding was quite specific—to provide child care while parents worked, with minimal requirements for what the care would be like and little to ensure that what the child learned during the care would be beneficial. The care typically was described as day care. Those hired often were assumed to be unskilled, minimum-wage earners, with little or no experience or education. As a result, rolled out under the guise of "day" care, such services were seen to be outside the realm of education.

In contrast, policymakers in Reggio Emilia, a city in northern Italy, faced similar conditions of economic growth and a similar influx of women in the workforce. In postwar Italy, families were emerging from the devastation of a horrendous war fought on their soil. Determined that their children would not have to face the wartime horrors that shadowed their lives, a group of mothers started a preschool, with money raised from the sale of battle tanks left behind in the fields (Barazzoni, 2000; Ghirardi, 2002). Over subsequent decades, with dedicated work from the community, a large, city-run system of infant centers and preschools emerged, serving children from birth to 6.

Under the leadership of educator Loris Malaguzzi (2012), these early childhood services linked care and education, putting the educational experience of children and the possibilities it might hold for the future benefit of society at the center of funding discussions. What emerged was a publicly funded child-care program designed to ensure that working parents of young children had ready access to affordable child care; that young children in these programs were cared for and supported in learning; and that teachers in these programs were well prepared and compensated fairly for their work (Ghirardi, 2002; Lally, 2001). More than a half century later, the Reggio Emilia early childhood schools have been proclaimed as among the best schools in the world (Kantrowitz & Wingert, 1991).

For the past half century, the experience of being an infant, a family with an infant, or a teacher working with infants has differed dramatically in these two contexts, with care and education treated and funded as separate entities in one context while seen as inextricably entwined in the other. The accumulation of evidence from research science during this same period clearly shows that children are learning from birth on. As summarized in a report of the National Research Council Committee on Early Childhood Pedagogy (2000): "Children come into the world eager to learn. . . . Right from birth a healthy child is an active participant . . . exploring the environment, learning to communicate and, in relatively short order, beginning to construct ideas and theories about how things work" (p. 1).

The unprecedented participation of women with young children in the labor force creates a pressing demand for child care. Couple this with the research on the early years as foundational for brain development and learning, and the message for policymakers is clear (National Research Council, 2000):

> The time is long overdue for society to recognize the significance of out-of-home relationships for young children, to esteem those who care for them when their parents are not available, and to compensate them adequately as a means of supporting stability and quality in those relationships for all children, regardless of the family's income and irrespective of their developmental needs. (p. 7)

Looking Back and Looking Forward

This book invites you on a journey to explore infants as robust researchers, as meaning-making subjects intent on making sense of the world. Throughout the book, you will explore policies that strengthen the triangle of relationships among infants, families, and teachers in infant-care programs. Each chapter introduces key evidence from science and explains practical application of these findings within the everyday experience of caring for babies. Through examples of practice from successful infant programs, you will be invited to reflect on what it means to teach and to learn when working with infants and their families. The next chapter provides an overview of how the brain works and the key role that relationships play in shaping the developing brain.

CHAPTER 2

Relationships Shape the Developing Brain

Too many babies . . . are now adults who cannot meet the challenges of the global competitive workforce. Too many have become parents whose brains were not prepared in early childhood to allow them to nurture their own babies' brains. If we do not act now, we will soon tip into a point of no return with too few healthy and well-educated adults in this country to protect it and keep it strong.
(Brazelton & Sparrow, 2013, p. xiv)

WHITMAN (1855/2005), in his poem, "There Was a Child Went Forth," describes the impact of everyday encounters on the child.

There was a child went forth every day;
and the first object he look'd upon, that object he became;
And that object became part of him for the day, or a certain part of the day, or for many years, or stretching cycles of years.
The early lilacs became part of this child.
And grass, and white and red morning glories, and white and red clover, and the song of the phoebe-bird, and the third-month lambs, . . .
All became part of him (p. 78)

These words capture the subtle potency of ordinary moments of childhood. Everyday experiences become a part of us, at first fleetingly, but when sustained over time or imbued with strong emotion, the sights, sounds, and smells that we experience endure within us. Ordinary moments become extraordinary, in terms of their enduring impact on the child (Pawl, 2003). In this chapter, we will look closely at how infants' everyday experiences influence the architecture of their developing brains. We will explore how the caregiver's touch, face, smell, gestures, voice, at-titude, and behavior become a part of the baby's brain, knit into developing structures that last a lifetime.

New technology has made it possible for scientists to look inside the brain and to measure brain activity as we use language to speak and read, or as we make a moral judgment, or as we feel empathy. This research has expanded understanding of how young children develop and learn. Among the most significant findings from neuroscience is that the brain of a baby is still largely undeveloped at birth and reliant on experience for how it will be built. Scientists (Committee on Integrating the Science of Early Childhood Development, Board on Children, Youth, and Families, National Research Council, 2000) describe this phenomenon as follows:

> Brain development is exquisitely attuned to environmental inputs that, in turn, shape its emerging architecture. The environment provided by the child's first caregivers has profound effects on virtually every facet of early development, ranging from health and integrity of the baby at birth to the child's readiness to start school at age 5. (p. 219)

Babies are exquisitely prepared at birth to gather information, organize it, store it in memory, and retrieve it for later use. Their eyes, ears, nose, skin, muscles, and organs gather copious amounts of information and relay it to structures within the brain. Although babies may appear idle or even passive, their brains are processing vast amounts of information during any single point in time. Gopnik (2009) refers to babies as the research and development department of the human species and attributes their prowess to the unique nature of the baby brain:

> Babies' brains seem to have special qualities that make them especially well suited for imagination and learning. Babies' brains are actually more highly connected

than adult brains; more neural pathways are available to babies than adults. As we grow older and experience more, our brains "prune out" the weaker, less used pathways and strengthen the ones that are used more often. If you looked at a map of the baby's brain it would look like old Paris, with lots of winding, interconnected little streets. In the adult brain those little streets have been replaced by fewer but more efficient boulevards, capable of much more traffic. (p. 11)

In this chapter, we will explore how these pathways form in the brain of a baby and how they make it possible for babies to accomplish so much in the short 3 years of infancy. This material builds an important foundation for the chapters that follow, as we consider what knowledge looks like from the infant's point of view.

SEQUENCE OF BRAIN DEVELOPMENT

The brain develops over a long period of time, from within a few weeks after conception through adolescence. During infancy, the brain is literally under construction. The brain of a newborn baby is about 25% of eventual adult size. From birth to the first birthday, this phenomenal growth continues (Schore, 2002). By age 3, the brain is about 90% of eventual adult size (Perry, 2002). After early childhood, brain growth slows. This slower pace continues through middle childhood and adolescence, with marked decreases during the adult years.

Perry (2002) describes four regions in the brain. These regions develop in hierarchical order, from bottom to top. This means that the lowest region of the brain matures first and the highest region of the brain matures last. Moving up the brain, from bottom to top, the organizational structure gets more complex, as does the work performed in those regions.

At the bottom of the brain is a region called the brainstem (Figure 2.1), above which lies a second region called the diencephalon. Above this is a third region called the limbic area. A fourth and uppermost region is called the cortex. These brain regions do not have marked boundaries, nor do they work in isolation. Each region assumes a particular focus, yet integrates its work with that of the others, gathering, organizing, interpreting, tracking, and acting on sensory and motor information coming from inside the body and from outside the body.

The brainstem is about 3 inches long, less than 1 inch across, and lies at the base of the skull. It is the first region of the brain to develop, during the prenatal period. The brainstem connects the spinal cord to the brain. The brainstem is the primary point of entry into the brain for incoming sensory information. As such, it manages connections with the exterior world, a function essential for survival. For this reason, the brainstem is well developed by the time most babies are born.

In addition to being the primary point of entry for incoming sensory information, the brainstem plays another important role. It regulates the rhythmic systems that keep us alive, like blood flow, swallowing, digestion, heart rate, sleep–wake states, and body temperature. The brainstem continually makes fine-tuned adjustments to these functions. These adjustments keep the body regulated in response to changing conditions from inside and from outside the body. It is thanks to the brainstem that we fall asleep and dream, that we squint in response to the bright light as we exit a dark room, that we shiver when we feel a rush of cold air, or that we cover our ears upon hearing a sudden blast (Perry, 2002).

While most babies have no problem breathing, circulating blood, digesting food, eliminating waste, or dropping off to sleep when tired, very young babies often need help keeping their systems working smoothly. Through a gentle touch, a reduction in surrounding noise, or the cadence of a rhythmic lullaby, caregivers help babies fine-tune the work of the brainstem, serving to co-regulate with the baby the developing brain.

Above the brainstem and closely tied in terms of functioning is a region called the diencephalon. The diencephalon is the second region of the baby's brain to develop. The diencephalon serves as a relay station between the brain and the spinal cord. Here multiple sources of sensory and motor information converge and make their first stop, as they enter through the brainstem. The diencephalon sifts through this information, sorts and organizes it, and sends it to other parts of the brain. It is here that babies construct sensory maps of their surroundings, based on what they experience. These sensory maps allow them to associate incoming sensations, connecting a sound sensation to a movement or a sight to a sound. For example, a young baby, upon hearing the voice of the caregiver from outside the room, may turn in the direction of the door, anticipating the caregiver's entry. The dien-

Figure 2.1. Regions of the Human Brain

The Human Brain

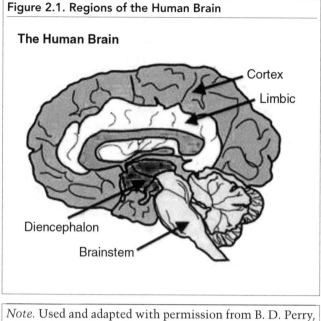

Note. Used and adapted with permission from B. D. Perry, MD., PhD, www.childtrauma.org

cephalon also houses a powerful, bean-size structure called the hypothalamus. This tiny structure is the visceral control center of the brain. It enables us to interpret sensory input from inside and outside the body and to relay a signal of hunger, thirst, chill, fatigue, anger, or sadness to sectors of the brain that prompt a cry, gesture, or movement (Perry, 2002).

Above the diencephalon is the limbic region. The limbic region holds structures that organize and integrate emotions. The limbic region alerts us to stimuli that might be either rewarding or threatening. This makes it the key brain region for processing, interpreting, and integrating emotional functioning. The limbic structures help us make sense of people, because it is from here that we organize and relay nonverbal social cues, like gestures and direction of gaze. The limbic region also houses a structure that is critical to the process of learning. This structure takes short-term memory and converts it to long-term memory (Perry, 2002).

It is fairly easy to see the development of limbic structures reflected in children's behavior. In the early months, newborns appear to vacillate between two emotions—"this feels good, or this feels bad." By their second birthday, however, they show a wide repertoire of emotions, delighting and challenging those around them with emotions like pride, joy, guilt, shame, and embarrassment. This leap in emotional competence is largely a reflection of more-developed limbic structures. The limbic region undergoes major

development between 6 months and 6 years of age, reaching maturity at puberty (Siegel, 2012).

The last brain region to develop is the cortex. Located highest in the brain, the cortex controls voluntary movement, thinking, reasoning, language, problem solving, and planning. The cortex is heavily convoluted, with many ridges and grooves that allow it to pack a lot of surface tissue into the small space of the skull. The cortex sits above and covers the inner brain. The forward-most region of the cortex, called the prefrontal cortex, is associated with attention, motivation, and goal-directed behavior and is the last region of the brain to undergo major development, with full maturation not reached until early adulthood.

Each brain region is important, and each is interconnected with the others, forming a complex and fine-tuned organization. This organization unfolds over time as the brain develops, from bottom to top, and is reflected in changes in children's behavior. For example, in the first 6 months following birth, young infants disturb easily, a function of a lower brain that still needs help regulating bodily systems. In time, the lower brain systems adjust to life outside the womb and infants get better at self-calming. Once they learn how to reach out and grasp objects, infants spend their days exploring, with eyes, ears, hands, and mouth, gathering information through their senses and organizing it as sensory maps within the developing diencephalon. As the limbic area and the cortex develop, infants show marked improvement in their ability to communicate, to remember events, to solve problems, and to plan. The cortex undergoes a major thrust of development between 3 and 6 years of age, when language, problem solving, and reasoning grow in complexity. New connections forming in the cortex result in a progression of more-complex motor skills, from rolling, to crawling, to sitting, to standing, to walking.

One of the most remarkable features of the brain is that it is malleable, that is, it adapts and changes in response to experience (Siegel, 2012). This allows the brain to absorb the wisdom accumulated across generations yet still retain the capacity to build new knowledge. While the brain of a baby is quite malleable, the brain of an adult is less so. Younger brains are more malleable than older brains, with infancy being the period when the brain is the most malleable (Perry, 2004). It is this malleability that allows the human species to customize a brain to fit the unique circumstances of life.

EXPERIENCE WIRES THE BRAIN

How the brain takes shape is dependent on two factors—genetics and experience. At birth, much of the brain is undifferentiated, meaning that specific structures have not yet formed and specific tasks have not yet been assigned. From bottom to top, brain regions transform as each undergoes development and differentiation along a predictable timeline.

Genes

The basic plan for human development is stored in the genes. Genes hold instructions for development. You can compare genes to blueprints used to guide construction of a house. Just as blueprints provide the specifications and measurements for a construction project, genes guide the basic design, sequence, components, and operation of the human being from conception to death. Genes are made up of DNA, long strands of tightly coiled molecules strung together in a precise order. The same package of genes is tucked inside each cell of the body. The DNA serves as a code that will determine the sequence and the components of development. This code can be compared to letters of the alphabet. Letters of the alphabet, when placed in a specific order, create a message that is read and understood as words that hold meaning. The strands of molecules that make up genes do the same. These strands of DNA work like strings of carefully ordered letters, creating messages that give basic instructions for how humans will grow and develop.

Some genes are identical for all humans. For example, the code that holds directions for how the heart is designed is identical in all humans. Other parts of the genetic code are unique for each individual, an example being facial features, skin color, or body build. A unique set of genes is created at conception, when mother and father contribute genetic information.

Genes encode information for how growth occurs and how structures become more differentiated. Genes carry a template of instructions that get passed on from one generation to the next. The body uses these instructions to manufacture a variety of proteins required for specific structures or functions.

Epigenetic Regulation and Experience

The genome refers to an individual's complete set of genes, which is preprogrammed at conception. During development, as cells divide, an identical genome is passed on within each new cell. How the code of instructions within a gene is activated, however, is largely dependent on experience (Siegel, 2012). Through the action of special molecules that sit on the surface of genes, experience determines how specific genes will be read and activated. These special molecules, called the epigenome, which means "above the gene," act like a dial, controlling how the genetic code gets expressed. A dial, when turned one way, increases the strength of a response, and when turned the other way, decreases the strength of a response. Depending on experience, the epigenome either "dials up," increasing how the gene is activated, or "dials down," decreasing how the gene is activated. In this way, the epigenome marks the genes with a chemical tag that influences instructions for development.

The epigenome plays a critical role in how cells differentiate and take on distinct tasks. For example, at conception, an embryo starts as a tiny clump of cells called stem cells. Stem cells are undifferentiated, not yet tasked with a specific function. Stem cells have the potential to develop into many different cell types that carry out different functions. As the embryo develops, some stem cells differentiate to become red blood cells, designed to carry oxygen, and other stem cells differentiate to become white blood cells, designed to fight disease. These variations are the result of changes in the epigenetic markers of stem cells, making possible a wide range of different types of tissue—skin, heart, lungs, and so on.

Genes are fixed at conception and do not change, whereas the epigenome is susceptible to change, based on experience. For the most part, the epigenome is durable, meaning that skin cells reproduce as skin cells and heart cells as heart cells, throughout the lifespan. However, experience, both prenatal and postnatal, can cause changes in the epigenome. These changes get passed on as a cell divides, creating lasting changes in the way cells work, from one generation to the next. Studies show changes in the epigenome in response to poor nutrition, stress, and pollutants.

Nutritional deficiencies can change the epigenome. If the raw ingredients for the epigenetic molecules are absent during critical stages of brain development, these molecules change, and these changes get passed on through cell reproduction. For example, if a pregnant mother's diet is lacking in folate, an essential nutrient found in many foods, the develop-

---

Research Highlight: How Poor Nutrition and Stress Change the Epigenome

Scientists study the nurturing behavior of mother rats to assess the impact of experience on the developing brain. In one study (Liu et al., 1997), baby rat pups were licked by their mothers in normal fashion. A control group was denied such licking. The baby rat pups who were regularly licked by their mothers were not easily startled, explored readily, and did not experience surges in stress hormones. The rats not licked as pups startled easily to noise, were reluctant to explore, and, when stressed, showed high spikes in blood pressure and level of stress hormone. When the brains of the rats raised under each condition were analyzed, the brains of rats that had not been licked had fewer receptors for regulating stress.

To test whether this was simply a difference in genes, the rat pups and mother rats were switched, so those born to the mothers who did not lick much were placed with the mothers who licked regularly, and vice versa (Caldji, Diorio, Anisman, & Meaney, 2004). The rat pups' behavior changed in response to being licked by the foster mother and so did their brains. The experience of being licked altered the epigenome, the molecular markers that activate genes needed for modulating stress.

---

ing cells of the fetus lay down an impaired pattern of epigenetic markers. This impaired pattern means that critical bone structures like the spine may not form properly. High consumption of alcohol during pregnancy may also cause epigenetic changes, resulting in fetal alcohol syndrome, associated with low intelligence scores and behavioral problems (Resendiz, Chen, Ozturk, & Zhou, 2013). Another factor that can cause changes in the epigenome is a high level of stress. These changes result in impaired functioning of brain structures that regulate attention, memory, and response to stress.

Since the epigenome can be changed by experience, the experiences we offer babies, whose brains are still forming, matter. Experience impacts which genes will be dialed up and expressed fully and which genes will be dialed down or silenced, a fact that can change the trajectory of a child's life. Longitudinal studies of children, from both nurturing and neglectful backgrounds, are underway to detect the impact of neglect on brain development. From postmortem studies of brains of adults who were victims of child abuse, scientists find changes in the epigenome of genes that help regulate stress. The genes charged with regulating stress failed to activate, silenced by changes in the epigenome (McGowan et al., 2009).

NEURONS AND HOW THEY WORK

The brain is only one component of the nervous system. The nervous system extends throughout the body and serves as the conduit for information and energy. The nervous system is made up of the brain, the spinal cord, the spinal nerves (which enter and leave the spinal cord and connect muscles, skin, and joints), and the cranial nerves (which enter and leave the brain, linking it with the internal organs of the body, like the heart, stomach, and lungs).

The basic building block of the nervous system is a special kind of cell called a neuron. Neurons have a specific job—to relay information and energy. Neurons communicate information into, through, and out of the body. Sensory neurons extend from sensory organs, like the eyes, nose, mouth, skin, and ears, as well as from internal organs, like the heart, lungs, and stomach, and carry information into the brain. Motor neurons carry information out from the brain and initiate commands to muscles and glands.

Neurons work together to form a complex information-processing system. For example, your nose detects a scent from the environment. A sensory neuron in the lining of the nose captures this scent and carries it to the lower brain, where it is encoded and associated with other sensations. In similar fashion, a sensory neuron from the eye brings visual sensations through the portal of the lower brain, where the visual input is compared with previously stored patterns of visual input. If the nose or the eyes have sensed something completely new, this novelty is encoded in new patterns of connections among neurons. In this way, the nervous system gathers information, integrates it, organizes it, processes it, and builds connections among neurons to hold new information and experience.

Over time, the brain of a baby develops into a vast and complex network of neurons that operate together. When an experience occurs repeatedly, the connections among neurons triggered by this experience strengthen. The more a connected pathway of neurons is used, the stronger and more efficient it becomes, a principle described as neurons that fire together, wire together (Hebb, 1949). In this way, a connected pathway of neurons literally holds an experience within the brain. What begins as a cluster of isolated neurons transforms, with experience, into a connected pathway that holds and relays information.

How Neurons Communicate

To understand how the nervous system works, it helps to understand the way a neuron is built and how one neuron communicates with another. In contrast to other cells of the body, which are tightly packed together, nerve cells are separated by a very tiny gap. This gap serves as a junction across which neurons relay information to each other. This junction is called a synapse. Thanks to synapses, neurons can send multiple messages in many directions simultaneously. When a neuron relays a message across the synapse, it does so by transforming the electrical message into a chemical message, made up of tiny particles called neurotransmitters. *Neuro* means brain and *transmitter* means message carrier, so the task of neurotransmitters is to transport messages from one neuron to another. Because neurotransmitters are chemicals, they flow readily into the synapse (Figure 2.2), cross this open space between neurons, and get absorbed by special receptors on the tip of the receiving neurons. These receptors transform the chemical message back into an electrical signal.

The core of a neuron is called the cell body. Figure 2.3 illustrates the parts of a neuron and how a message moves through a neuron. The cell body forms the central part of the neuron. Extending from the cell body are two types of branching fibers. These fibers send and receive information in the form of electrical energy. Dendrites are the fibers that extend from the cell body and receive information from other neurons. Axons are the fibers that extend from the cell body and relay information to other neurons. A signal received by the dendrite is delivered to the cell body. If the message is sufficiently important to relay on to other neurons, it is sent out through the axon. At the axon tip, the message transforms into neurotransmitters that cross the synapse to other neurons.

The beauty of neurotransmitters is that they can be configured and reconfigured in thousands of different combinations. This makes it possible for hun-

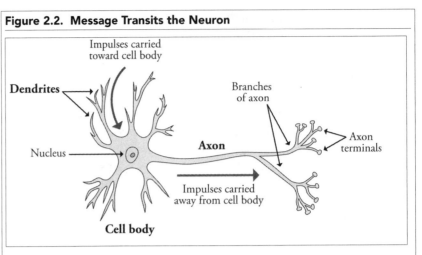

Figure 2.2. Message Transits the Neuron

Impulses carried toward cell body

Dendrites

Branches of axon

Nucleus

Axon

Axon terminals

Impulses carried away from cell body

Cell body

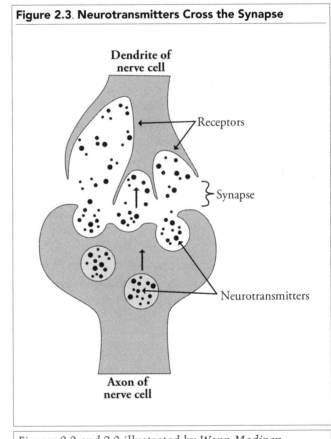

Figure 2.3. Neurotransmitters Cross the Synapse

Dendrite of nerve cell

Receptors

Synapse

Neurotransmitters

Axon of nerve cell

Figures 2.2 and 2.3 illustrated by Wenn Madigan.

dreds of messages to be sent to hundreds of different neurons simultaneously, resulting, over the course of infancy, in the formation of billions of synapses that hold and transmit information.

Each neuron potentially can communicate instantaneously with up to 10,000 other neurons (Siegel, 2012). Messages can enter and leave a single neuron on thousands of trajectories in a flicker of time. The production of billions of new synapses is what makes it possible for infants to remember, to know, to think, to reason, to feel, and to move in increasingly complex ways. As infants experience new people, objects, and events, synaptic connections get more elaborate. As an experience is repeated, day in and day out, the synaptic connection triggered by the experience strengthens. Over time, the brain of a baby transforms into a complex super highway of information storage and exchange.

At the peak of development, synapses form at an astonishing 2 million new synapses every second (Eliot, 1999). The first synapses form around 5 weeks after conception and form the spinal cord. Within weeks, the first synapses of the brain begin to develop. From 2 months gestation to around 1 year of age, a flurry of new synapses form. At 1 year of age, the number of synapses in the brain, the density of synapses, and the number of synapses per neuron peak (Huttenlocher, 1994).

Myelination

With synaptic connections forming and strengthening with use, the brain grows in size and complexity. Another factor that influences brain size is a process called myelination, which occurs once neurons establish their position in the brain and take on specific tasks. As this occurs, a dense, fatty substance called myelin begins to wrap the outer surface of the neuron. This fatty myelin coating serves as insulation. Just like the plastic coating that insulates an electrical wire, myelin makes message relay more efficient.

Myelination has barely begun in the newborn and proceeds throughout infancy. Some of the improvement in infants' knowledge and skills can be credited to myelination, because myelin speeds the conduction of energy and information and consequently makes all functions of the brain more efficient. Myelination takes place first in the lower regions of the brain. Not until much later do the upper, later-developing regions of the brain become myelinated. Some parts of the cortex that are used for higher-order reasoning are not fully myelinated until young adulthood (Eliot, 1999).

BRAIN PLASTICITY: BENEFIT AND RISK

At birth, a baby has an estimated 100 billion neurons, most of which are as yet undifferentiated, that is, not yet coded with a specific task or function. This large stock of neurons is more than the baby will ever need, yet having so many undifferentiated neurons on hand during infancy ensures that the brain will be sculpted in a manner that fits the unique experiences encountered by each baby. The brain of a baby is therefore quite malleable, a feature that scientists refer to as brain plasticity.

Sensitive Periods

One aspect of brain plasticity is the presence of a small number of sensitive periods during early development. During these sensitive periods, certain brain structures await specific types of stimulation in order to fully activate the instructions for development. If the specific type of stimulation is absent, those brain structures fail to develop or develop in an aberrant way. Vision has such a sensitive period, spanning the first months following birth. For proper development of brain structures responsible for processing vision, a newborn baby must experience sight, that is, the eyes must be stimulated by light waves. It is rare, yet possible, for an infant to be born with cataracts. Cataracts are webs of tissue that grow in the eye, preventing normal visual input from reaching the sensory nerves of the eye. If the cataracts are not discovered and removed soon after birth, genes with instructions for building brain structures for vision will fail to be activated and neurons that would otherwise fire repeatedly in response to visual input, fail to fire. The result is permanent loss of vision (Lambert & Drack, 1996).

Another example of a sensitive period is the organization of speech into coherent patterns. The ability to string words together in a meaningful pattern of speech requires brain structures designed to do this. These structures are not present at birth. During the early months of infancy, the brain awaits stimulation by auditory input from the human voice. If young infants fail to hear human speech, the genes that hold instructions for building brain structures that will organize speech sounds fail to be activated, and circuits of neurons that could potentially organize speech sounds fail to develop. The result is a permanent impairment in the ability to speak coherently (Eliot, 1999).

Fortunately, there appear to be very few brain structures with such restricted sensitive periods. For most genes, the experiences that activate their expression occur readily, as babies are held, talked to, and soothed, within everyday moments of care. Consequently, as babies experience similar patterns of behavior day in and day out, circuits of neurons wire together and over time fire together, strengthening synaptic connections. Since experience modulates how genes are expressed, what babies experience has the potential to either support or to compromise optimal development.

Pruning of Neural Connections

During peaks of synaptic production, a ready supply of neurons is an asset to the developing brain. However, once core brain structures are developed, an abundance of undifferentiated neurons is no longer needed. Through a process much like pruning a garden, the brain prunes back neural connections no longer used.

Pruning neural connections tends to occur following periods of rapid growth or new skill development. For example, in the period right before an infant starts to crawl, scientists detect a spike of electrical activity in the area of the brain associated with crawling (Huttenlocher, 1994), which they attribute to an abundance of synapses forming as the infant begins the work of mastering the new skill of crawling. Once the infant has been crawling for several months and is an accomplished crawler, the circuits of neurons involved in crawling become streamlined, and only the most efficient circuits get used. Those not used are pruned back. In essence, the brain performs periodic housecleaning, eliminating neural circuits that are no longer needed.

This process of overproducing synapses and then pruning them back reveals the dynamic, changing nature of the developing brain. The brain efficiently sculpts itself to respond to patterns of experience. Plasticity is a desirable feature when it comes to building a brain that fits well with the unique environmental circumstances into which a child is born. However, plasticity also brings risk, if desired experiences are absent. Infants are vulnerable to the negative impact of experience. Deprivation, neglect, and abuse will compromise the developing brain. When critical experiences are absent or when care is neglectful or abusive, connections either fail to form in the brain or form in maladaptive ways (Perry, 2007). Studies show noticeably smaller structures in the brains of children with a history of abuse, as well as abnormal patterns of electrical activity (De Bellis et al., 1999; Perry, 2008). Unless timely intervention occurs to remedy the neglect or abuse, the cost is high to the neglected

Research Highlight: Newborns' Acute Senses

Newborn babies have highly sensitive olfactory and auditory systems, making it possible for them to detect the sounds and smells of those who care for them. Consider the following research findings about newborn capacities.

- If placed between two sets of nursing pads, one used by the baby's mother and one used by another mother, newborns will reliably turn toward their own mother's scent (Porter & Winberg, 1999).
- A newborn, held between two conversing adults, one of them the newborn's parent, will selectively turn in the direction of the parent's voice, having been sensitized to the voices heard for months in the womb (Nugent et al., 2007).

Reflect on how these findings shed light on what structures in the brain are developed and functioning at birth.

infant, to the adult the infant becomes, and to society at large (Zigler, Finn-Stevenson, & Hill, 2003).

THE SOCIAL BRAIN

The brain of a baby is designed to detect, read, and relay information to and from others. For early humans, who moved as nomadic tribes from place to place, working together to forage and hunt for food was important. Equally important was the ability to recognize members of the clan and to stay together. Hundreds of generations survived draught, famine, and other onslaughts to master increasingly more complex ways of living, and they did so in large part because they relied on relationships with others (Perry, 2009). Staying connected to members of the clan ensured human survival and prosperity. Therefore, what has evolved over time is a brain dependent on connections with others, a brain shaped by interpersonal relationships.

Babies Read Others

Babies are born with the capacity to stay connected to those who will protect and nourish them. Newborns gather and organize sensory information about those who care for them. They have a repertoire of reflexes, many of which appear to be designed to keep them connected to others. For example, the grasp reflex results in the newborn clinging tightly to any object that touches the palm of the hand, and the rooting reflex will cause the newborn to turn in the direction of a touch to the cheek, an action that helps the newborn locate the nipple of the mother's breast.

Newborns' acute senses and their repertoire of reflexes connect them to those who provide food, warmth, and nurturance. Within the well-functioning lower brain, newborns connect circuits of neurons that hold patterns of expectation about people and events. These patterns become templates for what is familiar and consequently safe and what is unfamiliar and consequently not safe (Perry, 2006). This capacity makes it possible for babies to anticipate what others will do and how others will make them feel. In essence, babies have the ability to read others, to detect safety and threat, and to stay connected to their social group (Tronick, 2007).

Babies organize their brains in response to patterned, repetitive events (Perry, 2006). This begins prenatally, when a synchrony develops between the heart rate of the fetus and that of the mother (Ivanov, Ma, & Bartsch, 2009). The ongoing rhythmic sensation of the maternal heart rate entrains and organizes structures developing in the brain of the fetus. As Perry (2006) explains:

> Powerful associations are made during the prenatal development of the brainstem and diencephalon between rhythmic auditory, tactile, and motor activity at 80 beats per minute (i.e., the maternal heart rate heard and felt *in utero*) and the [circuits of neurons that mediate] the sensation of being warm, satiated, safe, and soothed. (pp. 39–40)

Once born, babies remain acutely sensitive to these internal and external rhythmic patterns. Studies of mothers and infants show a synchrony between the heart rhythm of the mother and that of the baby, one that increases substantially during episodes rich in smiles and vocalizations (Feldman, Magori-Cohen, Galili, Singer, & Louzoun, 2011).

Consider what happens when someone picks up a distraught baby. Most often, the person begins to rock the baby; to sway back and forth; and to hum, sing, or chant. This rhythmic pattern of movement and voice is evident across cultures and the cadence closely matches the beat of the resting human heart, about 80 beats per minute. Scientists (Malloch &

Trevarthen, 2009) track a similar synchrony in the cadence of spoken words used in traditional nursery rhymes, with the bursts and pauses of these nursery rhymes consistent across cultures and mirroring the rhythms of the resting human heartbeat. Long before infants have mastery of speech, their brains have been organizing in response to the rhythm and pattern of movement and sound that surround them.

Scientists have systematically analyzed the vocal patterns and movements of parent and baby during conversation (Beebe & Lachmann, 1988; Condon & Sander, 1974; Stern, 2000; Trevarthen, 2011). They detect a rhythmic synchrony between the baby and parent. A movement or a change in pitch of one sparks a corresponding and reciprocal change in movement or vocalization of the other. Baby and parent respond to changes in each other's phrasing or pitch with changes in gesture, expression, vocalization, and movement. For example, when a baby's vocalizations rise in pitch, the voice of the adult interacting with the baby shows an abrupt rise in pitch, followed by both baby and adult slowly adjusting the pitch downward. Trevarthen (2005) describes this as infants' intrinsic musicality, or time sense, and suggests that it connects the brain of the baby with the brain of the parent. In fact, such face-to-face vocal exchanges between infant and parent prompt a flurry of activity in the baby's brain and a corresponding flurry of activity in the identical region of the parent's brain, what Schore (1994) describes as "brain to brain resonance" (p. 77).

Research Highlight:
Mirror Neurons and Monkeys

To study how movement is processed in the brain, researchers placed an electrode in a motor neuron of a monkey's brain, so that they could track what movements caused this neuron to fire. Whenever the monkey picked up a piece of food and brought it to his mouth, the recording instruments showed electrical activity in that neuron. One day, by chance, one of the researchers entered the room eating a snack. The monkey, with brain still connected to the recorder, saw this. To the researcher's surprise, the electrode fired, causing a spike of electrical activity. Simply by watching the researcher feed himself, the monkey's brain fired in the identical way it had fired when the monkey had fed himself. This moment marked scientists' discovery of a special type of neuron called the mirror neuron.

Reflection: Your Mirror Neurons at Work

Reflect on what you do and how you feel when someone smiles at you. You probably sense a good feeling and smile in return. Or conversely, if you saw someone grimace, you might feel concern, or even fear, yourself. How do mirror neurons provide a clue as to how people can figure out others' intentions and feelings? How would you explain to someone else how mirror neurons work and how mirror neurons add to our understanding of interpersonal relationships?

Mirror Neurons

A clue to how such resonance occurs can be found in a special type of neuron called the mirror neuron. Mirror neurons were discovered quite by accident by a team of Italian neuroscientists (Gallese, Fadiga, Fogassi, & Rizzolatti, 1996) measuring brain activity in monkeys. Mirror neurons fire in our brain when we perform an action, but fire as well when we see someone else perform that same action. Moreover, mirror neurons are sensitive not just to actions, but also to emotions. Mirror neurons fire when we feel a certain emotion, and they fire as well when we see others feeling that same emotion (Wicker et al., 2003).

Babies Remember

Infants gather information about the world around them and store it in memory. It may seem odd to think of infants as having memory. Indeed, most of us are not capable of recalling events from infancy. We assume, therefore, that memory is not working during infancy. However, scientists have begun to unravel the complex web of memory and suggest that there are multiple types of memory. One type of memory, referred to as implicit memory, is present at birth. This early form of memory may be thought of as somatic or bodily memory (Siegel, 2012). Implicit memory is nonverbal in that we recall it as a sensation rather than as a story that we recount. It is distinct from memory of story or events in that it is based solely in sensations and feelings. It does not include recall of events, ideas, or experiences of self in time.

When a newborn, day after day, sees the caregiver's face, smells the caregiver's scent, and feels the caregiver's touch, the newborn holds within the brain an impression built from these sensations. These sensations form an implicit memory of the caregiver. Implicit memory is stored in the form of circuits of neu-

---

Reflection: Making Memories

Imagine an infant being startled by the sight and sound of a large, barking dog. Three years later, this same child, out on a walk with her father, encounters a neighbor who has a big, friendly dog on a leash. At the sight of the approaching dog, the child flushes, hides behind her father, and begins to cry. When her father asks her what's wrong, she has no answer for why she is so afraid of this neighbor's big, friendly dog (Siegel & Hartzell, 2003).

Will this 3-year-old be able to recall a scary moment that occurred when she was a baby? Will she have a memory of this earlier encounter with a big, scary dog? If so, describe the nature of this memory. Would you call it implicit or explicit memory? What about her feeling of fright? Is that connected to a memory? Is it possible for a young child to hold in memory sights, sounds, smells, and sensations? If memory is involved in this 3-year-old's encounter with the big, friendly dog, is there a story she can recount? Why? Why not?

---

rons that hold visual, tactile, olfactory, auditory, or visceral sensations. Each time a newborn experiences being with the caregiver, electrical currents travel the same circuit of neurons, holding auditory, visual, and olfactory sensations generated by the caregiver. These circuits fire together, welding into the baby's brain an implicit memory of the caregiver, a bodily based memory that endures over time.

Implicit memories are organized primarily within the lower brain, the parts of the brain that form earliest (Perry, 2008). Implicit memory is purely memory of movements, sensations, and feelings. The more emotionally charged an experience, the stronger the implicit memory. Implicit memory makes it possible for babies to store a vast array of sensory experiences and to organize these sensory experiences into sensory maps.

In contrast, scientists describe explicit memory as memory of events and memory of experiences that we can recount over time. Explicit memory is not present at birth, yet scientists have begun to detect some semblance of event-related learning as early as 3 months and to trace the emergence of an explicit memory system to around 9 months of age (Mullally & Maguire, 2014). Explicit memory is most easily recognized around 15 to 18 months of age, when infants demonstrate the ability to remember events or recollect stories. Explicit memory is most often associated with the hippocampus, a structure that develops in the limbic region of the brain.

FROM RESEARCH TO PRACTICE: BUILDING STRONG BRAINS

The moment-to-moment experiences that shape the architecture of the still-developing brain are literally in the hands of those who care for babies. When news reports first began to circulate about the spurt in brain development that occurs during infancy, many well-meaning parents and teachers responded by bombarding infants with stimulation in an attempt to build their brains. Electronic media, flash cards, and audiotapes were advertised as brain food in a box. Parents exposed their babies to videos and exercises intended to build the intellect, with the hope of taking advantage of what was described in the media as a limited window of opportunity that would soon close.

Developmental psychologists and neuroscientists (National Scientific Council on the Developing Child, 2007) leaped into the discussion to clarify the findings. They pointed out that although many brain structures are still forming during the first 3 years, the claim that the window of opportunity closes when a child reaches 3 years of age is unfounded, and for most brain functions the window of opportunity remains open well beyond age 3. They stressed that there is no evidence to support over stimulation of the baby brain nor is there evidence to support claims that educational videos or music recordings have positive, measurable impact on brain development. In fact, they suggest that "the more important influences [are] . . . attentive, nurturing, and growth promoting interactions with invested adults" (p. 7).

Looking Back and Looking Forward

Babies come into the world prepared to read and respond to the rhythmic patterns of movements and vocalizations of others. Their everyday experiences form patterns of expectation that are knit into circuits of the brain. Infancy is a period of rapid brain development. Babies' everyday experiences impact the developing architecture of the brain. How each baby experiences the world will influence how structures form in the brain, an aspect of brain development described as plasticity. Plasticity ensures a brain customized to the baby's unique life situation, but plasticity also means that the brain of a baby is vulnerable to the effects of neglect or abuse. The relationships that form between baby and caregiver sculpt the developing brain and influence lifelong learning. The next chapter explores how infants learn within these relationships.

CHAPTER 3

Knowledge from the Infant's Point of View

We as teachers are asked by children to see them as scientists or philosophers searching to understand something, to draw out a meaning. . . . We are asked to be the child's traveling companion in this search for meaning. (Rinaldi, 2006a, p. 21)

IN MANY WAYS, infants are small scientists (Gopnik et al., 1999). They actively gather information about what objects and people are like, and they investigate how one relates to another. Prominent scientists (Bruner, 1975; Stern, 2002) describe the central tendency of infants' mental life as an "active process of hypothesis formation and hypothesis testing" (Stern, p. 72). They experiment with and actively investigate objects and people. With focused attention, they gather information and then act on things to see how they react. Just like scientists, infants pursue a quest to move beyond what they know to discover what they do not know.

What does knowledge look like from the baby's point of view? What does it mean to teach infants? What do we teach them? How do we do it? And how do we know they are learning? This chapter pursues these questions, within the context of a broader quest—to explore the relationship between teaching and learning when working with infants and toddlers. Many equate teaching to instructing, that is, delivering facts, information, or activities aimed at developing discrete skills and concepts. The image of active, talking teacher and passive, quiet child fits this perspective. However, infants are not passive learners who simply wait to be taught. They initiate their own learning, and in simple but significant ways, they explore, investigate, form hypotheses, test them out in play, and construct concepts and theories. They do not do this in isolation. They look to others, primarily those who care for them, for information and assistance. Rinaldi (2006a) explains that infants ask us to be their "traveling companion[s] in [their] search for meaning" (p. 21).

The idea that infants experiment, investigate, and explore in order to build concepts and skills has roots in the theories of pioneering scientists Vygotsky (1986), Piaget (Singer & Revenson, 1978), and Bruner (1966), all of whom proposed theories of how young children learn. Although each developed distinct lines of thought about how young children think and how they learn, their work shares a common idea, that infants and young children actively construct knowledge, as they interact with objects and people, in a continuous process of organizing and reorganizing thoughts and ideas.

THREE TYPES OF KNOWLEDGE

To explore what knowledge looks like from the infant's point of view, imagine how this baby might be building knowledge. She lies on the floor, with several toys nearby.

Observation: Baby Tatyana rests comfortably on her stomach. She looks intently at the red basket several feet away. She reaches her arm toward the basket and, inching forward, she wraps her fingers around the edge of the basket. She rolls onto her side, holds the basket above her, and intently stares at it. She rolls all the way over onto her back and, clutching the curved basket edge with one hand, she waves it back and forth, eyes glued to the moving basket. She smiles and, as her face brightens, she kicks her legs. Suddenly, her arm stops moving as she peers at the basket edge. She adjusts her grasp to hold the basket with two hands. She scratches the open weave edge with two fingers of one hand. Then she pokes one finger into an opening on the basket edge.

This baby uses her senses and her actions to gather information about color, texture, and resilience. Within connected circuits of neurons, she holds in

Reflection:
Coming to Know the Physical World

Reflect on baby Tatyana's play. What information is she gathering with fingers, eyes, and mouth? Can you name the physical knowledge she is gathering as she explores these objects? What features will be known to her, and which will be new? As she plays, what knowledge is she building about angles and curves? What knowledge is she building about color or texture? Do infants build understanding of color, shape, or texture through playful interaction with objects and people, or must they rely on others to teach them about color, texture, or shape?

memory these sensations. As babies shake, mouth, and finger objects in play, they learn about the physical properties of objects, what they look like, feel like, smell like, and sound like. This baby notices the red color, the curved edge, and the smooth, slick surface. She also gathers information as she gazes at the person watching her, and later, when she reaches to touch the person's face, soaking in the unique physical features of the face and the sound of the voice. All of these sensations, associated within circuits of neurons, become a part of the baby, built into structures within the developing brain and forming the basis of knowledge.

After intently observing babies' play over time, scientist Jean Piaget suggested that there are three types of knowledge—physical knowledge, logico-mathematical knowledge, and social knowledge. We build physical knowledge as we interact with objects and people and experience their physical properties. We build logico-mathematical knowledge as we interact with objects and people and put them into relationships, like size, order, number, or pattern. We build both physical and logico-mathematical knowledge as we engage with and interact with our surroundings. The third type of knowledge, social knowledge, is distinct, in that we do not *build* social knowledge through active manipulation of the physical world. Instead, we *acquire* social knowledge as we engage with and learn from the people who make up our surrounding community (Kamii & DeVries, 1993; Singer & Revenson, 1978). Social knowledge, as a way of categorizing knowledge, can be thought of as the body of information we acquire from others, like language and expectations for behavior. All three types of knowledge have roots in infancy.

Infants Actively Build Physical and Logico-Mathematical Knowledge

By interacting with their surroundings, infants build a vast amount of information about the physical properties of objects and people. This includes shape, size, color, density, weight, texture, sound, smell, and taste, all of which are features that reside in the object itself and can be seen, felt, heard, or smelled. To discover how babies construct physical knowledge, imagine looking in on baby Tatyana's play once again. As follow-up to the prior play, her teachers decided to add to the play space a variety of new baskets that varied in color, shape, and texture.

Observation: Tatyana crawled toward the round red basket she had played with before. She grasped it and mouthed it, and then rolled onto her stomach and, spying the green square rattan basket, she inched toward it, red basket still in tow. As she grasped the edge of the green basket, she dropped the red one. From the teacher nearby, she heard, "Tatyana, you found the round red basket again, but you also found the new green square basket." She mouthed the green basket, pulled it back to look at it, and then waved it back and forth, before dropping it on the floor. She patted it with her hand, and it made a rasping noise as it slid from side to side. She stopped patting and listened, and then patted it again, repeating this action several times.

As baby Tatyana examines and handles these baskets with eyes, hands, ears, and mouth, she relates one to the other. She notices and feels how one basket has a curved edge. This is physical knowledge. She notices how one basket has a straight edge. This too is physical knowledge. However, when she looks at one and then the other and perceives that one is different from the other in shape and color, she constructs a relationship of difference. This is logico-mathematical knowledge. Relationships described as logico-mathematical knowledge exist in the mind, rather than in the physical world. With physical knowledge we see and we touch the physical property of curved or angled edge, or red or green color. With logico-mathematical knowledge, the relationship exists in the mind, not in the object itself. When Tatyana held the red round basket in one hand and the green square basket in the other, she built a relationship of difference. As she handled two objects simultaneously, one in each hand, she constructed a relationship of number, making "two." "Twoness" is not something we see or feel, like the color red or the curved shape. Number is a mental relationship, an example of logico-mathematical knowledge.

This baby used the physical knowledge she had gathered in play—the shape, color, and texture—to build logico-mathematical knowledge. As infants relate one experience to another, they organize and categorize. As they organize and categorize, they build the concept of classification—for example, these are red, so they go together, but those are green, so they go together. Classification, a form of logico-mathematical knowledge, means mentally putting together things that are alike and separating things that are different (Inhelder & Piaget, 1964). In time, through play with objects that vary in size, weight, or color, infants build the concept of seriation. Seriation means mentally ordering things according to their differences (Inhelder & Piaget, 1964). As infants explore how things fill, fit in, and move in space, they construct spatial relations. As they experience how things transpire over time, they build temporal relationships. As they relate one action to another, they build the concept of causality. Number, seriation, classification, and causality are all examples of logico-mathematical knowledge. Over time, with added experience within a variety of new contexts, infants construct more complex and coherent understandings of each of these concepts.

In simple moments of play, infants apply their expanding repertoire of physical knowledge to build an expanding repertoire of logico-mathematical knowledge:

- They build concepts of spatial relations and balance as they explore how a flat side has a unique advantage in staying put when placed on top of something else.
- They build relationships of cause and effect, when they bat at an object and make it move, learning that things move in response to force.
- They build relationships of number and quantity by putting objects together to get more or taking things apart to get less.
- They notice how some toys make sounds and others do not, constructing a relationship of cause and effect.
- They hold in hand two things that are identical, building a relationship of identity.
- They explore how one object fits inside an-

other, or on top of another, constructing spatial relations.
- As they experience hunger, are fed, and feel satiated, they experience a relationship of time.
- They might wrap their hands completely around the caregiver's finger but only partially around the caregiver's arm, a relationship of size.
- They construct spatial relations (inside and outside; on and under) and size (bigger and smaller) as they drop smaller objects into larger objects.
- They construct spatial relations as they explore how objects move in space, fill space, and fit in space.
- They build the concept of pressure as they explore how to get something to move or change shape.
- They construct number and understanding of quantity as they stack one, then another, and then a third object to make a single tall tower.

Through play with everyday, ordinary objects, infants gather information about the physical world of people and objects, and they relate one experience to another, building understanding of how things work and what they can make them do.

Infants Acquire Social Knowledge

Infants acquire a third type of knowledge, social knowledge, which refers to the names and cultural conventions invented by people, like language and expectations for behavior. Social knowledge includes the spoken and written language, rules of conduct, as well as stories told within the culture. Social knowledge is distinct from physical and logico-mathematical knowledge in that it is transmitted to the child, rather than actively constructed by the child through play or interaction.

We do not construct social knowledge in the same way we construct physical or logico-mathematical knowledge, both of which require us to actively explore and experiment with objects and people (Kamii & DeVries, 1993). We acquire social knowledge as we listen to what others say or watch what they do. As baby Tatyana played with the red basket, she heard the teacher describe it as the "round red basket." If the language in use were Spanish, she might have heard it described as "la canasta roja y redonda." So-

---

**Reflection:
Constructing Knowledge During Play**

Look for examples of children constructing knowledge in this observation.

Observation:

Toddlers Cecilia, Enrique, and Jamal have discovered the collection of large cardboard boxes and cylinders placed in the yard this morning. Enrique stacks several boxes to make a tower and then knocks them down. The three erupt in a gleeful round of applause and shouts and then begin to rebuild the tower. Through trial and error, they find boxes that will stack and balance. Jamal adds a cylinder to the tower, placing it flat side down, without hesitation. Enrique grabs another cylinder and adds it to the structure, but sets it curved side down. He watches it start to roll off the box, so he turns it upright to rest on its flat side. Cecilia pushes the structure and it topples again. The three laugh with delight. They build and topple their tower several more times, and the teacher watching from nearby comments, "Wow! You've made a tower of three boxes. Let me count them: one, two, three." As she says "three," the toddlers topple the tower again. From then on, as they start to push the boxes over, they chant, "One, two, three!"

Interpretation:

Consider what knowledge might be under construction within the minds of these toddlers. What physical knowledge are they constructing? What logico-mathematical knowledge are they building? Do you see any relationships of size, space, time, or number being built within the play? Is there an example of social knowledge being acquired in this play?

---

cial knowledge will vary with the linguistic and cultural context.

Social knowledge also includes acceptable modes of behaving and manners. For example, an adult might say, in response to seeing one child hit another child, "I will not let you hit him. Hitting people hurts them. You may ask him for the toy, but you may not hit him." The child hears the expected rule of behavior, and over time the child adds this understanding to his social knowledge.

Social knowledge is defined by the cultural context in which people live. What infants learn in regard to expected behavior, language, social roles, values, and manners varies widely, a function of their

experiences at home, in infant care, and in the community. Patterns of eye contact between adult and child, terms and gestures of respect and deference, ways of transporting infants (e.g., in slings, in strollers, in backpacks), or the pattern of discourse—all influence how infants behave and, in turn, how infants expect others to behave. The families served in group-care settings may come from a wide range of cultural and linguistic contexts, so teachers working with infants must support infants in making sense of the language and customs used at home as well as the language and customs used in the infant-care program.

LEARNING ACROSS THE DAY: CURRICULUM DEFINED BROADLY

With respect to how infants build and acquire knowledge, curriculum for infants cannot be interpreted as lessons aimed at delivering skills and concepts. To fit with what we know about how infants learn, curriculum must be defined broadly to include the many ways we invite infants to build and acquire knowledge. Lally (2009) argues, "What is happening in infant care today is a revolution in thinking about curriculum. The most critical curriculum components are no longer seen as lessons and lesson plans but rather the planning of settings and experiences that allow learning to take place" (p. 52). A broad definition of curriculum, when working with infants, includes three components—what teachers make available to infants in the play environment, the design of the care routines, and the expectations for conversations and interactions that involve infants (California Department of Education, 2012).

Play Spaces as Environments for Learning

With play central to the way in which infants construct knowledge about the world around them, an important aspect of curriculum planning is how teachers thoughtfully and purposefully develop play spaces. Play spaces are environments for learning. Within a well-designed infant program, the play environment holds immense possibility for concept development. Consider what learning might be underway in the photos in Figure 3.1.

The child in these photos was engaged in play that he initiated. His teacher noticed his play and took photos to capture evidence of what he appeared

Figure 3.1. Victor Reveals His Thinking

Reflection:
Play Space as Context for Curriculum

Study each photo in Figure 3.1. What do you notice? What knowledge does Victor reveal within this moment of play? What conditions made it possible for this play to occur? Is this curriculum?

to be thinking. She recorded her observation in written notes (Figure 3.2).

In this moment of play, Victor reveals his thinking, made evident by his selection and placement of toys. He notices the distinct features, that is, the physical properties, of the cars and vehicles available to him in the play space. He compares them and selects only those with common features, in this case, blue vehicles and cats. He relates one object to another, in a distinct order of color, size, and shape. He creates two sets of objects, a set of vehicles and a set of cats. These are all examples of Victor constructing logico-mathematical knowledge, that is, concepts of size, number, order, and type.

What made this moment possible was access to objects in the play space with which Victor could build these relationships of size, number, order, and type. His teachers outfit the play space just as carefully as scientists might stock their laboratories. They assemble an array of toys and materials that invite comparison and classification. They make certain that there are some objects that are identical and some that are similar, distinct in a particular feature. They do this in order to support toddlers' emerging concept of classification, that is, distinguishing one object from another. They include similar objects graduated in size, as a way to invite toddlers to notice and arrange objects by size. They make sure there are some objects that are identical, for making pairs, and that there are baskets with collections of similar objects, for assembling *many* rather than *few*, all of which supports emerging concepts of quantity and number.

The materials are easily available to the toddlers, on low shelves and in wide, shallow baskets and bins. Each container is labeled to hold a distinct type of object—toy vehicles in one, a collection of small animals in another, and a collection of small figures of people in another. This play occurs in what traditionally might be called the block area, but one these teachers choose to describe as the connections and construction area, since the focus for toddlers extends to much more than blocks. In this play space, toddlers find conical objects—simple plastic cups and cardboard cones—that will connect, one into the other, getting higher with the addition of each cup or cone. There are large Lego blocks that interlock. There are sets of blocks and sets of cardboard, metal, and plastic boxes, some identical in size and some varied in size, for balancing, stacking, and building. A large open floor space and a low, raised surface provide ample space for the toddlers to line up or stack objects.

In the course of spontaneous play, toddlers encounter these materials and build relationships of identity, order, size, shape, number, and space. Many of the materials, like the collection of small animals, are familiar to the toddlers, available in the bins of the play space many days running. Other materials, like the collection of blue vehicles, have been added recently, in hopes of extending and adding complex-

Figure 3.2. Observation and Interpretation: Victor's Play

Planning Question: What appears to be the focus of interest as Victor explores these small figures?

OBSERVATIONS	INTERPRETATIONS
For several days, Victor has spent considerable time gathering, carrying, and loading into containers a collection of small animals that we make available to the children in the connections and construction play area. Today, he returned to this play, but added to his play a collection of vehicles. • He selected only the tigers, lions, and blue vehicles. • He put one cat on top of each vehicle. • He experimented with several combinations, but in the end he had all three blue cars together, with the one blue truck in the front. • He placed the two striped tigers in the front and the two other cats in the back. • The cats and the trucks were lined up in order of size and were all pointed in the same direction.	Victor initiated this play on his own. He selected only the lions and tigers and only the blue vehicles from the collection of items on the shelf. He matched the smaller animals to the smaller vehicles, building categories of size, color, and shape. He experimented with placement of the objects before lining the cars to make a straight line, each pointing in the same direction, with two distinct types of cats on two distinct types of vehicles. He appeared to build a particular order and pattern in how he laid out the toys.

ity to the toddlers' play. The objects added to the play space are part of the teachers' curriculum plan. During their weekly planning, the teachers discussed how some of the toddlers, for several days in a row, had collected all of the small animals in canvas shopping bags and carted them from place to place. They wondered what they might do to prompt toddlers' building more complex connections with these collections. They decided to add the vehicles to prompt the toddlers' building new relationships of size, space, or identity. Their plan held a question, "Will the children relate the vehicles to the animals, with respect to type or size, prompting exploration of categories and classification?"

The teachers set the stage for learning but did not direct the learning. Victor constructed an ordered series of tigers and vehicles, without being prompted to do so by an adult. He constructed physical knowledge—gathering information about the various physical features of the objects—and he constructed logico-mathematical knowledge, relating one object in sequence and size to another.

By preparing play spaces as contexts for learning, teachers support infants as they actively construct knowledge. Play spaces for infants are their laboratories for learning, the places where they can explore, experiment, and research what things are like and how they work. Infants rely on families and teachers to thoughtfully select materials for their play spaces and to organize them in a way that draws the infants' attention and makes the materials easy to find and use. Early childhood educators Elizabeth Jones and Gretchen Reynolds (2011) use the term *stage manager* to describe this role. By this they mean that the early childhood teacher purposefully sets the stage for learning by selecting toys, furnishings, and materials that invite children to explore, experiment, and solve problems.

Care Routines That Invite Participation

The care routines provide a second context for learning. Infants enjoy pitching in as active participants in the care, ready to use their emerging skills and ideas (Rogoff, 2011). Meals, diapering, toileting, dressing, and hand washing are caregiving rituals that punctuate play and periods of rest. Pikler and Gerber (David & Appell, 2001; Gerber, 1998, 2002) encourage caregivers to see caregiving routines as rich opportunities to invite infants to be active participants.

Reflection: Involving Infants in the Care

Reflect on how the infant in this episode of diapering is invited to participate.

Observation

Thomas's primary care teacher squats in front of Thomas and catches his gaze, saying, "Thomas, I'm ready to change your diaper, now. I hope you're ready. What do you think?" Reaching toward Thomas, with palms turned up and pausing as he speaks, the teacher invites Thomas to notice that he is preparing to pick him up. Thomas smiles at his teacher, drops the toy he is holding, and reaches toward him. The teacher picks him up, saying, "I like that, Thomas. You told me you were ready," and as he carries Thomas to the diapering counter, says, "I'm going to put you down now," before gently lowering him onto the counter. Catching Thomas's gaze, he points to the baby's shorts and says, "First, we'll take your shorts off so we can change your wet diaper." Thomas lifts his hips slightly. "Thank you, Thomas. You're helping me! That's great. Next comes the wet diaper." Thomas shifts his weight slightly, and his teacher removes the wet diaper. Thomas hears, "There it goes, into the diaper bin." Thomas watches as the diaper drops into the bin. "And now I'm going to clean your skin. Are you ready? This is a wet cloth. I'll let you feel it." Thomas touches the cloth, held close to his hand.

Interpretation

What is this infant learning, as an active participant in diapering? What physical knowledge is being built? What logico-mathematical knowledge is being built? What does his teacher do to support such learning?

When care routines are seen as contexts for learning, adults involve infants with the same measure of respect and courtesy they would use if conversing with a friend. The caregiver uses the moment as an opportunity for the baby to listen to words in a meaningful situation, to anticipate the sequence of events, and to use emerging skills and concepts. By pausing to give the baby a chance to adjust posture, to notice something, or to take action in some way, the adult shows respect for the fact that the baby needs a moment to connect one action to another in order to build understanding. Chapter 12 explores how to invite infants' participation in each of the care routines—arrivals, departures, meals, naps, diapering, hand washing, toileting, and dressing.

Conversation and Story That Convey the Culture

Conversation and story—the narrative of the culture—provide a third context for learning. From those who provide their care, infants learn the expectations for behavior, as well as the language and the stories of the culture. Adults guide infants in knowing what they may do and what they may not do, within the limits of acceptable behavior. This is an important component of infants' social knowledge. When an adult nods or shakes her head, or gives words of encouragement or discouragement to an infant, these gestures and words help the infant make sense of what to do and what not to do.

Another component of social knowledge is learning the language code. Through conversations, songs, and stories, infants acquire language. Much of this comes through everyday exchanges around meals, diapering, play, and preparing to sleep. Language also is conveyed through regular retelling of shared stories and ritualized rhymes, chants, and games, rich in elements of repetition of the expected, interspersed with elements of surprise. The game of peekaboo is a classic example of such a ritualized game. In fingerplays and ritualized games, infants confirm the expected, while at the same time look for the unexpected (Bruner, 2008). Infants join in such play with delight, as they come to expect a ritualized turn-taking.

Through stories and conversations, adults transmit the customs, beliefs, and expected behaviors of the community, another important component of social knowledge. Through stories, infants learn the expected code for living within the culture. Storytelling, book reading, dramatic art, and visual arts transmit to infants and young children a shared sense of the ordinary. Bruner (2008) suggests that this shared sense of the ordinary is highly rewarding psychologically for infants and young children. It is the shared sense of knowing that comes through story that provides infants and young children with what they need to make sense of those who make up their community. Social knowledge, therefore, is important linguistically, and it also binds infants to others within the culture.

How infants acquire social knowledge is the subject of Chapters 9 and 13. Chapter 9 focuses on how adults support infants' language development, through conversation and story, and Chapter 13 explores how teachers help infants acquire the rules and expectations for behavior. Through everyday conversations and rituals of song, story, and interactive games, adults convey to infants the means for understanding the culture and the community in which they live. Accordingly, conversations and interactions should be seen as part of the broad definition of curriculum, when working with infants.

INFANTS LEARN THROUGH THE LENS OF CULTURE

Scientists who study child development across cultures (Levine et al., 1994; Rogoff, 2003) describe human development as a cultural process. Although babies develop along a predictable trajectory, what they learn is not universal. The skills, concepts, values, and beliefs held common and taught in one culture or community may differ from those in another. Over the course of history, beliefs, attitudes, and expectations transform as well. Therefore, the social knowledge that infants acquire is a function of where they are born, when, and to whom. What infants learn is influenced by the routine ways of doing things in the particular culture and community that surround them.

Divergent Values and Beliefs

There is tremendous variation in how people carry out the everyday routines that organize daily life. Only by taking into account the cultural context that surrounds the family and the child can we begin to make sense of variations in expectations and beliefs about how and what infants should learn. Culture influences in profound ways what we believe is right or wrong, how we expect others to behave, what we think children should learn, and how we think teachers should teach. Differences in values, beliefs, and attitudes about teaching and learning are common in early childhood settings.

Reflect on the values, beliefs, and attitudes in play in the story that follows. This story recounts an infant center director's experience. The infant center serves families employed in agriculture. The families whose infants attend the program are from rural Mexico, as are the teachers. The director, whose heritage is not Mexican, has a degree in child development.

One day I suggested a change in how we feed the infants who were starting to eat pureed food. I explained that many of the infants were capable of grasping the spoon and suggested that we offer the infants a spoon to hold during the feeding to encourage them to feed themselves. This made good sense in light of what I knew about emerging fine motor skills and the babies' interest in using simple tools. Of course, the babies would drop some of the food, which would get smeared on the table, but I saw this mess as insignificant, in light of the benefit of building self-help and motor skills.

What made sense to me, however, made little sense to the families and to the teachers. After our first attempt to let the infants hold a spoon during feedings, most of the teachers and parents saw this plan as messy, chaotic, and of little value. I heard the following complaints and requests: "The babies can't use a spoon without making a mess, so giving them a chance to feed themselves with a spoon is pointless. The babies just play with the spoons. It takes *so* much time to get through the feeding. And then it takes even more time to clean the table, the floor, and their faces! We're better off just spoon-feeding the babies."

Their comments helped me see that my "good idea" had robbed the teachers and the babies of an enjoyable, intimate moment of caring for and being cared for, of offering and receiving. It also had stripped the teachers of the pride and pleasure they felt in maintaining a neat table and a neat child.

Two value systems conflict in this scene. Depending on the value system chosen, one practice can be defended as being right, while the other is rejected as being wrong. On the one hand, infants' learning to do things on their own is valued, and, on the other hand, serving others a neat, tidy meal is valued.

What infants learn reflects the values, beliefs, and attitudes of those who provide their care. Values, beliefs, and attitudes can vary greatly from one person to another. It is not uncommon, within group care of infants, for attitudes and beliefs to diverge around such issues as how to put babies down to sleep, how to discipline them, or how to feed or talk with them (Gonzalez-Mena, 2007, 2013). Understanding how values influence expectations for behavior is a critical skill when working with children from multiple families and when working with other adults. Taking time to

Reflection: Divergent Perspectives—Wrong or Right?

What was your initial response upon reading this vignette? In this vignette, what values inform the beliefs of the director, the teachers, and the families? Do differing values influence what participants see as right or wrong? Consider independence as opposed to dependence. Is one valued more highly by some more than others in this vignette? Consider tidiness and order. Is this valued by some more than others in this scene? What values would influence your attitude and belief if you were the director? What experiences have you had when you felt uncomfortable with someone's behavior or expectations, simply because they were different from yours? Were you tempted to describe such behavior or expectations as wrong or inappropriate?

listen to others' concerns and not judging one idea as absolutely wrong and another as absolutely right give value to diverse perspectives (Derman-Sparks, 2013; Gonzalez-Mena, 2007). Educator and author Louise Derman-Sparks (Mangione, Lally, & Signer, 1993) offers this advice:

> The tendency as a caregiver or a teacher is to think that a behavior that makes me uncomfortable is wrong behavior, is developmentally inappropriate behavior, is unfair to children, or is harmful to children when a good deal of the time it's simply different behavior. It makes us uncomfortable because the power of culture—of our own culture—is so great that anything that isn't like it feels unnatural. (p. 11)

Culturally Respectful Negotiation

In caring for children from multiple families, conflicts inevitably occur. When we are mindful of the impact of deeply embedded cultural beliefs on values, attitudes, and behavior, we can engage in conversations about differences that respect others' ideas and beliefs and simultaneously allow an exchange of ideas that can lead to adaptation and change. Conflicts that arise in caring for babies can be opportunities to expand understanding of others' points of view.

Consider the case of a parent who comes to the teacher upset about paint on his toddler's shirt. The teacher values the painting activity as a learning experience, while the parent values protecting clothes from stains. The teacher does not want to restrict the

Figure 3.3. Steps to Culturally Respectful Negotiation

The following three steps, adapted from the Program for Infant/Toddler Care (Derman-Sparks, 2013), serve as a useful guide for conversations in which participants may differ on values or beliefs:

Acknowledge: Let the parent know that you understand his or her concern. For example, rephrase what you hear to be the issue that has led to the conflict and the parent's feelings related to the issue. "I can tell you are upset that Josiah had paint on his shirt when you picked him up yesterday."

Ask: Ask to find out more about why the parent feels the way he or she does. By asking, you gather information to clarify your understanding of how the parent feels. This must be a genuine request to hear more, as if interviewing the parent to discover his or her beliefs and the ideas behind those beliefs. "I realize that when the toddlers paint, they sometimes get paint on their clothes. I want to hear your ideas so that we can handle this differently in the future. Can you tell me more about your concerns?"

Adapt: Listen to what the parent says, and then ask to hear more. Look for areas of common agreement. Suggest possibilities for a win-win solution. "It sounds like what concerns you most is the cost of having to purchase new clothes when you are unable to get the stain out. Perhaps we could have him wear a large shirt as a smock to cover his own shirt. In your opinion, would that work? You may have some other ideas, so let's think about this together."

Figure 3.4. Knowledge from Infants' Point of View

Getting to Know Self and Others

- Expression of emotion: Engaging with and responding to others through gaze, gesture, or expression
- Relationships: Developing friendships with others
- Recognition of ability: Taking action to influence objects or events
- Empathy: Sharing in the emotional experience of others
- Emotion regulation: Coping with strong feelings
- Respect for limits: Complying with social expectations
- Shared social play: Participating in shared social rituals

Thinking and Reasoning

- Classification: Distinguishing differences
- Seriation: Relating things in order of their differences
- Causality: Detecting the relationship between cause and effect
- Spatial relations: Detecting how things fill, fit in, and move in space
- Representation: Using one thing to symbolize and represent another
- Number and quantity: Noticing differences in number and quantity

Language and Literacy

- Language: Comprehending words
- Expressive language: Using words and phrases to communicate with others
- Conversation: Engaging in increasingly complex communication exchanges
- Interest in print: Engaging with print in books and in the environment

Motor and Perceptual Knowledge

- Perception: Using the senses to track the social and physical environment
- Large-muscle coordination: Moving from place to place in increasingly complex ways
- Fine muscle coordination: Reaching, grasping, and using fingers and hands in increasingly complex ways

Note. Adapted from *California Infant/Toddler Learning and Development Foundations* (California Department of Education, 2009).

child's exploration of the paint, knowing that there is much to learn about the physical properties of liquids. The teacher accepts the risk that paint might get on the toddler's clothes. The parent, on the other hand, does not share this same value. The parent is concerned that he may not be able to get the red paint out of the shirt, and the stained shirt will make the child look unkempt. There may be a cost factor as well, because the parent may be concerned about having to replace a stained article of clothing. Two divergent points of view converge, neither one right or wrong, but this divergence presents an uncomfortable conflict that requires negotiation.

The Program for Infant/Toddler Care (Derman-Sparks, 2013) suggests a three-step process to culturally respectful negotiation. The three steps are illustrated in Figure 3.3. The first step is to acknowledge the concern. Next, ask to find out more about the parent's concern and listen with an open mind. This opens the conversation to all points of view and makes it more likely that ideas on both sides of the conflict will be understood and respected. This, in turn, leads to the third step, which is to adapt meaning to propose possibilities for resolution that may not have been considered before.

FROM RESEARCH TO PRACTICE: NAMING THE KNOWLEDGE—FOUNDATIONS FOR LEARNING

In recent decades, policymakers in education have created standardized descriptions of the concepts and skills children should learn in school. Standards for the birth-to-5 period sometimes are referred to as learning foundations (California Department of Education, 2009), since they describe the foundational knowledge needed for successful achievement in the subsequent years of school. Figure 3.4 (on page 31) provides a list of knowledge foundations commonly described for infants. These knowledge foundations summarize the concepts and skills that infants develop, within each domain—social-emotional, cognitive, linguistic, and perceptual-motor.

These concepts and skills are the foundation for learning in science, mathematics, language arts, fine arts, dramatic art, and physical education. When young children have ample opportunity to play in the company of friends, within a thoughtfully prepared play environment, and when they are invited to participate in daily routines rich in conversation and story, they build concepts, skills, and ideas that provide a foundation for success in school (Hirsh-Pasek, Golinkoff, Berk, & Singer, 2009; Jones & Reynolds, 2011; Zigler, Singer, & Bishop-Josef, 2004).

Looking Back and Looking Forward

This chapter reviewed the theoretical basis for a broad definition of curriculum that takes into account how infants gather and organize information, how they experiment and construct ideas, and how they acquire social knowledge. What infants learn is filtered through the lens of culture. They acquire knowledge about values, beliefs, behaviors, and attitudes from those who provide their care. Because values, beliefs, and attitudes can vary greatly across families, those caring for others' children must adopt a respectful approach to negotiating differences in perspective.

Seen through the eyes of those who study how infants learn, curriculum for infants and toddlers occurs throughout the day, within the play spaces as environments for learning, within care routines that invite infants' participation, and within conversations that make sense to infants.

The next chapter builds on this body of understanding about infants' ways of making meaning and this broad definition of curriculum. Chapter 4 focuses on how to support infants' learning through reflective teaching. Three components of reflective planning are explored—observation, documentation, and interpretation. Together they lead to a reflective cycle of teaching and learning that generates curriculum well-matched to infants' ways of learning.

Observing
Where Teaching and Learning Begin

Stand aside for a while and leave room for learning, observe carefully what children do, and then, if you have understood well, perhaps teaching will be different from before.
(Malaguzzi, 2012, p. 57)

THE PRIOR CHAPTER explored how infants learn much like scientists. They actively explore what objects are like and what they do. They notice small distinctions in the features of people and in their actions and intentions. They relate one thing to another and build concepts and ideas. They acquire the language and beliefs of their culture by watching and listening with focused attention.

Those who work professionally with infants also watch and listen with focused attention to discover what and how infants learn and what and how to teach them. When we take time to truly observe infants, infants readily reveal their thoughts, ideas, intentions, and feelings. Observing is where teaching and learning begin.

This chapter addresses how to systematically observe, reflect, and document in order to plan curriculum, to assess infants' learning, and to engage families. It describes a reflective approach to curriculum, assessment, and family participation, inspired by the philosophy of teaching developed in the schools in Reggio Emilia, Italy. Building on the ideas of leading scientists, educators, and theorists (Brazelton, 2006; Bruner, 1990; Lally, 2000; Rinaldi, 2006b), this chapter provides a road map for discovering what Lally (2000) describes as "infants' own curriculum" (p. 6).

OBSERVING, DOCUMENTING, AND INTERPRETING

Philosophers, psychologists, and educators have long theorized about how learning takes place. Pioneering scientists like Charles Darwin in the mid-19th century and Jean Piaget (Singer & Revenson, 1978) in the mid-20th century carefully observed the behavior of infants in order to explain the human capacity to acquire knowledge. They kept detailed notes about their own children's behavior. Piaget used these observation logs to develop his theory of how children construct knowledge. Observing children, whether within experimental situations in the laboratory or within natural settings, continues to be the primary way scientists learn about what children think, how they think, and why their thinking transforms as they grow older.

For families with infants and for early childhood teachers, observing children and reflecting on what transpires also hold great value. Noted researcher and pediatrician T. Berry Brazelton (2006) advises parents and those working with parents to observe infants in order to gain information about what the infants feel or want and to use this understanding to better inform their relationships with infants. When teacher and parent discuss and interpret what they are observing together, they generate ideas about what might be going on in the mind of the baby, what the baby is discovering, and what questions motivate the play or the interaction.

Infants are quite intentional in their actions and in their play. When we linger to watch their play closely, infants reveal to us, through gestures, expressions, and actions, their intentions, feelings, and ideas. To observe infants for cues as to what they might be thinking, we must be mindfully present. This is different from being actively engaged with a child in play, and it is different from directing the play. Whether for 1 minute or 20 minutes, it means lingering to see what unfolds in order to get a full picture of the play, described by Magda Gerber (2002) as follows:

> Let go of all the other issues that wander through your mind and really pay attention. Focus fully on everything your child does, trying to understand her point of view. Try to observe what interests her, how she handles frustration, solves little problems. Infants do not yet speak our language but they give us many, many signs. (p. 6)

When we are mindfully present as we observe infants' play, we discover that infants generously reveal their assumptions, thoughts, and ideas through actions, gestures, and expressions. We witness a nonverbal narration of intentions, assumptions, and experiments. We see them make predictions and generate theories about how objects relate or how people behave. An infant who shakes a rattle reveals an assumption, that this action will likely produce a sound. Very often it does, but sometimes it does not. Infants notice such differences, and as they notice differences, they evaluate what they assumed to be true with respect to what actually occurred.

We can watch this process in action during infant play. Infants investigate what objects or people are like. They peer at, mouth, and finger and shake objects. They stare and smile at people and gesture toward them to relay their thoughts and intentions. They compare what they find in one object or person with what they find in another. In doing so, they come to know the physical properties of objects and the behavior of people.

Infants pose silent questions, "So what does this feel like, look like, and act like? And what can I make it do? What will happen if I act on it like this?" These questions are hypotheses, much like those used by scientists as they investigate (Gopnik, 2009; Gopnik et al., 1999). An infant's hypothesis, if exploring a rattle, might be, "If I shake this, I think it will make a sound." Infants pose hypotheses, test them out in play, and make assumptions about how things work or why things happen. They form assumptions about how objects or people will respond when acted upon, assumptions that over time are used to construct theories.

Infants spend their waking hours making meaning (Tronick & Beeghly, 2011), that is, figuring out what things are like, what they do, or how they relate. They do this within simple moments of play or interaction with others. Moment by moment, day by day, infants experiment, invent, and construct knowledge. They invite us—those who provide their care—to notice their play and to support them in their experiments. By observing infants' play, we discover how we might support their learning, what Rinaldi (Lally & Mangione, 2006) describes as "possibilities for helping [infants] go deeper in their research." Rinaldi (2006a) explains this as follows:

> We as teachers are asked by children to see them as scientists or philosophers searching to understand some-

thing, to draw out a meaning. . . . We are asked to be the child's traveling companion in this search for meaning. We are also asked to respect the meanings that children produce, the explanatory theories they develop, and their attempts to find and give answers. When we honor the children this way, the children reveal themselves to us. We come to know how they perceive, question, and interpret reality, and to understand their relationships with it. (p. 21)

Teachers and families join infants on a journey in which they are actively getting to know the world. Infants are active participants in charting the course of the journey. The ideas of infants' families and the surrounding community also influence where the journey might lead. Infants, families, and teachers participate together in co-constructing the curriculum, the context for learning, through a process of observing, documenting, and interpreting (Rinaldi, 2006b).

Observing and Documenting

By observing infants, we discover how they gather information and make sense of it. Rinaldi (1994) explains that young children "ask us to listen, to observe, and support them and to render them visible" (p. 59). By rendering them visible, she means carefully documenting significant parts of what they do or say, using notepad and pen, tablet, camera, or recording device. Such documentation makes it possible for teachers and families to read, reflect on, and think together about what might be children's ideas, intentions, or feelings within an episode of play. With note-taking tools and camera, teachers are ready to document at a moment's notice. The value of a written note or a photo is that it holds traces of what children do or say, evidence of children's ideas and thoughts. This evidence, preserved as documentation, is easily shared later with others and mined for ideas on how to best support children's learning.

An effective written observation is descriptive and factual. It is legible in the sense that it paints a clear picture of what children do or say (Rinaldi, 2001), a picture that can be interpreted later as to how children might be building their knowledge or what strategies individual children might be using. A written observation provides a clear account of what occurs, an accurate description of actions, gestures, expressions, and words. The goal is to create an accurate record that can be shared later and discussed with others. Whether through written notes, photos,

or samples of what occurs, teachers preserve significant details of children's experience.

The following illustrates a clear, vivid description of what occurred in a moment of play:

> *Observation:* Patrick crawls toward one of the new baskets, grabs it, and waves it back and forth, watching it move. He mouths the curved edge and then drops it. It lands upright and wobbles on its circular bottom. Patrick stares at the basket as it wobbles round and round, carving a small circle, before slowing to a stop. He retrieves it, rolls onto his side, and with eyes glued to the basket, drops it onto the floor again. It wobbles in a circle as before and then slowly comes to a stop. With open palm, he taps the edge of the basket and sets it wobbling again. He watches it settle to a stop. Again he taps the edge, this time much harder, and watches as the basket flips over. Now upside down, the basket is motionless. Patrick slaps his hand onto the basket. It remains still.

A written record is one form of documentation. Another is to take a still photo or a video clip, which can capture expressions, gestures, timing, or movements, all of which can be significant in relaying a child's idea or intention. To document by means of photography, teachers need a small camera that records both still photos and short videos that can be downloaded for ease of viewing on a computer or tablet.

Reflecting and Interpreting

When written observations and photos are legible and rich in detail, they communicate for those who were not present a clear description of what was seen or heard. While observing, a teacher has impressions and interpretations of what children might be feeling or intending in the moment of play, but these are recorded later. It is important first to record as vividly as possible what children do or say, which can be shared and interpreted later with others.

When we interpret an event, we suggest possibilities for what the child might be intending, feeling, or thinking. For example, "I think he wanted to . . . ," or, "Perhaps he was frustrated because . . . ." As we interpret a child's actions, we reflect on and try to learn from what the child did or said, deducing what the child might be thinking or feeling. This is not always easy, yet legible and vivid documentation generates a wealth of questions and reflections that lead to thoughtful interpretation.

The interpretation below follows up on the prior observation of baby Patrick's play. Teachers discuss what might be Patrick's ideas and thoughts within the moment of observed play.

Interpretation: Patrick appears to be gathering information about the basket. He then experiments with what he can make it do—acting on it and watching it react. He tests to see whether he can repeat an action. It is as if he asks, "So what happens when I push down on the edge of this basket? It wobbles back and forth! Can I make it happen again?" Patrick is constructing a relationship of cause and effect. He appears to have an idea, "If I drop the basket or even just slap it, I can make it move in an interesting way."

When adults review together the photos or written observations of play, they engage in a reflective dialogue, sharing their interpretation of the documentation. Reflective dialogue is also a way for teachers to invite families to join them in support of children's learning. In reflecting together in conversation, they exchange impressions and ideas about what children are thinking and they explore possibilities for what contexts to prepare next to help children go deeper in their research. The goal is to build on what children already appear to be thinking and to invite them to explore related experiences in new contexts that offer new challenges.

Reflective dialogue around documentation occurs later, possibly days or weeks later, at scheduled times dedicated to interpreting the documentation and using it to inform teaching and learning. A reflective dialogue around documentation is not the same as a traditional staff meeting, where the focus is more on program operation. Instead, it is an opportunity to invite children into the process of curriculum planning, to explore what they are thinking, and to plan new contexts for learning.

Documentation preserves the story of how children build knowledge, that is, how they explore, experiment, investigate, analyze, and create. It is a record that can be revisited and shared among teachers, with families, and with children as notes, photos, or work samples. Documentation transports children's ideas, feelings, and thoughts beyond the moment of their occurrence and gives teachers and families access to them later.

Reflection: Work Sample as Documentation

Sometimes, documentation takes the form of a work sample, like a drawing, painting, or something the child has made. A work sample can be something as simple as a piece of paper on which a toddler has made marks. It can provide evidence of what a child might be thinking. Study this toddler's drawing. The child used a sheet of recycled paper, plain on one side and a grid pattern on the other. When she showed her drawing to her mother, she pointed to the circular image surrounded by a series of short lines and said, "This is my front." As she made a mark in the center of this image, she said, "This is my belly button." Then she turned the paper over, and as she did so, said, "And this is my back." On the reverse side, she had drawn a tiny circle with a dot in the middle.
What does this reveal about her thinking and her solution to the problem of how to render her image on a piece of paper?

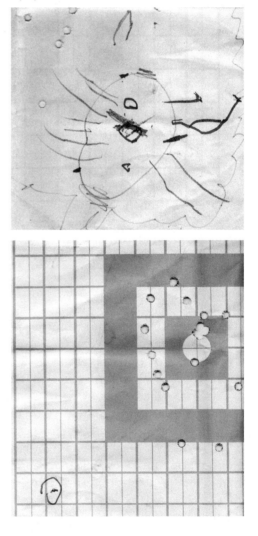

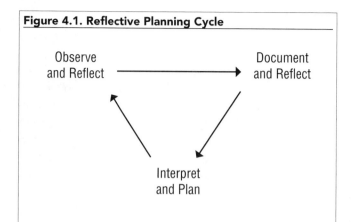

Figure 4.1. Reflective Planning Cycle

Observe and Reflect → Document and Reflect

Interpret and Plan

Rinaldi (2001) describes documentation as "visible listening, as the construction of traces (through notes, slides, videos, and so on) that . . . testify to the children's learning paths and processes" (p. 83). As such, documentation has multiple uses. It generates ideas for curriculum; it provides the data teachers need to assess children's learning; it serves as an invitation to families to think with teachers about how to support children's learning; and it can be shared as story with children, so that they can revisit their experiences.

CURRICULUM PLANNING

A reflective dialogue around documentation invites children's experiences, and consequently their thoughts, into the planning of the curriculum. When teachers study documentation in reflective dialogue, they adopt an attitude of curiosity and wonder, seeking what appears to be the intention or the focus of the observed play or interaction. This generates ideas for what new contexts to prepare next to support children's learning.

Reflective planning is cyclical (California Department of Education, 2012; Maguire-Fong, 2006). The cycle begins with observation and reflection, which generate documentation, that is, descriptive notes, photos, drawings, or other artifacts. Documentation prompts interpretation, from which emerge ideas for planning the next steps to support learning. As teachers implement a plan, the cycle begins anew. They observe what children do in response to the planned encounter, interpret what they see, document moments they wish to remember, and reflect on ways to add complexity or challenge to what they see infants do. Figure 4.1 illustrates this cycle. Although each component is described separately, it is important to

keep in mind that each responds to and builds on the others in a fluid, integrated cycle.

Observation, documentation, and interpretation are the three components of reflective planning. Each is part of a continuous cycle, informed throughout by reflection. As we observe, we reflect; as we document, we reflect; and as we interpret, we reflect. We reflect in the moment as we observe infants, and we reflect later, as we discuss the documentation with others and mine it for clues as to what to offer next to support infants in learning.

What follows is an observation of a moment of play, sparked by an art activity planned by a teacher.

Observation: Mariah squeezes a glue bottle tightly, watching the dribble of glue make a circle on a precut paper shaped like a bear. She sifts through an assortment of plastic eyes and yarn strands in a basket, but then grabs another bear shape from the center of the table, and just as she did with the first one, squeezes a large circle of glue onto it. She flips each of the glue-filled papers onto a large rectangular paper, pressing each with her palm. She drips more glue onto the large paper and uses both hands to spread the glue across the entire surface.

This observation captures how a toddler engages with the materials. It is significant in that it describes vividly what engages the child, that is, what the child does in response to what the teacher offers. It provides clues as to how the teachers can build on what the children know, to extend their learning and render it more complex. A vivid, clear observation generates ideas for what new contexts to offer next. Teachers revisit these notes later and discuss them. They wonder together what it is that this toddler might be thinking and intending. Figure 4.2 provides a glimpse into the reflective dialogue around this documentation. Two teachers discuss the documentation of this toddler's play with the squeeze bottles, glue, and paper. The ideas of one teacher inform and enhance the ideas of the other, leading to a deeper understanding of what might be going on within the mind of the child.

The teachers' conversation, a reflective dialogue, is framed around three key questions. These questions draw out each participant's unique perspective (C. Rinaldi, personal communication, April 15, 2010):

Figure 4.2. Reflective Dialogue:
Interpreting Documentation

Reflective Dialogue: Interpreting Mariah's Play

Teacher A: I think she was trying to make a picture of two bears, which are friends with each other.

Teacher B: But notice how she focuses the entire time on using the glue. She never lets go of the glue bottle. Is her interest really the bears, or is it the glue bottle and how it works?

Teacher A: I hadn't noticed that. When you think about it, she seems to be exploring the glue, what it does on her fingers and how she can move it on the paper.

Teacher B: In a way, she is conducting an experiment, figuring out what the glue is like and how the squeeze bottle works. This is a new tool for the toddlers.

Teacher A: She really is exploring cause and effect here. It might be fun to explore this more and look for some other squeeze tools to add to the play spaces.

Teacher B: And we also might consider more experiences with glue, because the toddlers may need more time to explore what it's like, without using it for a special purpose.

- What do you notice?
- How are the infants revealing their thinking?
- How does this inform the next steps in support of their learning?

In a reflective dialogue, teachers sift through the many layers of the experience, looking for core ideas that emerge in children's thinking. Doing so with others enriches the teaching and the learning. When we reflect with others on documentation and listen to multiple perspectives about what the children intended or thought, we enrich our own thinking with added dimension and clarity. Families bring an important perspective to the documentation as well. Reflective dialogue that invites families to view together a series of photos or a video clip of infants as they play is an engaging way to encourage family participation. Rinaldi (Lally & Mangione, 2006) describes the reflective dialogue as "a sort of metaphorical roundtable in which you want to offer children possibilities for going deeper and deeper in their research."

A reflective conversation around documentation will generate many possible ideas for what to pursue next, spawned by questions like, "What is it that appears to have captured the child's interest in this photo?" or, "What is the child telling me with his movements, gestures, or muscle tone?" or, "What questions appear to be driving the play as they explore these materials?" In observing and reflecting with care, teachers tune in to children's thinking and tie that thinking to what possibilities to offer next, in support of children's learning.

One way to record possible ideas is to write ideas as a web (Figure 4.3). A web starts with a question

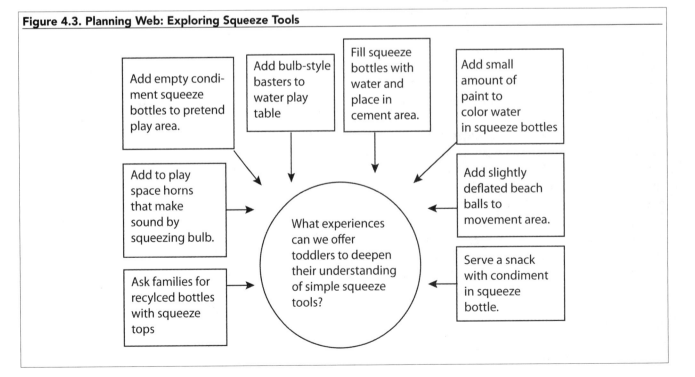

Figure 4.3. Planning Web: Exploring Squeeze Tools

Add empty condiment squeeze bottles to pretend play area.

Add bulb-style basters to water play table

Fill squeeze bottles with water and place in cement area.

Add small amount of paint to color water in squeeze bottles

Add to play space horns that make sound by squeezing bulb.

Ask families for recylced bottles with squeeze tops

What experiences can we offer toddlers to deepen their understanding of simple squeeze tools?

Add slightly deflated beach balls to movement area.

Serve a snack with condiment in squeeze bottle.

Figure 4.4. Plan of Possibilities: Exploring Squeeze Toys

Context: Add squeeze bottles near pans of water in yard and place some in pretend play area, as well.

Planning Question: What will happen when the children encounter squeeze bottles and dishpans of water in the yard and squeeze bottles in the pretend play area?

OBSERVATIONS	INTERPRETATIONS
J. wraps his fingers around the bottle, but no liquid comes out.	A struggle for J., due to his limited finger control. [fine motor] Adapt this? Add pliable bottle, easier to squeeze. This also adds an element of surprise for the others, as they figure out the pressure they need to make water flow.
E. forces a steady stream of water from her squeeze bottle. She looks at J., who frowns and begins to whine. E. reaches over and squeezes J.'s bottle for him. He smiles, but pushes her hand away, squeezes bottle again, but still no water comes out.	E. is aware of J.'s struggle. [empathy]
In pretend play area, R. directs A., "Like this! Put some in the soup."	A. and R. incorporate this simple tool into their pretend play, making soup. [causality; symbolic play]

---

in the middle of a blank page, a prompt to generate ideas for what new contexts might be offered next to help children go deeper in their research. Participants record possible ideas for what to plan next. Figure 4.3 illustrates how teachers use a planning web to record ideas discussed during a reflective dialogue around the documentation of the child's play with the squeeze bottle. The planning web shows possibilities for what they might offer next, as new contexts for play and learning, each connected to an idea revealed in the observed play.

Many ideas might be generated and written on a planning web, and as participants sift through the many possible ideas, they look for agreement on what to offer next, that is, what new context to plan, to engage children's thinking more deeply. In this way, reflective dialogue generates the curriculum.

Figure 4.4 shows the plan that emerged from the reflective dialogue around the documentation of the play with squeeze bottles and glue. It begins with a description of what teachers prepare in order to offer infants a new context for learning. The plan can be thought of as a plan of possibilities. It describes new contexts that the teachers will offer, but it does not dictate what the children will do in response. A planning question frames the experience as an open-ended investigation with phrases like:

- What might happen if we place (specified materials) in the play space?
- What will the infants do when they encounter (a change of some sort) in the play space?
- In what ways will the toddlers respond if we add (a new ritual) to the daily routine?

There are many possibilities for how children will respond to the experiences described in the plan. The children are invited to explore, investigate, invent, connect, transform, or represent as they choose within the new context.

Teachers decide on an idea, prepare the new context and, as they offer it to children, observe and document what the children do in response. The planning is cyclical—as teachers observe, they reflect on how children reveal their thoughts or what captures their interest within the play or interaction, they document this, and they use the documentation later as they reflect and plan new contexts. Children's ideas, expressions, and thoughts guide the curriculum.

A written plan includes a place where teachers record observations as well as interpretations, documenting infants' experience. In the written plan in Figure 4.4, one column is used to record the teachers' observations, that is, significant things to remember about what the children say or do; and a second column is used to record interpretations, that is, teachers' reflections, comments, or thoughts about what the children appear to be thinking, intending, or feeling. Interpretations include notes about concepts or skills that are revealed in the observations, as well as ideas for what to do next to support the children in their research.

The format for preparing a written plan adapts to fit the context. For example, teachers may want to track how individual children explore and work together as they encounter new materials. Figure 4.5 illustrates such a context, when teachers added tubes and balls to the play space, as part of an ongoing exploration of how balls fill, fit in, and move in space.

Figure 4.5. Plan of Possibilities: Investigating Balls and Tubes

Context: Add clear and opaque tubes of different dimensions to toddler play space, along with low baskets with collection of balls.

Planning Questions: How will the toddlers use a variety of balls and long tubes of different sizes? Will the play of one child influence the play of another child?

[4/18, 9 A.M. Inside, connections–construction area]

OBSERVATIONS				INTERPRETATIONS
Ivan	Julia	Ramon	Dyshay	

They wanted to track what individual toddlers did, and also how the play of one influenced the play of another. This format helps teachers record the behavior of each child over time.

Typically, one teacher assumes responsibility for documenting what infants do when a new context is offered. Later, in subsequent reflective dialogue with co-teachers or families, this teacher shares the written notes, photos, or samples of work generated. For the most part, teachers decide in advance what to systematically document within the daily experiences and which tools to use, that is, notes, audio recorder, or camera. However, there will be other moments of spontaneous learning that happen within the course of the day that teachers may wish to document as well.

Reflective curriculum planning is a dynamic search for ways to support children's meaning-making (Rinaldi, 2006b). In reflective planning, children take on the role of researcher, and teachers do so as well. Plans are not restricted to a designated set of actions or learning objectives. Instead, a plan holds open many possibilities for what infants will do as they gather information, relate ideas, and construct concepts, some of which could never have been anticipated by the teacher. Rinaldi (Lally & Mangione, 2006, Disc 2, Chapter 3) asks, "What kind of context, what kind of possibility can you offer to the children for the next step and the next step, not because you know the next step, but because you want to offer [them] a possibility for going deeper and deeper in their research?"

ASSESSING THE LEARNING

Documentation also gives teachers the evidence they need to assess children's learning. As teachers interpret the documentation, they mine it for evidence of concepts and skills revealed in a photo, video clip, or written observation. They note this, naming the concept or skill in evidence (see Figure 4.4). In the documentation of Mariah's play with glue, for example, teachers notice how she appears to be more interested in the squeeze bottle than she is in the paper cut into the shape of a bear. They interpret her exploration of the squeeze bottle to be evidence of the concept of cause and effect, that is, "When I act on it a certain way, I get a predictable reaction." They add a notation, "causality," to the written observation, in order to name the learning in evidence.

A single observation often will provide evidence for more than one assessment measure. In the case of Mariah, who was exploring the glue bottle, the observation reveals evidence for multiple measures of learning. She is building the concept of causality, she is persisting in her approach to problem solving, she is developing fine muscle control, and she is experimenting with pressure and gravity. Ongoing observation and documentation provide the evidence needed to support periodic, formal assessment. Many teachers, especially those working in publicly funded programs, are required to periodically complete a formal child assessment, which is kept in each child's portfolio of development. A portfolio is a file with notes, photos, and samples that provide authentic assessment data and document the story of a child's progress.

The multiple uses of a single piece of documentation can be seen in the example of Mariah's play with glue. The same written observation that the teachers used to plan the next context for curriculum was copied and slipped into Mariah's portfolio as evidence that she is developing a concept of causality, that her fine motor skill allows her to be successful in using a simple tool, and that she is persisting in solving problems. When child portfolios are kept digitally, teachers can easily link written observations or photos to relevant assessment measures for each child.

When working with infants and young children, documentation as a tool for assessing learning has a clear advantage over traditional assessment tools. Traditional assessment tools are composed of a battery of test questions or problems that children must answer or solve. However, they are difficult, if not impossible, to administer with infants and young children. The data captured may not give a true picture of what the child knows or can do (Kamii, 1990). In contrast, systematic documentation, when done regularly, generates multiple examples of children building desired concepts and skills.

ENGAGING FAMILIES

Documentation also serves as an invitation to families to notice and value the skills or concepts made visible within the observed play. When teachers share documentation with infants' families, they invite families to think with them about what their children are learning and possible next steps to extend the learning, whether at home or in infant-care settings. Through observation, documentation, and interpretation, teachers, infants, and their families co-construct the curriculum.

FROM RESEARCH TO PRACTICE: CURRICULUM AS CONTEXT

Teaching in the early years is most effective when children have ample opportunities to engage in meaningful play, well supported by materials and experiences that fascinate them and engage their natural ways of making meaning (Giudici, Rinaldi, & Krechevsky, 2001; Hirsh-Pasek et al., 2009; Singer, Golinkoff, & Hirsh-Pasek, 2006; Zigler et al., 2004). When viewed from this perspective, curriculum is best understood as a context for learning, rather than as simply a lesson or a series of lessons or activities based on a theme. The reflective approach to curriculum described in this chapter takes full advantage of infants' natural urge to explore and investigate. This sets it apart from curriculum composed of lessons or activities intended to teach a specific skill and also distinguishes it from curriculum designed around themes.

The following excerpt from an interview with a teacher in a Reggio Emilia infant center (Gandini, 2001) illustrates the dynamic and contextual nature of reflective curriculum and provides a good contrast to activity-based curriculum or theme-based curriculum. The teachers are discussing an investigation they did with a group of toddlers. After visiting the ocean with his family, a toddler brought sea urchins to school to share with friends. In this excerpt, the teachers discuss what contexts they might provide to support the children's curiosity about these new and different creatures.

> We thought to offer the children some magnifying lenses so the children could see more closely and look inside the sea urchins. We also decided to place some mirrors of different dimensions on the table to change the points of view and to look at the sea urchins from different sides. In a sense, we were rendering the situation more complex. When it was placed on the mirror, the sea urchin was indicating the multiple aspects of its one image to the children. We teachers experimented together about a graphic language that small children could use to interpret the sea urchin. We opted for thin black markers and white paper. (p. 63)

This investigation is sparked by documentation of a chance encounter with an item that one child brought from home. The teachers noticed how the item captured the children's interest, and they built on this interest.

This example points to a clear distinction between reflective curriculum and theme-based curriculum. In theme-based curriculum, teachers plan activities that relate in some way to a prechosen theme. Children do the activities, but how they respond to the activities has little bearing on what gets planned next. Imagine how sea urchins would fit into theme-based curriculum. In a theme-based approach to curriculum, the teachers might reserve any mention of sea urchins for a predetermined week in which the chosen theme was oceans and marine life. With this theme, they might plan a finger-painting activity with blue-green paint; add plastic sea animals to a water table; sing a song about slippery fish; and read a story with a fish as the main character. In the minds of the teachers, each activity relates in some way to oceans. However, in the mind of a child, this connection may not yet exist. While the children might enjoy each experience, most likely they would end the week having learned little about creatures living in the sea. If the goal is to support children in getting to know creatures living in the sea, an investigation like the one described by the Reggio Emilia teachers is a better curriculum fit.

Reflective curriculum differs from theme-based curriculum with respect to the use of time, as well. Teachers doing theme-based curriculum typically cycle through a new theme each week, irrespective of children's growing interest, mastery, or understanding of the topic. In contrast, teachers who use reflective planning observe children's play to guide the schedule of events. Some investigations last a few days and others a few weeks. In essence, teachers co-construct the schedule with the children by observing the play to discover how the children are engaging with the materials, how they are making and solving problems with the materials, how they are building more complex or coherent understanding, and whether they enjoy what the materials offer.

In settings where teachers are expected to work with predetermined themes, the creative teacher can still adopt an attitude of reflection and create investigations within the themes. For example, a predetermined theme of plants and how they grow might play out as, "How might infants respond if, each day, we put in the play space a different kind of herb, using bundles of pruned stems from an herb garden, one day lavender, another rosemary, and another spearmint? Also, in what ways might we draw the families into this investigation?" An attitude of investigation and inquiry is maintained, even within an overall frame of predetermined themes.

Looking Back and Looking Forward

Curriculum for infants and young children is a journey that can and should follow diverse and equally scenic paths. The journey for each group of children in infant care is unique, designed to match the pursuits of the infants, families, and teachers who make up that group. Rinaldi (1994) explains that when teachers see their role as wise traveling companions to meaning-making children, they are able to weave the desired learning foundations into everyday pursuits. As artful navigators, they know how to observe and listen to children's play in order to plan the curricular route and to construct contexts rich in possibilities for building foundational knowledge.

Reflective planning aligns teaching and learning with infants' ways of making meaning. It supports infants in pursuing their innate urge to explore, experiment with, and construct understanding of the world around them. It is co-constructed among infants, teachers, and families. Teachers and infants' family members observe and listen to discover infants' ideas, feelings, and interests. They document their observations, and by reflecting on what was observed, they prepare new contexts for learning. They look for patterns of play that emerge in a group, and they chart individual children's progress. Each child's journey takes a distinct path, and each group of infants enjoys a unique journey. To serve the interests of diverse families and communities, the curriculum is not prescribed in a set series of activities. Instead, it is responsive to the group of infants, teachers, and families who form the infant community.

Reflective curriculum is more than a selection of activities slotted into boxes on a lesson plan, and it is more than a smattering of activities related to a theme. Carefully planned, reflective curriculum is dynamic and flexible, open to change in response to children's pursuits. Chapters 5 through 9 include examples of how teachers engage in reflective planning to support infants' learning across all domains of development—emotional, social, motor, cognitive, and language.

Part II

WHAT INFANTS LEARN

THE PRIOR PART of the book established a foundation for how infants learn. This part examines what they learn. This series of chapters explores what knowledge looks like from the infant's point of view, using key research as a foundation. Chapter 5 explores what infants learn through the lens of emotional development, with an overview of infants' first feelings. Chapter 6 expands this discussion to look at how infants learn about self and other, the genesis of social understanding, using key research from studies of infants' social development. Chapter 7 provides a framework for understanding motor development and movement patterns, how infants organize their bodies to take action. Chapter 8 examines infants' cognitive development, with descriptions of how infants build concepts and ideas. Chapter 9 concludes this part by examining how infants acquire language, within a shared social context.

CHAPTER 5

First Feelings
Emotional Development

How is it that some children become happy and curious, whereas others become sad and withdrawn, and still others become angry and unfocused? My answer is that these different outcomes are related to . . . the balance of the child's success or failure during his or her social-emotional interactions.
(Tronick, 2007, p. 172)

T HERE ARE MANY things that make babies special, and primary among them is the fact that they have a way of endearing themselves to even the most stoic. With open gaze, expectant smile, and pleading cry, infants have the power to engage hearts and minds, weaving an emotional bond of connection with those who provide their care. This chapter focuses on how infants build this emotional bond of connection and explores how they make sense of feelings, their own and those of others, and how they form patterns of expectation about how others will make them feel and how they will feel about others.

Underlying the vague concept of feelings is a physiological process. When infants are rocked, hugged, smiled at, spoken to, and seen with love and affection by the caregiver, they experience, through touch, smell, sight, sound, and movement, physical sensations that Perry (2014a) describes as a "somatosensory bath." The sight of a face, the touch of a hand, and the sound of a voice are sensations that babies knit together, through connected circuits of neurons. These circuits generate feelings of safety, security, and calm. A baby who feels seen and soothed builds neural pathways of safety and security, and a baby who is neglected and whose cries bring no relief builds pathways that expect rejection.

ATTACHMENT

The emotional tie that forms between baby and caregiver is often described as attachment. Attachment is

Research Highlight: When Relationships Are Absent

Dr. Rene Spitz (1949), a psychiatrist inspired by Bowlby's work, studied the fate of orphaned and hospitalized children, who were reared without the close physical contact of a parent or trusted caregiver. During the 1940s, many hospitals adopted policies that reduced human contact for hospitalized or institutionalized infants. This policy was intended to limit the transmission of germs and disease. Many hospitalized or orphaned infants were fed and clothed, kept warm and clean, but were never played with or held. Spitz filmed some of these infants in their cribs. The film footage depicts desperately sad infants, some crying incessantly, some withdrawn and rocking repetitively, and all clearly revealing the traumatic impact of abandonment and emotional loss. Many of these infants became ill and some died. Spitz, like Bowlby, concluded that to survive and prosper, infants need an emotional bond with a caring adult.

an enduring relationship that binds infant and caregiver together in time and space (Ainsworth, Blehar, Waters, & Wall, 1978). Scientist John Bowlby was one of the first to use the term attachment for this relationship. As a research scientist, Bowlby was interested in the environment that surrounds the baby and suggested that the instinctive patterns of behavior that babies are born with serve an important purpose—to keep the baby emotionally attached to the parent, which ensures protection and survival. Bowlby's ideas became the basis for a theory known as attachment theory (Bretherton, 1992).

Secure and Insecure Attachment

Researcher Mary Ainsworth (Bretherton, 1992), a colleague of Bowlby, studied the conditions that lead to attachment between infant and parent. Ainsworth recruited families who agreed to have researchers observe their caregiving at regular intervals in their homes during the year following the baby's birth. Observers recorded detailed narratives of face-to-face exchanges, separation situations, and episodes of crying, as well as how the baby explored and how the baby approached the parent.

Analysis of the observations showed a clear pattern with respect to the way parents noticed and responded to babies' signals. Some parents picked up their infants fairly soon after the babies began to cry. Others were less responsive, either waiting before responding or responding unpredictably. This pattern yielded an interesting result. Young babies whose cries were responded to swiftly tended to cry less at 12 months of age, when compared with babies whose parents were less responsive (Bell & Ainsworth, 1972).

When the babies in her study reached 1 year of age, Ainsworth created an experiment to find out whether the patterns of care she saw in the home influenced how infants played and explored and also how they influenced the baby's response when separated from the parent. Her experiment is known as the Strange Situation. She invited each parent–infant pair to a playroom. From an adjacent room with a one-way window, a researcher observed and recorded how the baby played, with the parent present. Then a stranger joined the baby and parent in the playroom. In a few minutes, the parent was asked to leave briefly. The parent returned and then the stranger left. This separation sequence revealed an interesting finding. The majority of children in the study responded as you would expect. While the mothers were out of the room, the infants stood near the door, some of them crying. When the mothers returned, the infants approached and sought contact, with outreached arms. Once comforted, the babies quickly resumed play with the toys in the room.

However, not all the infants showed this pattern. Some, described by Ainsworth as avoidant, snubbed the mother upon her return to the room, looking or turning away or refusing to interact with her when she attempted to engage the child in play. Another group, described as ambivalent, protested loudly when the mother left, but seemed angry with her when she returned, while at the same moment trying to seek contact. When picked up, these infants were difficult to soothe and often pushed away from the mother while in arms or pushed away toys she offered (Ainsworth et al., 1978).

Ainsworth coded these patterns of attachment as secure, insecure avoidant, and insecure ambivalent. When she compared these patterns with the parents' responsiveness at home, she found that secure infants had experienced responsive interactions; avoidant infants had experienced less responsive interactions, some characterized by resistance to close body contact; and ambivalent babies had experienced inconsistent responses when they tried to engage, sometimes getting a response and sometimes being ignored.

Ainsworth suggested from her findings that patterns of everyday care establish enduring bonds of attachment. If the bond of attachment is secure, it establishes in the infant an expectation that there will be a secure base to rely on and return to, when in need of help or solace. This sets up a pattern of harmonious interactions. If the bond of attachment is insecure, the infant comes to expect that he or she cannot rely on the caregiver as a secure base and cannot predict that the caregiver will offer help, comfort, or solace. This establishes a pattern of problematic interactions.

Attachment as Secure Base

Infants who have secure relationships with those who provide their care use them as a secure base from which to explore and as a safe haven to return to when tired, frustrated, or afraid (Powell, Cooper, Hoffman, & Marvin, 2009). This is easy to see when infants are contentedly playing on their own. They periodically make eye contact with the caregiver or return briefly to check in with the caregiver (Mahler, Pine, & Bergman, 1975). One way of interpreting this pattern of reconnecting and using the caregiver as a secure base is to see it as the infant getting emotionally refueled with the feeling of goodness that comes in the caregiver's presence. Once refueled, the infant is prepared to move away and explore, knowing the emotional tie to the caregiver remains.

Infants appear to be acutely aware of the presence of the one who will keep them safe and secure. In a study of 14-month-olds, Johnson, Dweck, and Chen (2007) wanted to find out whether an infant's attachment status influenced the infant's perception of the caregiver as a secure base. The researchers found that infants assessed as insecure in their attachment to the caregiver appeared to expect the caregiver to move *away* from a distressed infant, rather than move *closer* and give comfort to a distressed infant. The researchers interpreted this to mean that in the short

Reflection: Difficult Behavior—Seeking Safety

When infants or young children throw temper tantrums or hit others in a fit of anger or defiance, sometimes they hurt others and sometimes they hurt themselves. Caregivers often label such behavior as "unsafe" and restrict, chastise, or punish the child in response. However, is it possible that for some children, defiance and anger are a way to stay safe, that is, a way to protect themselves? When those charged with protecting children fail to protect them, or scare them rather than comfort them, is it possible that children have no one to turn to but themselves for protection or comfort? When a young child lashes out at others in anger, is it possible that the child's prior experiences have made this a reasonable response? If a child has learned to expect rejection rather than consolation in the face of distress, pushing people away prevents the overwhelming fear and sadness that come from being rejected. Children who have learned to expect rejection in the face of distress protect themselves from being rejected by lashing out at others or ignoring them. Defiant behavior can be a child's disguised plea for help.

span of a year, infants who experience unresponsive or inconsistent care learn that, when distressed, the *expected* experience is to be ignored or rejected by the caregiver. In contrast, infants who experience a pattern of responsive care expect the caregiver to approach and offer comfort to an infant in distress.

Such studies provide a cautionary lesson for those caring for infants and young children. When a child shows a pattern of difficult behavior, it may be a consequence of the child having a distorted expectation about how others will react in response to the child's need, desire, or intent. If, when in need, a child expects to be rejected rather than helped by others, it makes sense that the child would push others away or reject overtures to help. Difficult behavior may be a disguised plea for help in the face of fear, sadness, rejection, or anger, that is, a "lost" child simply seeking a safe haven. With thoughtful intervention and guidance, these patterns can change. Chapter 13 reviews strategies for guiding children's behavior when patterns of difficult behavior emerge.

Research shows a clear connection between attachment patterns formed early in life and difficulties with interpersonal relationships later in life (Schore, 2002; Siegel & Hartzell, 2003). This underscores the importance of teachers and families incorporating social-emotional concerns into the broad definition of infant curriculum.

HOW BABIES RESPOND TO STRESS

Babies rely on a relationship with a trusted caregiver to help them navigate the emotional ups and downs of life. However, their reliance on relationships with others makes them vulnerable when the experiences they encounter with others bring undue stress instead of satisfaction. Babies face moderate levels of stress on a regular basis, like the discomfort of a wet diaper, a hunger pang, or fatigue. However, high or prolonged levels of stress can unleash a cascade of stress hormones that threaten the baby's developing brain. This is of grave concern, considering that babies are busy building brain structures that will last a lifetime.

Stress Response System

Just like adults, babies have a stress response system designed to alert them and to help them take action in response to threat. The stress response system of the brain is made up of an integrated complex of neurons

Research Highlight: Impact of Stress on Babies' Brains

At moderate levels, cortisol helps us cope with stressful situations. However, when secreted at high levels, it has negative effects (Gunnar, 1998).

- Weakens the immune system, which increases risk of illness.
- In laboratory animals, damages cells in a brain structure called the hippocampus. In humans, the hippocampus is involved in learning and memory. It develops during the first year of infancy. Infants with higher cortisol levels show reduced activity in the hippocampus.
- Impacts the part of the brain that allows us to selectively pay attention, putting child at risk of impaired ability to regulate attention.
- May lower the activation threshold of the amygdala, the "fire alarm" of the brain, making it more likely that a child will lash out at others when uncertain or afraid.
- May compromise the ability to act appropriately in social situations, due to impact on brain regions that process information about people.

that work closely together. Some of these neurons originate in the brainstem and extend upward to higher regions of the brain, and others extend downward to the heart and other organs. These neurons make it possible for a message that enters the brain to be relayed instantaneously to many different parts of the body.

Sensations from within the body, like hunger, or sensations from outside the body, like a loud, angry voice, are relayed to a structure in the limbic region of the brain called the amygdala. The amygdala is referred to as the fire alarm of the brain, because it monitors incoming sensory information for signs of danger or threat. If danger or threat is detected, the amygdala signals a release of stress hormones into the blood stream, carrying the message, "This is important! Pay attention! Something is not right!"

One of the stress hormones released is called cortisol. At moderate levels, cortisol supports the ability to pay attention and to cope with everyday challenges. However at high levels, it can negatively impact brain structures that are developing during infancy (Gunnar, 1998).

Relationships Buffer Stress

Of concern to scientists who study the developing brain is what happens when babies experience frequent and prolonged bouts of stress. In stressful situations, the baby's nervous system reduces output of energy for exploration and learning, in exchange for increased energy to regulate the internal organs in response to threat. This is illustrated in a classic experiment called Still Face (Tronick, 1989). A mother is asked to play face to face with her baby, while a camera records the mother's face. Another camera simultaneously records the baby's face. After several minutes of play, the mother is asked to adopt a still face and look down. This experiement, conducted with a wide variety of infants and parents, reveals a clear pattern of infant response. In response to the mother's still face, the baby squirms, cries, and reaches and points to the mother in a desperate attempt to get her to re-engage. After a few minutes, the mother is asked to resume play with the baby as normal, and the baby recovers.

Two findings stand out in the Still Face research. The first is the remarkable, rapid disorganization of the baby's physiological system. The second significant finding is how well babies recover and resume play, as soon as the mother drops the still face and

Research Highlight:
Infant Response to a Still Face

Using two cameras, one to record the infant's expression and one to record the parent's expression, researcher Ed Tronick (1989) recorded engaged face-to-face play between parent and infant, and then he asked the parent to adopt a still face for several minutes. The findings were the same across many pairs of infants and parents. The infants worked hard to capture the attention of the parent, using big smiles, gestures, and very intent gazes, but the parent did not respond to the infant in any way. The infants began to fuss, to look and turn away, to clasp their hands together, to suck their thumbs, and to show changes in skin color. Some began to drool and hiccup. These are all signs of stress. After several minutes of maintaining a still face, the parent returned to engaged play with the infant. The infant showed clear signs of relief and happily resumed play.

begins to respond to the baby's overtures to engage. The Still Face experiment illustrates babies' resilience in the face of the ordinary messiness of infant–caregiver interactions (DiCorcia & Tronick, 2011; Tronick, 2007). In a typical pattern of interaction, sometimes caregiver and baby are in synch with each other, and sometimes they are not. For example, when the baby fusses and the caregiver responds with an expression of empathy, this is a match. However, a mismatch is also common, as when the baby looks to the caregiver, yet in that moment the caregiver is looking away. In most instances, the caregiver looks back, and once again there is a match.

Tronick emphasizes that it is the overall pattern of mismatch followed by repair that matters. This pattern of rupture and repair helps babies learn that losing contact with the caregiver is not a cause for alarm. Babies learn to cope with the messiness of social interaction. Although the baby's stress level may increase a bit on the mismatch, it decreases on the match, always staying within a healthy, manageable range. It is the oscillation that occurs within the everyday course of responsive care that helps babies build resilient stress response systems. Tronick uses the term *mutual regulation* to describe this infant–caregiver dynamic, in which the feelings and states of the caregiver influence the feelings and states of the baby, and vice versa. Through mutual regulation, the caregiver helps the baby organize and regulate physiological systems, like breathing, blood flow, and heartbeat.

One explanation for how mutual regulation works may be found in a specialized nerve called the vagal nerve (Porges, 2001). This specialized nerve speeds the relay of sensory information and allows us to take action in response to threat. The vagal nerve has long fibers that innervate the eyes, ears, face, and vocal cord, and these long fibers extend through the brainstem all the way down to the heart and other internal organs. In the face of threat, the vagal nerve transmits sensory signals quickly to the heart and other organs of the body, triggering immediate response. When a baby sees a facial expression, hears a vocal pattern, or senses a touch, the baby's nervous system quickly analyzes it for safety or threat. If coded as a threat, the baby's nervous system quickly relays a signal to the heart to either beat faster or slow down, in order to calm or to alert.

In less than a fraction of a second, the vagal nerve can send a signal to the heart to change pace in order to respond to the source of challenge. The vagal nerve acts on the heart much like a brake acts on a tire. When the brake is on, the vehicle slows down. When the vagal brake is on, the heart rate slows, keeping a sense of calm. When we experience unusual or prolonged stress, our vagal brake is released. With the brake off, our heart rate increases, our breathing and blood flow accelerate, our body temperature rises, and our skin tone changes, in response to stress and to prepare for action.

Relationships that infants form with trusted caregivers buffer the full impact of stress. When infants experience predictable, reliable relationships with caregivers, they use what they feel, hear, and see to build their capacity to regulate the amount of stress hormone produced by their bodies. This means that when they are upset or frightened, they are able to respond without triggering secretion of high levels of stress hormones. For example, the experience of be- ing poked by a sharp needle tends to trigger a flood of stress hormones into the blood stream. However, during a baby's routine immunization, if the baby is held in the arms of a trusted caregiver, the level of cortisol in the baby's system does not increase markedly (Gunnar, Brodersen, Nachmias, Buss, & Rigatuso, 1996). The presence of a trusted person, with whom the baby has a secure relationship, buffers the impact of stress hormones on the developing brain.

Of concern is what happens when babies experience neglect and do not have the benefit of the mutual regulation that happens within predictable, reliable relationships. If babies experience frequent or prolonged bouts of stress, the integrity of brain structures that are undergoing development may be compromised. Of additional concern is that brain structures formed early in development are very resistant to change (Perry, 2008; Perry & Marcellus, 2013). When babies build into their brains patterns of behavior that are maladaptive, these patterns endure, with consequences that can persist throughout life. The earlier a structure forms in the brain, the more difficult it will be to modify or repair later, through therapy.

A baby who experiences frequent activation of the stress response system may build brain structures that are accustomed to high levels of stress. A child may be so sensitive to the negative emotions of others that he may anger easily, react impulsively, or hit others without provocation. Also, too much stress in the early years, without the benefit of strong relationships, may compromise a child's ability to engage with others, to build healthy relationships with others, to pay attention, and to learn (Perry & Marcellus, 2013; Siegel & Hartzell, 2003).

PLANNING FOR INFANTS' EMOTIONAL DEVELOPMENT

Helping infants cope with strong feelings is a big part of teaching and learning when working with infants and their families. For infants immersed in learning about themselves in relation to others, coping with strong feelings *is* their curriculum and it should become part of the planning. There are many possibilities for infants to build trust, self-confidence, and a broad array of emotions that include joy, satisfaction, and pride in accomplishment. Infants learn about emotions—their own and those of others—within ordinary moments and from simple interactions and

---

Reflection: Butterflies in the Stomach

Think of a time when you may have seen something or heard something that made you uneasy and nervous. You might recall feeling a sensation in your stomach at the same time. You may have heard the phrase, "I have butterflies in my stomach," or, "I feel it in the pit of my stomach," connected to this sensation. Consider these phrases in relation to the work of the vagal nerve. Keep in mind how the fibers of this nerve innervate the eyes, nose, ears, and skin, and extend down to the organs in the chest and the abdomen.

conversations. Observing when infants are sad, joyous, or anxious and documenting the situation that prompts these feelings is the starting point for creating contexts to support infants' learning about their feelings and those of others.

Separation and Sadness: Opportunities for Learning

One of the most emotionally difficult transitions infants face is separating from those they love. For many infants, sadness, confusion, and fear are overwhelming when those they love leave for extended periods of time. These feelings are made worse when family members depart without the infant seeing them leave. Infants scan the room in search of familiar family faces or voices. Finding none, they may erupt in frantic tears and cry for hours, preoccupied with a search for their family.

Family members, as well as infants, experience sadness and uncertainty when faced with the ordeal of departing and leaving their infants with others. They may want to avoid seeing their infant's sadness and fear, and may think that if they sneak out, the infant will not see them leave and therefore will not be sad or afraid. These are understandable responses, because parents want to protect their children from sadness and fear, yet they are problematic. The problem arises in that babies *do* notice the family's absence, once family members are gone, and *do* notice that those caring for them are not the same as their family. Sneaking out confuses infants and erodes trust.

Moments of separation can be trying and awkward for teachers, as well. Teachers may want the infant to get over the sadness quickly, in order to join activities. They may resent the time required to soothe the upset child who cries incessantly following the family's departure. However, departures present rich opportunities for learning.

Much infant distress can be alleviated when infants and their families are allowed to transition gradually from home to group care over the course of days or weeks. When given the chance to spend time with the parent in the group-care setting, infants get used to the new faces and the new environment, within the safe arms of those they know and trust. Program policies should be designed so that teachers invite parents to spend whatever time is necessary with their infant in the group-care setting before departing.

Reflection: An Italian Model for Adjustment to Group Care

An inspiring model for transitioning infants and their families to group care can be found in northern Italy (Bove, 2001), where an infant's adjustment to being cared for by others is regarded as a delicate period of transition. This period spans several weeks, giving the infant time to become accustomed to the new setting. When the family and the teachers first meet, they spend a few hours together at the center during the first days. The infant observes and plays, the parent observes and talks with the teachers, and gradually the parent and infant increase the duration of their daily stays, during which time the parent participates in the care routines. Teachers observe to learn the patterns of care between infant and parent. When the parent is ready, the baby begins to stay on his or her own with the teachers at the infant center.

Consider what this experience might feel like for infants, for their families, and for the teachers. What might be the barriers to instituting such a policy? What thoughts do you have for confronting those barriers?

Good-Bye Rituals

It is helpful to plan with the family a departure ritual, one that is repeated each day, inviting the infant to actively participate. In reflective dialogue with families, teachers can acknowledge the families' perspective with a phrase like, "It is hard to think about your baby being upset when you leave." They can bring the baby's perspective into the dialogue as well, by saying, "Babies are often sad when they see their parents leave. This sadness cannot be avoided. Let's explore how we might help your baby learn to make sense of your leaving. If we do, over time, she will come to associate the sadness of seeing you leave with the joy that comes when you return."

The goal of such a reflective dialogue is to acknowledge a family's desire to protect the baby from sadness and to invite the family to consider how the baby is trying to make sense of this emotionally trying experience (California Department of Education, 2010). After acknowledging the parents' feelings, teachers ask the family for ideas on how to handle the departure. Families propose ideas, as do teachers, making sure that the baby sees the parent wave good-bye and hears the parent say good-bye, as the parent exits. Teachers can reassure parents that although the

---

Figure 5.1. Plan of Possibilities: A Good-Bye Ritual

Planning Question: Will J.'s anxiety on separating from his family be reduced by adopting a good-bye ritual? (8/12–15)
Context: Morning separation: J.'s father says good-bye and that he will be back, as he waves to J., making sure J. is watching as he does this. During the day, offer J. a photo of his family to keep with him. Reunion: J.'s father says, "I'm back!" as he greets J.

Observations	Photos	Interpretation

---

baby is sad, the baby is actively making sense of the experience, seeing and hearing the departure and, in time, relating the departure to the reunion.

By being part of the good-bye ritual, babies have the certainty of knowing that the parent has departed. They associate the phrase, "Good-bye. I will be back," with, "Hello! I came back!" The sadness of departure is real, but if given the experience of a departure ritual, babies begin to make sense of it. Separation rituals also support infants in building trust. Figure 5.1 illustrates how teachers and parents together develop a plan to support infants in coping with separation.

When parents and teachers acknowledge sadness, instead of ignoring it or trying to change it, they help infants cope with the overwhelming nature of sadness and help them make sense of it. By recounting the story of what happens when the parent leaves and returns, parents and teachers provide a coherent narrative of separating from loved ones, a narrative that toddlers literally keep in mind throughout the day. This story helps toddlers make sense of and cope with separation.

Once a parent has departed, teachers help infants confront their sadness and cope with the uncertainty of being in the hands of someone who looks different, sounds different, and responds in different ways. A respectful way to help infants through this transition is to avoid looking the baby in the eye, to read the baby's nonverbal cues as to whether the baby wants to be held, and to acknowledge the baby's sadness: "I can tell you are really missing Mom. She just left, didn't she? That makes you sad." These words name the strong feeling of sadness and give it value. By describing the departure, before the parent leaves as well as after the parent has left, the teacher tells the story of what is happening in a way that helps the infant hold this story in mind. Even for very young infants, this is important.

For some infants, the sadness of separation can last for hours. When the teacher acknowledges the child's plight, the child feels "felt," a resonance that calms the child (Siegel & Hartzell, 2003) and in turn calms the teacher, an example of mutual regulation. The frantic sense of peril that comes with the abandonment of separation gives way to sensations of safety and security.

Simple conversations help infants hold their families in mind when the families are gone (Pawl, 2006). Talking with the child about the family's absence lets the child know that his family holds him in mind, too, when family members are away. This can be done in a variety of ways. For example, a sad young toddler might enjoy sitting with the teacher and writing a note to the parent, a note that holds in words what the child says or might be feeling, like, "Shall we write that Jerome is sad and that he misses his Dad?" Inviting the child to think with the teacher about what to do with the note, where it might be kept, and to whom it might be given is an additional way that the teacher makes it possible for the child to hold his family in mind and in so doing, to keep the overwhelming impact of sadness at bay. A laminated photo of family members that a child can carry with him provides a ready, reassuring reminder for the child who is missing his family.

Reflection:
Protective Urges and the Ritual of Saying Good-Bye

In infant-care settings, it is not uncommon for departing parents to be reluctant to call attention to the fact that they are leaving. Why do you think this is so? When parents want to depart quickly, unseen by the baby, what consequences are there for the parent? What consequences are there for the baby?

Reflect on how you might wonder with the parent about what the infant might be experiencing, when the parent leaves unseen. When the baby suddenly looks around and does not find the parent there, does this impact the baby? If so, how? How might you acknowledge the parent's protective instinct to shelter her child from experiencing the sadness of seeing her depart? What are some possibilities you would suggest for a good-bye ritual?

Figure 5.2. Planning Web: Ideas to Help with Separation

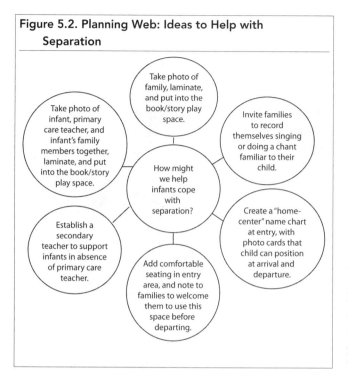

Some children appreciate being held or physically comforted when sad, while others resist such contact. Through nonverbal cues, infants alert the caregiver as to when to approach and when to stay back. Some children need time to assess the new situation and are more relaxed when the adults do not attempt to engage them in play. A way to respectfully engage a sad child in play, especially one who is entering group care for the first time without the parent, is to use indirect contact (Lally, 2011b), a strategy in which the teacher begins to play quietly with a toy placed between the child and the teacher. This often engages the child's interest in the toy as well. When the child appears ready, the teacher begins to engage with the child, as well as with the toy. The toy becomes the indirect point of contact between the child and the teacher. The child feels more comfortable playing with the toy than he does looking at or listening to a stranger. Time spent exploring a toy that attracts the interest of the teacher as well, and gives the child a chance to adjust to being with this new and strange person.

Figure 5.2 provides an example of how teachers use a planning web to propose possibilities for how to ease the sadness and dismay infants encounter as they adjust when left in the care of others. Some ideas on the planning web propose possibilities for arranging the environment; some for adapting a care routine; and some for providing or modifying a recurring interaction or conversation. Each idea represents a possible direction for what to offer next and places infants' attempts to make sense of strong emotions at the center of the curriculum plan.

FROM RESEARCH TO PRACTICE: INFANT MENTAL HEALTH

Infants cared for by responsive caregivers tend to grow into children who are happy, socially competent, resilient, empathic, persistent in solving problems, and willing to seek help when needed. Infants cared for by cold, unreliable, or erratic caregivers tend to grow into children who are distant, hostile to authority, more inclined to be mean, reluctant to ask for comfort, lacking in self-confidence, and dependent on others for help in solving problems (Siegel & Hartzell, 2003). Although *mental health* is not a term often associated with babies, infants and young children are vulnerable to the adverse effects of parental mental health problems, poverty, and domestic violence (Committee on Integrating the Science of Early Childhood Development, Board on Children, Youth, and Families, National Research Council, 2000).

The research reviewed in this chapter shows clearly that even very young infants are able to react to the intentions and emotions of others (Brazelton, 2006; Tronick, 2007). When relationships are strong, infants build a healthy emotional foundation. When they are weak, that foundation is imperiled. For a variety of reasons, infants may come to see themselves as helpless and hopeless and withdraw (Tronick & Beeghly, 2011), becoming apathetic and depressed. Other infants, who have regularly experienced threat or danger, may become hypervigilant, anxious, hyperactive, or perseverative. Still others may show patterns of dysregulated behavior or have difficulty making sense of themselves in relation to others (e.g., those with autistic spectrum disorders). These aberrant forms of meaning-making disrupt an infant's ability to master many emerging developmental skills, especially those related to social or emotional development (Harrison, 2005; Tronick & Beeghly, 2011).

A field known as infant mental health, or infant–family mental health, has emerged to address the growing concerns related to aberrant social-emotional development during infancy. Infant and family mental health programs have been established in many communities to support strong, flexible, secure, stable, and responsive relationships between infants and caregivers, whether within infants' homes or within group care.

Reflection: Missing Someone Special—
Being Held in Mind

Reflect on how teachers support this toddler as he makes sense of the sadness that overcame him when his primary care teacher left for the day. How do the teachers turn a moment of sadness into a context for learning? The teachers posted this documentation near the entry in hopes that it would help reveal to parents how coping with strong emotions is one of the earliest and most important contexts for learning.

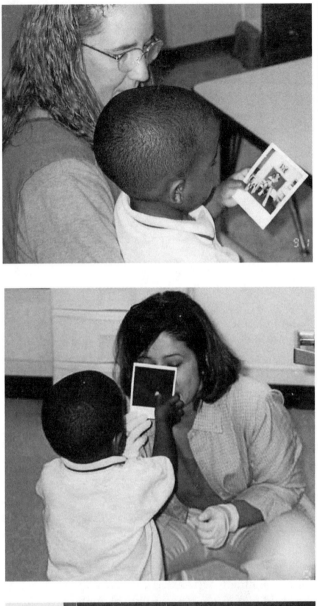

Missing Someone Special—Being Held in Mind

Teacher Colleen was leaving for the day. One of the infants in her primary care group cried when he saw her prepare to leave. The next day, the teachers took a photo of the child together with his primary care teacher. With the child's help, the teachers laminated it and gave it to the child when Colleen departed. After she left, he stared at it for a long time, kissed it, showed it to one of the other teachers, and motioned for her to kiss it too. He carried it tightly in hand for the rest of the afternoon, quietly making sense of sadness, while at the same time using the photo to tell the story of his friendship with Colleen. This story of missing someone special can now be read and revisited in the infants' book and story area.

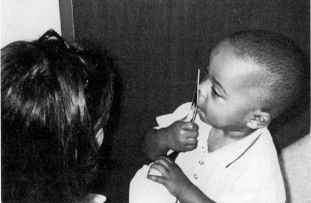

The focus of infant mental health is to protect every child's right to get off to a healthy start in life, with respect to mental health as well as physical health. Two types of infant mental health programs are designed to strengthen infant–caregiver relationships and to ensure every infant's right to optimal development. One is called home visiting, and the other is called early intervention.

Home Visiting

To support all parents and infants in getting in tune and building strong relationships of trust and care, the concept of home visiting has taken root within many communities (Harden, 2012). The goal is twofold: to enhance the ability of those caring for infants at home to read and respond contingently to their babies' cues and to support families in creating healthy environments for learning in the home. For the first 2 years following a baby's birth, a family receives periodic home visits from a professional with specialized knowledge of child development, health care, and education. These are either free or at low cost and affordable to all families.

Home visiting includes attention to the full range of concerns faced by a family with a baby. A visit includes guidance in nutrition and health care; counseling on early emotional, social, language, intellectual, and perceptual/motor development; and screenings for signs of developmental delay (Lally, 2013). As needed, the home visit includes assistance in transitioning babies into early education and care programs. A typical schedule of visits begins within 5 to 7 days following hospital discharge and continues as follows: 2 weeks, 1 month, 2 months, 3 months, 4 months, 6 months, and 9 months.

Early Intervention

Early intervention refers to programs designed to find and remediate, early in infancy, problems related to an infant's development. Early intervention specialists work with families and with teachers to identify and address developmental concerns as soon as they arise. The central idea of early intervention is to identify problems early, through regular screening, and to provide the appropriate intervention and therapy, as needed. Early intervention specialists work with families in the home to help establish routines of support that address a developmental delay or concern. They also work closely with teachers in group-care settings to assist infants and young children with identified issues of concern.

An important component of professional development for early childhood teachers is knowledge of how to work with infants who have special needs, with respect to development. Teachers working with infants are often the first to see signs of developmental delay. Knowing what to look for within the broad spectrum of typical development prepares them to recognize when there is cause for concern. Equally important is knowing how to raise these concerns respectfully and responsibly with infants' families and knowing how to refer families for early intervention services.

Looking Back and Looking Forward

For centuries, babies have been assumed to be devoid of emotions and not yet capable of conscious awareness. The studies reviewed in this chapter shatter this long-held belief. Infants, once seen to be devoid of emotions, are now seen as active protagonists in an emotional dialogue with those who provide their care (Brazelton, 2006; Tronick, 2007). The emotional context we offer infants, whether within the home or within group-care settings, influences how they come to know themselves in relation to others. It also influences how they learn and what they learn. Chapter 6 extends what we know about infants' emotional development to their understanding of self and other.

Sense of Self and Other

Social Development

The most important thing to understand about babies is that they are born looking for us—and what that means. Only one thing is more important to a baby than food, and that is human contact. Babies are born utterly motivated to engage in social interaction. (Pawl, 2003, p. 3)

EDUCATOR AND AUTHOR Vivian Gussin Paley (2011) suggests that two questions predominate in the minds of young children, "Where's my family?" and "Who's my friend?" These questions extend to babies as well, because, for babies, the people who care for them and the people who make up their immediate community are a primary interest. Infants are biologically primed at birth to go in search of others like themselves, a life-sustaining dance to stay connected through social interaction. They are ready to engage in a synchronized exchange of social cues between themselves and others. At times, an infant will lead the exchange with a cue of expectation about what others should do, and at times an infant looks to others for direction on what will come next. Through this social exchange, infants come to know others and come to know themselves in relation to others. This chapter explores infants' social development, with a focus on how infants form a link between self and other.

BORN LOOKING FOR US

Babies are born looking for those who will provide their care (Pawl, 2006). Even prior to birth, the fetus is seen to react to the sound of voices outside the womb (DeCasper & Fifer, 1980). A review of studies of newborn competence (Nugent et al., 2007) shows that newborns prefer to look at a face rather than an object; a face with open eyes, rather than closed eyes; a direct gaze rather than an averted gaze; and a smiling face rather than a fearful face. When given a

> **Research Highlight: Newborns Imitate Others**
>
> Within hours after birth, newborns imitate a facial expression. Scientists Meltzoff and Moore (1977, 1983) tested babies ranging in age from .7 to 71 hours old on their ability to imitate the facial expression of the person holding them—one expression, lips open and puckered in the shape of an O, and the other expression, a protruding tongue. If given time, the newborns reliably imitated these expressions.

choice, babies just 1–3 days old prefer to look at videos of their mother's face rather than videos of the face of a stranger. They show a similar sensitivity to the human voice, preferring to listen to the voice of their mother rather than the voice of another woman. Infants' preference for things human—voices, faces, scents, and moves—primes them to distinguish among people right from the start, and to seek out and connect with those who will provide warmth, nourishment, and protection.

Babies look to those who care for them for information about what to do and how to do it. Through their participation with others in everyday events, they learn skills, knowledge, attitudes, and beliefs that are valued by their family and community (Rogoff, 2011). Once babies adjust to life outside the womb, they begin to exchange intentional smiles and loving looks with the caregiver. Around 3–4 months of age, they begin to actively pursue two-way, purposeful communication, what Greenspan (1999) calls circles of communication.

Circles of Communication

A circle of communication might be thought of as the baby's first attempts at conversation, with the communication for the most part a nonverbal dialogue. A circle of communication is a full back-and-forth exchange between infant and caregiver. This might consist of the caregiver smiling at the baby and the

Figure 6.1. Disengagement Cues

Subtle Disengagement Cues		Potent Disengagement Cues
Brow lowering	Head lowering	Back arching
Cling posture	Hiccoughs	Coughing
Diffuse body movement	Increase in sucking noise	Crawling or walking away
Dull-looking face/eyes	Increased feet movement	Cry face
Eye blink	Join hands	Crying
Eyes clinched	Leg kicking	Fussing
Facial grimace	Looking away	Halt hand
Fast breathing	Pout	Lateral head shake
Finger extension	Pucker face	Maximal lateral gaze aversion
Frown	Rapid wrist rotation	Pale/red skin
Gaze aversion	Self-clasp	Pulling or pushing away
Hand-behind-head	Shoulder shrug	Saying "no"
Hand-to-back of-neck	Sobering	Spitting or spitting up
Hand-to-ear	Straight arms along side	Tray pounding
Hand-to-eye	Tongue show	Vomiting
Hand-to-mouth	Turning head	Whining
Leg tense	Whimpers	Withdrawing, from alert to asleep
Lips compressed	Wing palm	
Lip grimace	Wrinkled forehead	
	Yawn	

Source. Sumner & Spietz, 1994.

baby smiling back, or the reverse. Initially, these simple reciprocal exchanges consist of gestures, facial expressions, postures, and vocalizations of delight. Over time, infants build their repertoire of social signals. By 9 months, their circles of communication have become quite elaborate, marked by long strings of reciprocal back-and-forth exchanges: "I look at you, and you look back. I wave my arms, and then your eyes widen. I smile, and you smile back." These shared moments of interacting knit together circuits of neurons that organize infants' expectations about how others behave and how others make them feel.

Engaging and Disengaging

Infants are active partners in these circles of communication. They have the capacity to engage to keep the communication going, or to disengage, when they need a break. When an interaction becomes overwhelming, infants will look away, turn away, or in other ways give a clear message that they need a break. When ready to engage again, they use a range of nonverbal cues to signal, "I'm back, let's keep going."

Researchers have developed a tool for coding this primarily nonverbal repertoire of engagement and disengagement cues (Sumner & Spietz, 1994). Some cues are obvious and quite potent in relaying a desire to either engage or disengage. The most obvious way infants disengage is by falling asleep. Falling asleep allows the infant to disengage from ongoing stimulation and in so doing to replenish important energy stores. Other potent disengagement cues include crying, fussing, turning the body away, pushing outward with an open hand, or arching backward.

Other disengagement cues are subtle, like looking away, drawing a hand up behind the ear, yawning, and extending the fingers straight from the palm, called "wing palm." Figure 6.1 provides a list of commonly seen disengagement cues, some subtle and some potent. Knowing how to recognize disengagement cues is useful when working with infants, who may not be able to clearly communicate their feelings or needs verbally. Potent disengagement cues are a sign that the child is stressed and a signal to the caregiver to slow down, move back, be silent, pause, or wait, thereby reducing the level of external stimulation and helping the infant calm.

Figure 6.2. Engagement Cues

Subtle Engagement Cues	Potent Engagement Cues
Brow raising	Babbling
Eyes wide and bright	Facing gaze
Face brightens	Feeding sounds
Hands open, fingers slightly flexed	Giggling
Head raising	Mutual gaze
	Mutual smiling
	Reaching toward caregiver
	Smiling
	Smooth cyclic movements
	Talking
	Turning head to caregiver

Source: Sumner & Spietz, 1994.

In contrast, engagement cues mean the infant is ready for interaction. Some engagement cues are robust and easy to read, like a direct gaze, a broad smile, or an arm extended toward the caregiver. Other engagement cues are subtle, like lifting the eyebrows, widening and brightening the eyes, opening the hands with fingers slightly flexed, or simply raising the head. Figure 6.2 lists examples of subtle and potent engagement cues (Sumner & Spietz, 1994).

If all goes well, babies routinely experience positive, engaged interactions with caregivers, ones that follow a rhythm of engagement and disengagement and then re-engagement. For example, a baby who gets overwhelmed with excitement in face-to-face play might avert her gaze for a moment and look down at her hands. This gives her a chance to recoup her energy in order to return to engaged play. Such pauses are important in the back-and-forth pattern of infant–caregiver exchange. Babies disengage in order to calm and recoup energy. When caregivers respect these breaks and wait before responding, they help babies self-regulate.

When there are no reparative pauses within an interactive exchange, babies become overstimulated and begin to show signs of physiological disorganization. For example, a baby might look away and turn his body away. If, in response, the caregiver immediately moves into his line of vision, relentlessly talks to him, and continues to handle him, despite his turning away, the baby has little time or space to recoup his energy and get back into sync with the caregiver. If this happens on a regular basis, the baby develops a pattern of avoiding the intrusive caregiver, averting

his gaze or turning away. Such disengagement comes at a cost, because the baby is turning away from his only potential source of comfort and support (Tronick & Beeghly, 2011).

Infants also might develop a pattern of disengagement if caregivers are often distracted and not responsive. When distressed, such babies still *want* to be comforted by the caregiver, but they have learned, from experience, that they risk rejection and deep sadness if they attempt to engage the caregiver. Facing this dilemma, babies may develop a pattern of disengaging from the caregiver and seeking ways to self-soothe, like fingering the edge of the blanket or engaging in repetitive play with a toy. Although these babies may appear to be immersed in play, at a distance from the caregiver, it is distracted play, with the focus of their energy less on exploration and play and more on coping with the stress of not being "seen" by the caregiver (Powell et al., 2009).

HOLDING OTHERS IN MIND

At around 9 months, infants enter a new phase of social development, what scientist Philippe Rochat (2009) describes as the birth of co-consciousness. At this age, infants become more aware of what others are thinking. This advance, from a focus on what others *do* to a focus on what others *think*, occurs around the same time that infants begin to crawl and to walk. As infants crawl or walk into the surrounding world, they experience the joy of discovering new things, but this newfound freedom and excitement present an emotional dilemma. When they move out to explore, they end up distancing themselves from the one who provides safety, solace, and security (Rochat, 2009).

Joint Attention

Infants invent a clever way of resolving this emotional dilemma. They master several new skills that allow them to share with the trusted caregiver what they discover as they venture into the surrounding world. The first of these skills is called joint attention. Joint attention is when an infant looks at what the caregiver looks at and vice versa. The intentional shift of the gaze helps infants gather information about what others think is important. The message in the gaze is, "I want you to pay attention to what I am paying attention to."

The first inkling of joint attention can be seen when babies turn to follow the gaze of the caregiver. The adult looks at an object. The baby looks at the adult's face and then turns to look at the object the adult is looking at. Joint attention requires a bit more skill than just engaging face to face. The emergence of joint attention at around 9 months is a sign that babies are genuinely interested in what interests others. A baby this age appears to be thinking, "When you look at something, I should look at that thing too, because it must be important."

Pointing

Another new social skill that emerges at around 9 months is pointing. Infants begin to point at objects as a way to share an interest with someone else. By pointing, infants are able to get someone else to jointly attend to an object of interest. Babies are quite intentional in their pointing. They keep pointing until the person they are with turns to look at the object to which they are pointing, the implication being, "I am looking at this, and I want you to look at it, too."

Pointing is also a powerful communication tool when it comes to making a request. For example, a toddler might point to the refrigerator as the adult walks by, grab the adult by the hand, and say, "Doose." The adult might say, "Oh, you want some juice. You must be thirsty! Come, let's see if we can get you some juice." With a one-word utterance, coupled with a series of synchronized points and gestures, the toddler influences the mind of the other and enlists the help of the adult to accomplish his goal.

By their first birthday, babies have figured out that pointing is a gesture that connects them to other people's minds. For example, when they see someone pointing at an object and follow the direction of the pointed finger, they surmise that the object being pointed at is important to, or desired by, the person pointing. Pointing can be a request for help, an offer of help, or a sharing of useful or interesting information. How babies interpret the motive within the gesture of pointing depends on the social relationship established with the one who points. The pointed finger could mean to notice or to enjoy something together, but it could also mean to retrieve. Pointing requires that the baby read the social context for clues as to what might be going on in the other person's mind.

To most adults, the emergence of pointing as a communication skill may not seem highly significant, since adults point without giving it a second thought. However, for infants, this skill marks an important cognitive and social advance (Gopnik et al., 1999; Rochat, 2009). When infants begin to point, it means they have begun to be aware of what the other person thinks is important, a sign that they are

---

Research Highlight: "Like Me" Theory

Scientist Andrew Meltzoff (Gopnik et al., 1999) investigated whether infants look to others for clues as to how to behave. His findings show how infants learn simply by observing an adult's facial expression. Meltzoff recruited babies near their first birthday for an experiment in which the parent and baby sat facing the researcher. In front of the researcher on the table were two boxes. The baby watched as the researcher looked into the first box and showed an expression of joy. Then the baby saw the researcher look in the second box, with an expression of disgust. The researcher pushed the boxes toward the baby. The baby had not yet seen inside the boxes. The baby happily reached into the box that made the adult happy, but did not reach into the box that provoked disgust.

In another experiment, the baby watched as the researcher leaned forward and touched his forehead to a box on the table. The box suddenly lit up when he did this. The baby was not allowed to touch the box. A week later, the baby returned, but this time the researcher did nothing with the box other than push it across the table for the baby to explore. Without hesitation, the baby touched his forehead to the top of the box, just as he had seen the researcher do a week prior.

**Research Highlight: Social Referencing—
To Cross or Not to Cross**

A classic experiment called the Visual Cliff (Sorce, Emde, Campos, & Klinnert, 1985) provides clear demonstration of social referencing, a social skill that emerges near the first birthday. Researchers invite infants to crawl across what appears to be a drop-off of the floor, but is really just a continuous sheet of thick, clear plastic, half of which is painted black and half of which is left transparent. For the baby, crawling along the painted surface is like crawling along a solid surface. Infants prior to about 9 months of age stop and do not continue, when they reach the painted edge, the visual cliff. Older babies, however, pause and look toward the mother, standing at the end of the transparent surface. The mother has been instructed to say nothing and responds with either a facial expression to signal, "Go ahead," or "Stop!" These older infants will check in with their mothers on how to proceed, and, if the mother smiles, will continue crawling across the clear surface. If the mother shows a look of alarm, the baby will not cross.

---

developing their ability to take the perspective of the other. Joint attention and pointing create connections to others, even while at a distance, giving infants a sense of security. Rochat (2009) suggests that pointing and shared attention are the first inkling of infants' ability to share.

Social Referencing

Infants pay close attention to what occurs between people and objects, and they make an important assumption about people—people are "like me" in a way that objects are not. This "like me" assumption (Meltzoff, 2007) enables babies to observe the behavior of others and use it to learn about their own powers and possibilities.

At around 1 year of age, infants begin to reference others for advice. They do this by using the gaze and expression of others as a reference for how to behave in uncertain situations, what scientists call social referencing. A typical example of this can be seen in a moment where a 1-year-old encounters a new object for the very first time. Rather than engaging directly in play with the object, the baby will look to the caregiver before approaching the novel object. If the caregiver smiles, the baby approaches, but if the caregiver frowns and looks concerned, the baby does not budge.

If all goes well, by their first birthday infants have advanced to a fairly sophisticated understanding of how to figure out people and are adept at pointing, joint attention, and social referencing. As they move into their second year, they also begin to exhibit more complex emotions like embarrassment and shame, emotions not seen during the first year. The emergence of these emotions indicates that, as toddlers, they become noticeably self-conscious. It is interesting to speculate on why this is so. Toddlers are excited to explore the surrounding world, away from the safe harbor of the trusted caregiver. However, they face a risk in doing so, in the form of scrutiny and disapproval by others. They might experience a frown or a harsh voice rather than a smile and words that calm. Consequently, they feel rejected, and this rejection gives rise to shame and embarrassment (Rochat, 2009).

A shamed toddler shows signs of stress—heart racing and skin flushing—and will quickly disengage—looking or turning away, lowering the head, or running away to hide and escape scrutiny. Rejection is a highly disturbing experience for children of any age. Chapter 13 explores guidance strategies designed to avoid subjecting toddlers to unnecessary embarrassment, shame, or public scrutiny.

THE WITHDRAWN INFANT

Infancy marks an important period for identifying developmental lags and taking steps to give infants special support as needed. Techniques for identifying delays in social-emotional development have improved, along with strategies for intervening when there are signs of concern. When infants approach the first birthday and show no signs of pointing, joint attention, or social referencing, this is cause for concern,

---

Research Highlight: Embarrassment and Shame

A classic study sheds light on how shame emerges in toddlers. Experimenters (Lewis & Brooks-Gunn, 1979) put a dot of red rouge on the nose of a young child. As the child looks in the mirror, they record the response. One-year-olds simply look in the mirror and respond as if noticing another baby with a red dot on the nose. When this experiment is done with 2-year-olds, the response is very different. As soon as these children see their image in the mirror, they look embarrassed, turn away, and begin to rub where the red dot is.

Research Highlight:
What I Want as Compared with What You Want

To find out whether infants were able to detect the desires of others, researchers (Repacholi & Gopnik, 1997) studied two different age groups, 14-month-olds and 18-month-olds. The infant sat across from the researcher, who first showed the infant two bowls of food, one with crackers and another with raw broccoli. The researcher then offered each bowl to the baby. All the babies in the study selected the crackers rather than the broccoli. Then, as the infant watched, the researcher tasted the food, making a delighted face and saying, "Yummy!" in response to one food and a disgusted face and saying, "Yuck!" in response to the other. The researcher put both bowls of food near the baby, held out her hand and asked, "Could you give me some?" If the researcher had indicated she liked the crackers but not the broccoli, all babies, 14- and 18-month-olds, gave her a cracker. However, if the researcher had indicated that she liked the broccoli and not the crackers, the babies 14 months old gave her the crackers, and the babies 18 months old gave her the broccoli.

an indication that there may be underlying developmental problems.

The term *autism spectrum disorder* (ASD) describes a group of complex disorders characterized by difficulties in social-emotional interaction and verbal and nonverbal communication, and in some cases by repetitive behavior. ASD is sometimes associated as well with intellectual disability, motor coordination difficulties, attention maintenance difficulty, or physical health issues, like disturbances of sleep or gastrointestinal functioning. ASD incorporates a vast range of symptoms and manifests in a wide range of social-emotional challenges. Since ASD appears to have its roots in very early development, early identification and intervention to support the withdrawn infant are important.

Research is underway to identify early signs of ASD and intervention strategies. Dr. Stanley Greenspan (Greenspan & Wieder, 2006), a pioneering researcher in infants' emotional development, created a program called Floor Time, designed to support families and teachers who work with withdrawn infants and children. The focus of Floor Time is to help children experience safe, comfortable ways to engage socially with others. In Floor Time, adults deliberately follow the child's lead in play and simultaneously encourage chains of social interaction, that is, circles of communication, between child and adult, so that the child experiences a connected and coherent exchange of gestures, vocalizations, and movements while engaging with others. Floor Time is a very focused type of play that helps infants and toddlers gradually engage with others and simultaneously builds on a child's strengths through play strategies tailored to the child's unique sensory or motor processing challenges. Chapter 7 explores sensory motor processing in more depth, with ideas for reflective planning for children who show signs of persistent withdrawal.

CARING AND COOPERATING

At one time, infants were thought to be egocentric, not yet able to read others' desires or intentions and not yet able to see something from the perspective of another. However, studies suggest otherwise. Infants notice the impact of others' actions on objects, and as toddlers, they notice that others have desires different from their own.

Research Highlight:
Toddlers Help Others in Need

Scientists Warneken and Tomasello (2007) created several experiments in which infants watched someone who appeared to need help. Toddlers watched as a person hung clothes on a clothesline. The person accidentally dropped a clothespin. Although the person made no request for help, nearly all of the 18-month-olds in the study retrieved and returned the clothespin to the person. In a variation of the scene, the toddlers saw the person intentionally throw the clothespin to the ground. In response, most of the toddlers did not retrieve the thrown object.

In another experiment, toddlers watched as a person placed one book on top of another, but misaligned one of the books, causing it to fall from the stack. Nearly all the toddlers, upon seeing the book fall, picked up the fallen book and handed it to the person who had dropped it. The experimenter carried the stack of books with both hands to a closed cupboard and repeatedly bumped up against the closed cupboard door with his body, trying to open it, as the toddlers watched. Nearly all the toddlers walked to the cupboard door and opened it for the person, doing so within about 10 seconds, with minimal hesitation.

Research Highlight:
Infants Discriminate Friend from Foe

As babies 5–12 months old sit on their parents' lap, they watch a puppet stage scene in which a puppet tries but fails to open a box. A different puppet comes on stage and helps the first puppet open the box. Then the babies see the original scene again, with the puppet trying and failing to open the box, but this time a third type of puppet comes on stage and flops down hard on top of the box, preventing the box from being opened. Then the researchers offer the babies a choice of two puppets lying on a tray. One is the puppet that helped and the other is the puppet that hindered. Overwhelmingly, the babies choose the puppet that helped (Hamlin & Wynn, 2012).

In another experiment (Hamlin et al., 2011), the researchers gave babies 19–23 months old a chance to provide rewards to two different puppets, one they saw acting to help another and one they saw acting hurtfully. The toddlers were more likely to give rewards to a puppet previously observed as helpful and to take rewards from a puppet previously observed acting hurtfully.

To test whether such prosocial tendencies are present earlier in infancy, researchers (Hamlin & Wynn, 2010) placed 3-month-olds in front of an animated scene. The animated scene consisted of a circular shape attempting to move up a steep hill. Then a triangular shape moved toward the struggling round shape and pushed it to the top of the hill. The scene repeated until the baby tired and looked away. Then the scene changed. This time, as the round shape struggled to get up the hill, a square shape appeared at the top of the hill and pushed the round shape down the hill. In the first scene, the baby saw prosocial behavior, and in the second scene, the baby saw antisocial behavior, but would the baby favor one over the other? To find out, the researchers gave the baby a chance to select one of the objects, either the helpful triangular shape or the hurtful square shape. The babies overwhelming chose the object that helped.

Midway through the second year, toddlers' awareness of others' feelings and wishes improves. For example, they will initiate activities aimed at comforting a distressed person (Radke-Yarrow & Zahn-Waxler, 1984). Their care and concern for others are influenced, to some degree, by the kinds of conversations and social interactions they have had with the adults who care for them (Thompson, Laible, & Ontai, 2003). If parents regularly converse with young children about the day's events, including episodes of misbehavior as well as good behavior, young children learn to show care and concern for others.

Warneken and Tomasello (2007) created a series of experiments in which young toddlers watch someone who appears to need help. Their results show a consistent pattern of toddlers helping others in need, without any request to do so. Simply by watching an event transpire and seeing a person struggle to get something out of reach or to open a closed door, toddlers act to retrieve the desired object or to open the closed door.

The characteristic of acting for the good of others, called altruism, is a complex prosocial skill that appears to have roots in infancy (Thompson & Newton, 2013). To find out whether infants prefer helpful over hurtful actions, researchers have infants watch animations of puppets behaving in ways that are helpful and ways that are hurtful. Using a research design called habituation, researchers can determine whether infants detect the difference between behavior that helps and behavior that hinders. Studies show that infants as young as 3 months old, who watch a scene in which one figure helps and another figure hinders an action, do notice the difference. Then, by offering the infant a choice of grasping the figure that helped or the figure that hindered, the researchers check to see whether the infants prefer one behavior over the other. Infants as young as 3 months old are significantly more likely to select a puppet they saw in a helping role over a puppet they saw in a hurtful role (Hamlin & Wynn, 2012; Hamlin, Wynn, & Bloom, 2010; Hamlin, Wynn, Bloom, & Mahajan, 2011).

TEMPERAMENT: A GOODNESS OF FIT

Another important aspect of who the child is in relation to others is temperament. Temperament refers to persistent patterns in how people show feelings and respond to the world around them (Chess, 2011). Stud-

Reflection: Reading Others' Intentions

Reflect on the research studies related to infants' awareness of others' intentions or needs. What explanation can you give for how infants and toddlers respond when seeing others in need? What implications does this research have for understanding issues like justice and morality?

ies have identified nine temperamental characteristics, which cluster in three temperamental types. Temperamental characteristics include activity level, regularity, readiness to approach or withdraw, adaptability, sensitivity, intensity of reaction, mood, persistence, and distractibility. The three temperamental types are commonly described as easy, cautious, and feisty.

Most children fit the profile of having an easy temperament. Children who have an easy temperament are adaptable and fairly regular in their biological rhythms of sleep, elimination, and hunger. When excited or upset, their reactions are moderate, and they tend to approach new situations readily, with a positive attitude, and adapt easily to change. When working with infants who have an easy temperament, it is important to provide special attention, so that they do not get ignored in the midst of caring for a group of children. Checking in with them from time to time is important.

A second type of temperament is described as cautious or slow-to-warm. Children who have a cautious, slow-to-warm temperament are somewhat shy. They tend to watch before engaging readily in new situations. They require more time than others to adapt to change. Whether upset or happy, their responses are noticeably mild, and they are often more sensitive than others to noise, touch, food textures, and temperature. For children with a slow-to-warm temperament, the following is recommended:

- Don't pressure.
- Give them time to adapt.
- Draw them in and stay nearby for a moment.
- Ensure consistent caregivers.
- Give them their own space.
- Be patient with resistance to something new.

A third type of temperament is described as difficult. These children tend to be feisty and to react slowly to new situations, with reactions of high intensity. They tend to be highly sensitive to noise, touch, food texture, or temperature and may exhibit a more negative disposition. Recommendations for working with infants who show a difficult temperament include the following:

- Be clear with limits and redirect.
- Be flexible.
- Prepare them for changes.
- Make the most of quiet times.
- Provide opportunities for active play.

> ### Reflection: Putting a Sensitive Baby to Sleep
>
> Consider what it must feel like to be an infant who is unusually sensitive to sights, sounds, and tactile stimulation. Consider what a caregiver faces when putting such a sensitive baby down for a nap. The baby appears drowsy and begins to fall asleep, but as the caregiver leans over the sleeping mat to put the baby down to rest, the baby's eyes open. As soon as the baby's back hits the mat, the baby begins to cry. What suggestions would you offer in handling such a situation, keeping in mind this baby's temperament?

Not all children fit readily into one of these categories. For each temperament, there are interaction strategies that generate a goodness of fit, so that the social-emotional needs of every child are met.

It is important to understand that temperament is not destiny (Kagen & Snidman, 2004). Cautious children are not destined to be shrinking violets, and they adapt well when drawn into new situations gradually, at their own pace, with the support of a sensitive caregiver. Infants who have a feisty temperament, and who may be highly reactive, benefit when their teachers give them extra time and keep levels of stimulation low. This helps them regulate their energy in new and uncertain situations and still retain their vibrant, robust personalities. In this way, they reap the advantages of their temperament, rather than being tied to it as a burden. Both feisty and cautious infants can be fussy and may cry for long periods, but when caregivers realize that such infants are easily disturbed by small changes in the environment, they can look for ways to reduce the impact of such changes.

TOUCHPOINTS

Over the course of decades of work as a pediatrician and researcher, T. Berry Brazelton (2006) identified predictable points during childhood that are marked by a sudden burst in development and accompanied by stressful changes in behavior. Although such sudden bursts in development are normal, the accompanying changes in behavior are unexpected and can be troubling for the parent. When parents are unaware of these points in development—what Brazelton calls touchpoints—they worry that something is wrong with their child or with them, creating tension between child and parent and rendering the relationship vulnerable. Brazelton has demonstrated that when

Research Highlight: Touchpoints and Sleep

Brazelton (2006) identifies these touchpoints related to sleep.

- 4 months: Babies learn to extend their sleep cycles in order to stretch them to 8 hours. This requires learning how to get themselves back to sleep, despite alerting at the end of a 3–4 hour light sleep cycle.
- 8 months: Babies awaken at night and as they move around, they resume what they were fascinated with learning during the day, that is, crawling and practicing pulling to standing. Acutely aware of being separated from loved ones at this age (an awareness not present earlier), they also may cry out for their parents in the middle of the night.
- 10 months: Babies learn how to pull to standing several months before they are able to lower themselves down, so, if they pull to standing in the middle of the night, they may send out a disturbing call for help.
- 12 months: A 12-month-old who is learning how to walk may awake at night, remember the excitement of practicing this new skill, and begin to do so again instead of returning to sleep. Also at this age, babies want to be independent, yet they still enjoy the comfort of being dependent on the parent, a potential source of conflict between parent and child.

families are aware of these delicate points of transition, they worry less and adapt their responses to the child, which, in turn, strengthen the child–parent relationship.

Brazelton's work is based on an important principle of child development, that the developmental trajectory of a child is not a smooth process marked by gradual change. A more accurate description of development is that advances occur in sudden bursts at fairly predictable points. Whenever an infant approaches one of these points of sudden developmental advance—like beginning to pull to standing and walking—the act of learning this emerging skill comes at a cost to the infant in terms of expenditure of energy. Infants will spend a large portion of their limited store of energy mastering the new skill and reorganizing bodily systems to accommodate the new skill. Consequently, the energy remaining to spend on other tasks may be reduced. This may result in children

resisting or fumbling through what they used to do with ease. To the parent or the caregiver, it may look like the child is moving backward, that is, regressing. However, the developmental burst that caused the confusing behavior is actually a sign that the child is progressing, not regressing. The parent or caregiver who can recognize this can relax and see the behavior in a positive light, knowing that what feels like a disturbing bump in the road is normal and to be expected within the course of development.

Touchpoints occur at predictable points during infancy. At each touchpoint, the caregiver–child relationship is vulnerable. To help caregivers anticipate and successfully weather these potentially stressful times, Brazelton suggests observing the baby, as a way to build understanding about the baby's behavior and a parent's concern. Teachers and other professionals working with families use touchpoints as opportunities to engage parents in observing and learning from their babies' ways of making meaning of the experiences they encounter. By observing with others, parents begin to see the effort babies put forth mastering emerging skills and concepts. As parents take this effort into account, they begin to comprehend how this burst of effort can result in disturbing changes in behavior that are normal, and most likely temporary, as the baby moves through this natural period of transition.

FROM RESEARCH TO PRACTICE: REFLECTION IN THE WORKPLACE

Observing for temperament and for touchpoints requires an attitude of reflection. Brazelton's Touchpoints model is an example of how professionals use reflective practice to work through and to understand how to best navigate an experience with children and families. To support every infant's development and to build a strong triangle of relationship among infant, family, and teacher, one factor is essential when working with babies and their families—reflective practice. Reflective practice means stepping back and looking at the relationship between how one feels in a situation, what led to the situation, and what possibilities there are for the future, with respect to this situation. Reflective practice is essential when working with infants and their families, because the context of caring for and caring about children and their families can bring out very intense emotions. Without engaging in reflective practice, it is far too easy to simply react, without thinking, which can lead to misguided assumptions, misunderstanding, anger, and frustration.

Chapter 4 introduced the concept of reflective planning as a frame for creating contexts for children's learning and sharing those contexts with families. Reflection is also a critical tool in supporting professionals who provide services for infants and families. The term reflective supervision refers to the regular, collaborative reflection between a clinician or teacher and the supervisor. The collaborative reflection builds on the supervisee's thoughts, feelings, and values that emerge during his or her work with children and families. Reflective supervision can be applied in early childhood settings. It requires a system in which each member of the staff working with children and families is assigned a trusted colleague and assured a regular time and place to reflect on their interactions with families, children, and co-workers (Lerner, 2006). By taking a reflective look at their work, in conversation with a trusted colleague, adults can thoughtfully examine the issues that concern them, from their own perspective, but also from the perspective of the child, the family, or others involved. Reflective supervision is especially helpful when facing emotionally charged and challenging situations. Through reflective supervision, teachers and family support staff learn from even the most trying situations and better prepare themselves to respond sensitively to similar encounters in the future. Whatever the setting—curriculum planning, family support, or professional growth—reflective practice encourages mutual respect, collaborative relationships, and thoughtful problem solving.

Looking Back and Looking Forward

Infants have amazing potential to develop into caring, cooperative, and productive human beings, yet they are vulnerable. Caregivers have profound influence over whether infants learn to trust or not to trust; to protect or to harm; to treat fairly or to cheat. Infants develop patterns of expectation about how they will be cared for by others, and, in turn, these patterns influence how they will care for others. These patterns have the potential to last a lifetime.

Jeree Pawl (2003) sums up what we might hear if we could listen to the thoughts of a baby cared for within a responsive relationship:

> She waits while I swallow. She smiles in my eyes. She likes what she sees. She talks a little while I rest and entertains my ears. She notices when I have had enough. She thinks I'm important. She cares what I want. She figures out what I want. She is people. People are good. (p. 20)

CHAPTER 7

Taking Action
Motor Development

In the course of her motor development, a baby . . . learn[s] how to turn over onto her belly, to roll over, crawl, sit, stand and walk, [but] she also learns how to learn. She learns to tackle something on her own, to take interest in something, to try something out, to experiment. She learns to overcome difficulties. She experiences the joy and the satisfaction that comes with success, the result of her patience and perseverance. (Pikler, 1994, p. 16)

A BABY ROLLS OVER for the very first time and is greeted with cheers of delight. Although a cause for celebration, the more fascinating story is what occurred in the weeks prior to this new move. The study of infant movement is more than just a list of motor skills that develop during infancy. It is a window into babies' ways of making meaning about themselves in relation to the world around them. Movement is integrally tied to infants' ways of perceiving and thinking. This chapter provides an overview of the patterns and progressions of motor development in infancy. It also explores how teachers and families can support infants' sense of balance, strength, and grace as they develop their muscle systems.

PATTERNS OF MOTOR DEVELOPMENT

Watch infants at play and their actions reveal clues about what might be going on in their minds, that is, their thoughts, feelings, and intentions. Infants' actions and movements are closely connected to their ideas and concepts. Both influence their ways of making meaning. Scientists describe the intimate relation between how infants move their bodies and how they build their minds as embodied cognition. A baby playing with a toy mouths, fingers, shakes, and bangs it. Simultaneously, the baby stretches and flexes with

Research Highlight: Newborns Reflexively Seek Nourishment

In an unmedicated birth, a newborn baby, placed on the mother's abdomen, will inch reflexively and gradually to the mother's breast, pushing alternately with the feet in a reflexive stepping pattern (Widström et al., 1987). When the baby's cheek touches the mother's breast, the baby will turn in the direction of the touch, as if going in search of the nipple, a reflexive action called rooting. As the baby's lips touch the nipple, the baby's sucking reflex is triggered, pulling milk into the mouth. As the milk hits the back of the mouth, the baby reflexively swallows.

arms, legs, and torso. These actions and movements are accompanied by expressions of satisfaction and interest. This chapter addresses the cascade of changes that occur as babies move, navigate through, and act on their surroundings.

Infant Reflexes

Newborns arrive with a package of innate movements called reflexes. Reflexes are movements that occur without conscious intention or planning. Blinking is an example of a reflex that stays with us throughout life. Other reflexes, infantile reflexes, appear only in the first months following birth, after which time they disappear. The short duration of infantile reflexes may be related to the fact that they assist in keeping newborns connected to the nurturing adult during a vulnerable period of transition.

Infant reflexes, like rooting, stepping, sucking, and swallowing, appear to help babies seek the nourishment they will need in order to survive outside the womb. Other infant reflexes may assist the newborn in staying physically connected to the nurturing adult. A newborn's hand tends to be kept reflexively clenched, and an object touching the baby's palm results in the fingers closing tightly around the object. A sudden drop in the newborn's head position or a loud sound nearby elicits a reflexive inward pull of arms and legs, called the startle reflex.

When pediatricians perform behavior tests on newborns to assess brain development, they check newborn reflexes. Over the course of the first few months, in typically developing infants, infantile reflexes become less evident. Eventually, they can no longer be elicited, having been replaced by voluntary actions. Pediatricians monitor the disappearance of these infantile reflexes as a sign of healthy development. A reflex that persists well beyond the average age for disappearance may be an indication of disrupted brain development.

Self-Organizing Systems

A simple motion, like lifting a cup to drink, involves continuous cycles of information being relayed back and forth between the brain, the muscles, and the surrounding world. Because even simple movements involve complex actions within the systems of the body, the brain dedicates a special structure to keeping all the movements of the body coordinated. This structure is called the cerebellum. The cerebellum sits at the back of the head, behind the brainstem and below the cortex, and performs a job not unlike that of an air traffic controller. The cerebellum receives input from the cortex—about ongoing movements—as well as input from all the sensory systems—vision, hearing, proprioception, and balance.

Given the complexity of the movement system, it is not surprising that babies take months to accomplish what appear like fairly simple feats. As babies experiment with how to move their bodies in an expanding array of motions, the cerebellum helps to organize joints, muscles, tendons, and sensory and motor neurons into complex systems. These are self-organizing systems, meaning that as babies repeat motions and combine them, they create new ways of moving through space and more refined ways of manipulating objects. As they play and move freely, babies self-organize their motor system, fine-tuning moves to achieve balance and grace. Although at first their movements are awkward and disorganized, with continued effort, they become smooth, effortless motions. For example, a young infant bats at objects over and over without connecting, but with time and practice, this motion becomes an effortless grasp.

Directional Trends

Two patterns emerge in the development of the motor system. These patterns serve as useful guides when planning environments for infants and selecting toys and furnishings. The first pattern—head to toe—is called cephalocaudal development. This means the muscle system matures and organizes following a head-to-toe directional pattern, from the brain down through the core of the body. This progression of movements is evident in large-muscle development. A baby first develops the ability to control the neck muscles; then the ability to push up with the muscles of the shoulders; followed by maturation of the muscles of the torso, needed to roll over; followed by the muscles of the hips, needed to sit up; followed by the muscles of the legs and then the feet, needed for standing.

The other directional trend in motor development is from inside to outside. This is called proximal–distal development. Muscles organize first within the body core, followed by muscles organizing progressively outward, through arms and legs, and eventually hands and feet, and, in the end, fingers and toes. An example of this developmental trend is found in the infant's grasp. Initially, an infant bats at an object with a movement of the whole arm, rarely making contact. Then, once the muscles of the hand become organized into a smooth system, the infant reaches and successfully grasps, using the whole hand. As the muscles of the fingers get recruited, with additional practice, the infant deftly picks up an object, using thumb and index finger. Motor development is not simply a matter of maturation, that is, waiting for the right connections to form. Experience plays a role in creating complex systems. During waking hours, babies are almost constantly in motion, practicing new moves. By the end of the first year, babies have mastered many new postures.

LOCOMOTION: FREEDOM TO MOVE

By observing large groups of infants over the course of infancy, researchers have created scales that describe the range and the average age for accomplishing motor skills. These scales are used to describe the normal course of development and to identify infants who may be at risk of developmental delay. The premise of these scales is that babies will achieve the same

Figure 7.1. Development of Large-Muscle Systems

Motor Skill	Average Age (Months)	Range (Months)
Rolling from back to side	4.4	2–7
Rolling from back to stomach	6.4	4–10
Crawling	7.1	5–11
Getting into seated posture on own	8.3	6–11
Pulling to standing on own	8.1	5–12
Pulling down from standing on own	9.6	7–14
Walking without support	11.7	9–17

Source. Bayley, 1969.

motor milestone at generally the same age. Measures taken from the Bayley Scales of Infant Development (Bayley, 1969) are referenced in this chapter as a guide to typical development, with the intention of providing professionals working with infants a framework for tracking potential developmental concerns. Figure 7.1 presents an average age and a normal range for when key motor skills appear.

Although useful in tracking development, scales of motor milestones do not reveal what transpires in the period leading up to the attainment of each of these motor skills. Pediatrician Emmi Pikler (2006) recorded in great detail infants' transformation of postures from back to stomach, from creeping on belly to crawling, to sitting up, to pulling to standing, and to walking. Her research provides detailed descriptions of the progression of infants' postures and movements. She studied babies' spontaneous efforts to get into a posture, to achieve balance in that posture, and eventually to master moving into and out of that posture with ease and grace. She observed as babies moved freely within thoughtfully designed play spaces. Her records of each phase of motor development show a purposeful sequence of movement transformations, with one movement giving rise to another, as babies actively experiment with how to use their bodies. As Pikler (1994) explained:

> [An infant dedicates himself] with extraordinary interest and amazing patience. He attentively studies one movement innumerable times. He enjoys and becomes absorbed in each little detail, each nuance of a movement, quietly taking his time in an experimenting mode. Perhaps it is the very repetitiveness of this study that brings such delight to a child. During the first two years, she is busy—or better, she is "playing"—with each movement for days, weeks, sometimes months. Each movement has its own history of development. Each one is based upon the other. (p. 12)

Pikler's research defined an important principle of motor development. Time spent in self-initiated practice results in balance, confidence, and grace in posture and movement. When free to move, to experiment, to try and fail, to try again, to test a variation, and to slowly and surely reach a posture of balance and grace, infants thrive.

Newborn Movement Patterns

Newborns, rested and free from hunger, will lie on their back with legs and arms bent, with head turned slightly to the side. This posture is determined by a reflex, called the tonic neck reflex, which keeps the baby's head turned in the direction of the outstretched arm. In a few weeks time, this reflex disappears. As they lie on their back, newborns move their arms and legs in motions that are at first erratic and choppy. As days pass, these movements self-organize into smooth, rhythmic patterns.

During the first 2 months, newborns are adjusting to life outside the womb, what Montagu (Mendizza, 1994) characterizes as a "womb with a view" (p. 2). Very young babies need very little in the way of toys and furnishings, because they are experiencing simple things for the very first time—the caregiver's face, the feel of the blanket, the chorus of sounds around them, the pattern of air flow on skin, or changing smells in the air. In addition, the baby's own body, how it moves and works, provides the baby with a wealth of material to investigate.

Newborns are most at ease in the protection of the caregiver's arms or within the calm surroundings of a crib. On a firm mattress and in clothing that does not restrict movement, newborns are free to move arms and legs naturally. In time, they begin to follow the movement of their own hands with their eyes. A newborn's hands also may find their way to the mouth for sucking. Pikler advised caregivers working

Figure 7.2. Rolling from Back to Side

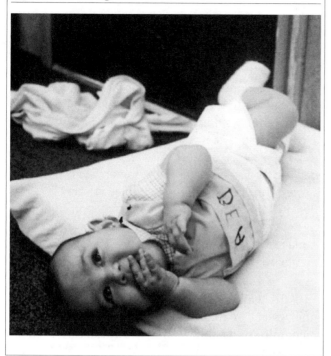

with newborns to honor this period when babies are becoming familiar with their own bodies and to avoid bombarding them with surrounding toys (David & Appell, 2001).

At about 3 months of age, infants' sleep–wake cycle stabilizes, with longer periods of alertness. At this point, most babies will enjoy a comfortable, protected play space on the floor. A blanket-covered wooden or flat floor surface, partitioned safely from areas used by active crawlers or walkers, provides a comfortable, safe, protected play space. When lying on their back, infants will actively move arms and legs and flex and stretch the torso. Until babies can freely lift the head with muscles of the neck and shoulders, they will be more at ease resting on the back than on the stomach. When lying on the back, infants are balanced and secure, and they are able to feel and see their arms and legs in motion. They also can freely flex and stretch, preparing for the next move, which is rolling onto the side, a prelude to rolling over onto the stomach.

Rolling Over

When babies lying on their back begin to reach in the direction of an object, they stretch their entire body during the reach, an effort that may coincide with a turn of the pelvis, which tilts them onto their side. This is a challenging posture, one that requires effort to stay balanced. Babies in this position will tense

their full body to stay in a side position (Figure 7.2). To relax and rest, they return to their back, but soon will return to balancing once again on their side. With repeated tries, their balance improves in this side posture and they can stay on their side for long periods of time, which Pikler (1988) points out gives babies a whole new perspective on their surroundings. The Bayley Scales show that on average a baby turns from back to side at 4.4 months of age, and within a range as early as 2 months and as late as 7 months.

Babies who have learned to turn from back to side are content to play on their side for weeks. On average, 8 weeks will pass between the point when a baby learns to roll from back to side to the point when the baby masters rolling all the way over, from back to stomach. The average age for turning from back to stomach is 6.4 months, within a range of 4–10 months of age. Once babies accomplish rolling fully over from back to stomach, they often choose to spend increasing amounts of time lying on their stomach. This gives them an opportunity to experiment with lifting the head, then using hands and arms to lift the torso. Flexion of the torso facilitates stretching toward objects in an attempt to reach them. Some babies transform this stretching into inch-by-inch movements in the direction of a desired object. Pikler (1988, 2006) emphasizes the importance of the bending and stretching movements that take place as babies lie on their stomach. As babies bend and stretch, these natural movements elongate and straighten the spine, while the torso simultaneously becomes elastic and flexible.

Crawling

What follows from all this stretching and flexing is that babies figure out how to roll from place to place, which for some babies might be their first form of locomotion. Locomotion refers to any movement that allows the baby to move from place to place, most often in search of objects of interest. True to the pattern of cephalocaudal development, the torso and hips organize prior to the legs and feet. When babies are 5–11 months of age, and on average 7.1 months old (Bayley, 1969), they begin to crawl. Many begin to crawl by pulling themselves along the floor on their stomach. Initially, they may slide backward rather than forward, but forward movement gradually improves. Often the arms take the lead, propelling the baby along the floor. This action serves to strengthen the coordination of arms, torso, and legs, with the result that the baby lifts onto hands and knees or feet and rocks back and forth.

Crawling takes much practice over the course of weeks. Prior to crawling on hands and knees, many infants belly crawl on their abdomen, pulling along the floor. Others hitch along the floor in a seated position, propelling forward by flexing the front leg. Some move along the floor on their back, with outstretched limbs. Some roll from place to place. Sometimes the push is with just one limb or the pull is with just arms, dragging the legs behind. The variations are many (Adolph & Berger, 2006), but in time babies begin crawling in some fashion.

Once they begin to stretch out in an effort to move their bodies along the floor, infants need a firm surface that provides easy traction for pushing with hands, knees, feet, or belly. As crawlers gain more confidence, objects like pillows to crawl over, boxes or short tubes to crawl through, or low platforms to climb onto offer engaging challenges. Stable surfaces placed in the crawler play space invite pulling up to standing. Low rungs secured to the wall, table legs, or overturned sturdy boxes provide other spots where crawlers can pull to standing. As they practice how to pull to standing, babies work their upper body muscles—shoulder, arms, and torso—more than they work their legs.

Equipment described as baby walkers send thousands of children to hospitals every year, with reports of babies in walkers tumbling down stairs, getting burned, drowning, and being poisoned. Such accidents occur even when the babies in the walkers are being watched. A baby in a walker can move more than 3 feet in 1 second, so an adult simply cannot respond quickly enough to prevent accidents. The American Academy of Pediatrics (2013) warns parents not to use baby walkers, because they put children at risk and offer no benefits.

Reflection: Risks of Baby Walkers

What happens when babies not yet able to crawl and not yet able to get into a seated position on their own are placed in equipment marketed as baby walkers, activity centers, bouncers, or other such devices that sit them upright, with feet pushing onto the ground? Consider the direction of development, and decide which motor systems would be organizing at this age. Would these systems include the arms, shoulders, torso, hips, legs, or feet? With respect to cephalocaudal and proximal–distal development, which muscle systems are preparing these babies for crawling and pulling to sitting or for balancing in an upright posture? Are these muscle systems worked when a baby is placed in equipment of this type? Does such equipment impede or help motor development?

Baby walkers, like much equipment marketed as infant seats or infant exercisers, restrict an infant's freedom to move, but they also stimulate movement patterns that are not consistent with cephalocaudal development. For example, in devices marketed as baby exercisers or walkers, infants are busy moving their legs up and down, but they have minimal opportunity to use, and consequently organize and develop, the muscles of the upper body. The upper body muscles are what infants need to use and strengthen in order to push up to sitting or to pull to standing. In contrast, when infants are free to move in a protected floor space, they work their upper body muscles in ways that allow them to pull themselves along the floor in a crawl and to pull themselves to seated or standing positions.

Infants who master pulling to standing enjoy lingering in this new posture. Any raised surface they pull to becomes a potential place to explore. When a variety of engaging toys are placed on top of a sturdy overturned box or bench, crawlers delight in the challenge of pulling themselves up and standing with balance to explore what they discover there.

Sitting

Crawling strengthens the muscles of the back, torso, arms, and hips. When these muscle systems have strengthened and organized, babies will pull themselves into a seated posture. This movement occurs within a range of 6–11 months, and on average at 8.3 months (Bayley, 1969). It may take 5–6 months from the time babies turn onto their stomach to the start

Reflection:
Sitting Up—Propped or Free to Move?

Observe a baby who has been propped in a seated position. Most likely, you will see a curved spine, rather than an erect spine. The weight of the baby's body centers on the tailbone, rather than the buttock, forcing the baby to curve the spine unnaturally forward in order to resist falling backward. The baby's chest sags inward, compacting the lungs and other organs. Bones and muscles are misaligned. For a baby who cannot yet get into a seated posture on his own, sitting is a strain, even when propped.

Some argue that babies enjoy being propped in a seated position. What advantages or disadvantages do you see of babies being propped to sit? What impact might this have on the muscle systems that organize in preparation for crawling or pulling to standing?

of their attempts to pull to a seated position (Pikler, 1988). At first, babies roll onto the side, then prop themselves in a half-seated posture. This leads, in time, to a fully seated posture.

Pikler (1988) and Gerber (1998) urge caregivers to let babies get into seated or standing positions on their own. They discourage caregivers' propping babies in seated positions or holding them in standing positions if the babies cannot yet get into that position independently. Pikler notes that babies who get into a seated position on their own will quickly adjust their balance and learn to sit with confidence and ease, relaxed yet still moving freely. They are able to shift their body weight onto the buttock bones, with torso upright, aligning head and spine. Once babies learn how to get into and out of a seated posture, they explore variations of sitting, including kneeling and sitting on their heels, on their feet, or between their knees on the ground.

Standing

On average, babies pull to standing at around 8.1 months, and within a range of 5–12 months (Bayley, 1969). Pulling to standing tends to coincide with getting into a seated position independently. Often infants approach the task from a kneeling position and use rungs, knobs, or table edges to pull themselves up. Watch a baby who has managed to pull to standing and observe how the baby manages this posture, not so much by the support of the legs but by the support of the arms, with hands clasping tightly a sup-

porting surface. This is another example of cephalocaudal development.

The act of lowering to the ground is largely the work of the leg muscles, which are still organizing. The average age for independently getting down from a standing posture is 9.6 months (Bayley, 1969). This is more than a month after the average age for independently pulling to standing, 8.1 months. The baby who has just figured out how to pull to standing may whimper, bounce up and down in frustration, and look around for help. If no one comes to the rescue, the baby will tire and fall awkwardly to the floor.

Walking

Once able to stand, babies will spend considerable time practicing how to move from place to place while standing and holding on. By holding whatever supports they can find, babies take sideways steps to move from place to place. They cover a fair distance in this mode, so providing a variety of low, sturdy supports for them to grasp while standing and stepping sideways is an effective way to create contexts that support motor development. A variety of stable surfaces can be assembled near one another, such as upturned boxes, low benches, play slides, and large buckets. These create an engaging pathway that offers infants a chance to hold on while walking from place to place.

The average age for walking without support is 11.7 months and occurs within a range of 9–17 months (Bayley, 1969). Walking independently, with ease and confidence, takes time. Babies take their first unsupported steps uncertainly, with legs and arms spread wide for balance and toes gripping the floor. It will take several years for their gait to become a smooth, swaying gait (Smitsman & Corbetta, 2010).

When infants master walking without support, they take on the challenge of perfecting their walk, but they soon turn to a new challenge, climbing. Low,

Reflection: Stuck in Standing

Compare the average age for independently pulling to standing with the average age for independently sitting down from standing. Is it much? If you have ever watched an infant pull to standing and then seem "stuck" and begin to cry and look to the caregiver, this statistic might explain the baby's cry. What role does cephalocaudal development play in this? Can you recall from Chapter 6 how this dilemma is considered a touchpoint related to sleep?

Figure 7.3. Plan of Possibilities: New Contexts for Movement

Context: Add sturdy cardboard fruit packing boxes to the play spaces, inside and in the yard.
Planning Question: Will the boxes invite crawlers to pull to standing? Will toys placed atop the boxes attract crawlers to reach up and pull up? Will the toddlers use the boxes to climb into, on, or through?

Date: 3/17–21

OBSERVATIONS	INTERPRETATIONS

---

raised surfaces for climbing attract the toddler. These can be simply a row of upturned sturdy boxes or a pile of low, wide pillows. Open-topped boxes provide spaces to climb into, as do low, wide utility basins or dishpans. Slightly graduated ramps and inclines add a unique challenge for the young walker, who must learn anew how to move up and down a sloped surface. Slightly graduated stairs, both with and without sides, also attract young toddlers.

Planning Play Spaces with Movement in Mind

Free to move, infants delight in having time and space to practice their motor skills. They expand their repertoire of movement and learn to move with balance, strength, flexibility, and grace. Pikler (1994) offers this advice, with respect to what adults can do to support infants' active movement and motor development:

> The question is not how we can "teach" an infant to move well and correctly, using cleverly thought up, artificially constructed, complicated measures, using exercises and gymnastics. It is simply a matter of offering an infant the opportunity—or, more precisely, not to deprive him of this opportunity—to move according to his inherent ability. . . . If one does not interfere, an infant will learn to turn, roll, creep on the belly, go on all fours, stand, sit, and walk with no trouble. This will not happen under pressure, but out of her own initiative—independently, with joy, and pride in her achievement. (pp. 6–12)

Teachers support infants' motor development by adapting the room, the yard, and furnishings to accommodate infants' developing movement skills. Figure 7.3 provides an example of how teachers use infants' developing motor skills to plan new contexts for learning.

Reflection:
Movement as Provocation for Curriculum

In the Plan of Possibilities shown in Figure 7.3, teachers in a family–childcare home propose a planning question related to motor development. There are two crawlers in the program, both of whom are just starting to pull to standing, and there are two toddlers, who have learned to walk and have begun to enjoy climbing onto low surfaces. The teachers propose a planning question to explore what new movement contexts to offer these children.

They were curious to know whether the sturdy boxes used to pack fruit, when turned upside down in the play space, would serve as an invitation to the crawlers to pull to standing. They wondered whether the crawlers, once they were standing, would use the boxes as an engaging work surface where they could explore toys. They saw the round holes in the box surface as invitations to use developing fine motor skills to poke objects through. They decided to put some of the sturdy cardboard boxes in the toddler play area, as safe surfaces for climbing. The boxes stayed in the play spaces for several days. The teachers made periodic notes of what they saw, adding these to the observation section of the plan. As they read through the notes at their next planning meeting, they decided to deepen the investigation with a new planning question and an emergent new context for learning: "If we rearrange the boxes in the room, will the babies who are starting to pull to standing use them to cruise from place to place?"

Reflect on how observations of infants' motor development can generate ideas for enhancing the play space as an environment for learning. How do such plans help broaden the definition of curriculum, when working with infants and toddlers?

PREHENSION: REACHING AND GRASPING

As babies practice moving from place, they are also organizing small-muscle systems. Over the course of the first year, reaching transforms to batting, to grasp-

Figure 7.4. Stages of Prehension: The Voluntary Grasp

Stage	Hand Position	Average Age (Months)	Range (Months)
Bats at object	Arm and whole hand, fingers together	5.6	4–8
Palmar grasp	Fingers together in opposition to palm	6.8	5–9
Partial pincer	Fingers together in opposition to thumb	7.4	6–10
Neat pincer	Index finger in opposition to thumb	8.9	7–12

Source. Bayley, 1969.

ing, and finally to picking things up precisely with finger and thumb. By the first birthday, infants are artfully manipulating and inspecting whatever they find.

Prehension means reaching out to grasp an object. It is a process that takes months to develop. A phenomenon described by researchers as prereaching is seen in infants as young as 5–9 days old. It is different from goal-directed reaching, which does not show up until about 4 months of age. Prereaching occurs when an infant fully extends the arm and opens the hand toward an object, without making contact. Prereaching is thought to be a precursor to what eventually will become the grasp (Smitsman & Corbetta, 2010).

By around 4 months, a baby's hands have become a primary object of interest. Infants this age spend hours in close inspection of the movement of their hands. A baby might spend long periods of time opening and closing the hand and watching this move closely. This intense focus of interest gives way, in time, to objects beyond the infant's body. Infants begin to reach out in an attempt to grasp objects and will reach with the whole body in the direction of an object of interest.

Learning to successfully reach and grasp is a process that requires several months of practice. Figure 7.4 shows the sequence of hand and arm movements that take place as babies master a mature grasp. By around 4 months, babies begin to bat at objects using a whole-arm movement. At first, they have little success. Repeated practice, however, helps babies synchronize the muscles of the hand and arm with the muscles of the head, neck, and torso. In time, on average at 6.8 months of age, and within a range of 5–9 months of age (Bayley, 1969), as they bat at objects of interest, infants begin to reliably connect with objects in a whole-hand grasp.

From Palmar to Pincer

The development of the ability to successfully grasp voluntarily is an example of proximal–distal development. The shoulder and arm muscles organize first to accomplish prereaching and batting. Next the wrist and whole hand get involved, followed by the fingers. Once babies can reliably grab an object of interest, they inspect it with eyes, fingers, and mouth.

The first grasp is a whole-hand grasp, called the palmar grasp. With the palmar grasp, the baby clasps an object between the palm of the hand and the four fingers together. The thumb is not yet involved. In the palmar grasp, the four fingers are restricted to working as a unit, because the finger muscles have not yet organized to be able to work separately. Infants practice the palmar grasp repeatedly, as they pick up toys, mouth them, inspect them, and then drop them, only to look around for more things to pick up.

With practice, a more refined grasp emerges. Instead of using the fingers together as a unit in the palmar grasp, infants begin to separate the fingers and will pick up an object using several fingers together in opposition to the thumb. Occurring on average at 7.4 months of age and within a range of 6–10 months of age, this is called a partial pincer grasp, because it leads in time to the final form of the grasp, called a neat pincer grasp, clasping an object between the index finger and the thumb (Figure 7.4). The neat pincer

---

Reflection: What the Newborn Sees

Newborns coordinate their eyes to work together and focus within a limited range, about 10–12 inches from their face. By 2 months, they discriminate color. Sometime between 3 and 5 months of age, infants develop depth perception. By 4 months of age, infants have fairly reliable depth perception and are able to bring objects at any distance into clear focus. By 6 months, infants' visual perception has improved markedly to the point where they have clear input for gathering information about the world around them (Slater et al., 2010).

Is there an advantage to restricting the newborn's visual acuity to this range? What value might there be for the newborn to see the face of the caregiver in full focus, yet perceive things at a distance as an unfocused blur?

Figure 7.5. Objects to Invite Baby's Reach and Grasp

occurs on average at 8.9 months of age and within a range of 7–12 months of age (Bayley, 1969).

Selecting Toys with Prehension in Mind

Infant toys should not be restricted to commercially manufactured objects sold as toys. Many of the most popular infant play objects are ordinary objects, like boxes, bowls, swatches of fabric, containers, or tubes. Knowledge of stages of prehension is especially helpful in deciding how to select play materials. The line of sight for babies lying on their back is about a 45-degree angle from the floor. Therefore, toys with a bit of height, rather than toys that rest flat against the floor, work best for the youngest babies. The features for selecting play materials for 4- to 8-month-olds are summarized here and described in more detail in Chapter 11, where the focus is on setting up play spaces for infants:

- Supple rather than rigid
- Lightweight
- Easily held in one hand
- Handholds to grasp
- High enough to be seen when baby is lying on back

Figure 7.5 shows examples of play materials that have these features.

Avoid objects that roll or move away when touched, like round balls with smooth surfaces. Features that invite a baby's still fledgling grasp include handles of some sort that the baby can easily grasp; parts that serve as handholds, like the leg of a stuffed toy dog or the edge of a lightweight basket; objects with openings in the surface; and objects that have resilience to the touch. Since young babies have limited arm muscle control, objects should be lightweight. For a baby's first toy, Gerber (1998) recommends a stiff cotton scarf that can be propped into a small peak, with features that make it both visible and graspable (see Figure 7.5).

Objects with edges that can be easily grasped using several fingers clasped together against the thumb (see Figure 7.5) give 6- to 9-month-olds opportunity to practice the partial pincer grasp and to refine the neat pincer grasp. Baskets and boxes, made from sturdy cardboard, fabric, or metal, attract the baby's emerging grasp and invite the fingers and thumb to work together. They should be lightweight, because babies will wave, bang, drop, or fling them, as babies gather information about their physical properties, using mouth, eyes, hands, and arms. Cloth or woven baskets, jar lids, wooden embroidery hoops, and metal bracelets are examples of ordinary objects that have edges that accommodate infants' partial pincer grasp.

The final phase of the voluntary grasp, the neat pincer, enables the infant to pinch, poke, and investigate the small openings and crevices of objects. When infants are mastering the pincer grasp, a feature to look for in play objects is the presence of holes and openings that invite infants to use the pointer finger (see Figure 7.5). Ordinary objects that have this feature are metal canning jar rings, egg cartons, whisks, ice cube trays, and measuring cups and spoons.

PERCEPTUAL AND MOTOR CHALLENGES

How infants perceive and experience the world around them will influence how they move through the expected sequence of motor milestones. For some infants, their perceptual systems may distort patterns of action and movement, making simple acts of movement difficult and awkward. They may become agitated with exposure to sights and sounds that for most children would be fine. Therefore, knowing how to recognize signs of perceptual or motor challenge is important when working with groups of children. Such children rely on the adults in their lives to modulate the intensity and the timing of sensory input. This means making subtle but significant changes in the sensory or the physical environment that enable all children to move and act comfortably and thereby to learn through play and interaction with objects and people. If this does not occur, children's movements and actions are compromised, as is their learning.

Sensory-Processing Challenges

Sensory processing refers to the particular way in which the various senses are tuned to take in and process incoming information. For some babies, sensory processing is more challenging than for others, because their perceptual systems are tuned in such a way as to cause them to be either overwhelmed or "underwhelmed" by typical levels of sensory input. When sensations are more than what a baby can handle, they surpass that baby's sensory threshold of comfort. For other babies, the opposite is true, and sensations that typically would arouse an infant are of insufficient intensity, with the baby not even noticing or alerting to the sensation.

Imagine a baby in a state of quiet alert. The baby catches the gaze of the caregiver. The caregiver sees this as an invitation to play and tries to engage the baby with a brightly colored toy. The toy also makes a sound when shaken. At first, the toy captures the baby's attention, but after a brief moment of interest, the baby looks away, turns away, and begins to fuss, as if to say, "Stop talking so much! Stop making that noise! Stop touching me so much!" If, in response, the caregiver quiets and stills, the baby calms. From the perspective of sensory processing, this baby may be experiencing sensory overload in this simple moment of play. The baby disengages as a way to self-regulate. The downside of such a response, however, is that by disengaging, the baby is no longer actively

> ### Reflection: A Toy in Hand
>
> It is not uncommon for an adult to dangle a toy near a newborn or place a toy into a newborn's clenched fist, in expectation that the baby will play with the toy. However, for newborns and babies just 1–2 months old, grasping objects and exploring them is not yet their agenda. Newborns have other work to do. They are organizing the muscles of shoulder, arm, and hand to work together to reach and grasp. Not until they do so will a toy in hand make any sense to them. Gerber (2002) urges caregivers to restrain from putting a toy into a young baby's hand. Instead, she suggests placing it nearby and letting the baby grasp it when ready to do so. This supports babies' mastery in learning how to reach and grasp, a voluntary act, not something imposed before they can voluntarily handle, reach for, or release a toy.

engaged in play or actively engaged in learning. If this happens on a regular basis, it could be troubling.

Sensory processing can be seen as a continuum. Babies highly sensitive to sensory input are on one end of the continuum. It takes very little stimulation from the surrounding environment for such babies to reach the threshold beyond which they are overloaded and visibly uncomfortable. To defend themselves, they disengage from the environment, as best they can, which appears as a strong disengagement. Therapists describe such behavior as hyper-reactive (Williamson & Anzalone, 2001). Children who are hyper-reactive tend to be very sensitive to touch and may even dislike sitting on someone's lap to be cuddled. Their sensitivity may extend to textures of food or to fabrics that irritate their skin. If they have high sensitivity to touch, they may resist playing with water, sand, clay, or paint, materials commonly offered in early childhood settings.

Some hyper-reactive children protect themselves against sensory input by remaining vigilant throughout the day. This makes them appear anxious and fearful. In reality, they are simply trying to keep from having their sensory systems overloaded. The downside, with respect to learning, is that in their constant vigilance, they show little interest in play and are easily preoccupied by seemingly trivial things, like the irritation of labels in clothing, or overhead lights, or the accidental touch of a passerby.

On the opposite end of the continuum of sensory processing are children who are hyporeactive (Williamson & Anzalone, 2001). These children have a high threshold of arousal, meaning they require a lot of sensory input before they notice or respond. In essence, they have a high sensory appetite. To be satisfied, comfortable, and engaged, they need highly stimulating sensorial experiences. When a high-sensory diet is lacking, they may disengage from people and play and become isolated.

Hyporeactive children may hardly notice when they are touched, or may not be aware when they are bumping up against something themselves, because the sensory input is insufficient to reach their threshold of sensory arousal. Their high-sensory appetite means they must seek sensory-stimulating experiences. They may enjoy richly sensorial materials like sand, clay, and paint. However, a high-sensory threshold may put such children at risk when playing with others. They may not even notice when other children are trying to engage them in play. This might isolate them from social play with peers. Caregivers aware of the higher sensory appetite of these children can provide them with sensory-rich play materials, interact with them more frequently, and help them to enter play with other children.

It is important to note that children with sensory challenges may appear socially withdrawn, but there may be two entirely different reasons for this. A child who is hyporeactive simply may need a higher level of sensory input in order to engage with others. A child who is sensory avoidant simply is disengaging socially in order to keep from being overwhelmed by sensory input. Both children may appear to be socially unavailable, yet, just like all children, they too want to engage with others and have friends. They rely on their caregivers for help in modulating sensory input to help them engage socially with others.

Children who have high sensory thresholds may be very active and moving constantly, in their search for high levels of sensory stimulation (Williamson & Anzalone, 2001). They are sensory seekers looking for intensive sensory experiences. Ensuring their safety is important, because they are attracted to situations that offer high sensory stimulation but high risk of danger, like high surfaces or big heavy objects. They also may be at risk of emotional meltdown, when they become overly stimulated during play. Caregivers can offer sensory seekers play contexts that satisfy their sensory diet, yet keep them safe, like hammock swings, in which they can wrap themselves in tactile and movement stimulation; cloth bags filled with sand or rice,

---

Reflection: Sensory-Processing Challenges— At Risk of Being Left Out

Some babies who are hyper-reactive cope by spending all of their energy avoiding situations that might overload their sensory systems. They appear fearful or anxious. Other babies might be on the opposite end of the continuum, hyporeactive, and may not notice an invitation to join others in play. They may on the surface appear sad or uninterested, but, in reality, the sensory input is simply too low and they are not even aware that others are trying to connect socially with them. Although they appear quiet and disengaged, they still want to play with others. They simply need a higher dose of sensory input in order to notice and respond to the invitation to play.

What suggestions do you have for caregivers who encounter babies with these sensory-processing challenges? How would the suggested intervention for the hyper-reactive baby compare to the intervention for the hyporeactive baby?

---

sewn shut, and available to carry from place to place; and safe opportunities for indoor climbing.

Motor-Planning Challenges

Some sensory-processing problems reveal themselves in how children move, what experts call motor-planning challenges. Motor planning is the process of figuring out how to accomplish a goal that involves sequential actions. It requires an awareness of sensations going on within the body. Typically, when we consider the senses, we think of the five senses that bring in information from the outside environment—seeing, hearing, feeling, tasting, and smelling. However, we have additional senses that allow us to detect sensory input from within the body. These include the proprioceptive system, which generates sensation from muscles and joints, resulting from active movement of body parts; and the vestibular system, located in the inner ear, which responds to movement of the head and body in relation to gravity, giving us our sense of balance and equilibrium as well as our sense of movement in space. As we move, we continuously generate feedback from our proprioceptive and vestibular systems. We can thank proprioceptive feedback for our ability to effortlessly climb stairs, without having to be consciously aware of the height of each step. Encounter one step that is of greater height, however, and our proprioceptive system will immediately alert us.

For most children, moving in space becomes seemingly effortless, thanks to the tactile, proprioceptive, and vestibular systems that guide them through the process of mastering motor milestones. However, for some children, these systems do not work smoothly together. For children with motor-planning challenges, a simple act like climbing stairs is awkward and energy consuming, irrespective of how many times they have done it before. Their proprioceptive feedback system fails to provide the needed feedback. Children with motor-planning deficits also may have difficulty controlling direction of movement and may clumsily bump into things.

In some children with motor-planning challenges, their vestibular system may warn them of danger too quickly, so they may be very sensitive to being moved, react intensely, and feel out of balance with even just a simple change of position. They might appear less active than other children, and a simple experience like swinging could overwhelm them. In some children, their vestibular system is calibrated in the reverse direction, and they may not even notice when they are about to lose their balance. They may crave active, rambunctious play and may delight in being swung to great heights.

Caregivers can help such infants engage with the environment in ways that modulate stimulation, minimize threat, and sustain play. A key planning question is, "What activities or events organize or disorganize the child? What does the child appear to need in terms of sensory diet? Does the child need a little bit less, a little bit more, a lot less, or a lot more sensory input?" These questions lead to an intervention plan that provides a goodness of fit in the play environment and in the daily routines.

Infants Born Prematurely

Infants born prematurely encounter sensory-processing challenges as well, but within a limited timeframe, during the weeks or months following birth. These babies must cope with stress that comes from being born too soon. Premature infants are still developing critical systems for regulating sensory input. Without the protection of the womb, they are vulnerable to an onslaught of lights, sounds, and touches. Premature babies spend most of their energy on regulating body systems, like breathing, digestion,

---

Research Highlight: The Challenge of Being Born Too Soon

Heidelise Als (Als et al., 2004), a pioneer in improving hospital environments for premature babies, advises caregivers to pay close attention to how a baby moves or looks in order to know how to respond. Skin color, body temperature, breathing patterns, movement patterns, and body position can be monitored to determine how well a premature baby is coping with the surrounding environment. A very young baby who is coping well with sensory input will show organized movement patterns, stable breathing, and no stark changes in skin color or body temperature. In contrast, a baby not coping well will show disorganized movement patterns, irregular breathing, poor blood circulation revealed through blotchy skin color, or temperature differences between trunk and extremities. These are signals to the caregiver to reduce the baby's sensory load by quieting the room, lowering sounds and lights, minimizing touch and handling, and simplifying visual surroundings (VandenBerg et al., 2009).

---

and elimination. They have little energy left to engage in play. A fleeting glimpse in the caregiver's direction may be all that a premature baby can afford.

Premature babies are easily disorganized by sights, movement, or sound (VandenBerg, Browne, Perez, & Newstetter, 2009). Touch that is too strong can overwhelm. However, moderate pressure massage can be calming for premature babies and facilitates improved growth and development (Field, et al., 1996). Massage has the effect of providing an even blanket of rhythmic pressure on the infant's body, much like the even blanket of rhythmic sound in a lullaby or the even rhythm of motion in being rocked.

FROM RESEARCH TO PRACTICE: MOTOR DEVELOPMENT THROUGH A CULTURAL LENS

Although motor development scales suggest that motor skills emerge along a similar trajectory for all children, there is tremendous variation in how infants move through their surroundings and with what degree of freedom. This is evident in studies of child-rearing across cultures and across time (Levine et al., 1994; Tronick, 2007). Infants develop motor skills within a social context that is informed by the values, beliefs, attitudes, and behaviors of the culture. A family's culture and the desired caregiving practices influence the objects made available to the infant, the context offered for movement, and the emergence of movement patterns.

The contexts that influence the emergence of motor skills vary widely. In some communities, babies are carried close to the caregiver's body, in variations of a sling, and the babies may be somewhat restricted in movement for many hours of the day, during the early months. Brazilian babies, 3–5 months old, were found to develop the grasp and to sit at an age significantly later than average (Santos, Gabbard, & Goncalves, 2001). The researchers attributed the difference, at least partially, to the traditional caregiving practice of holding infants almost constantly for the first 5 months.

In some cultures, babies are swaddled when put down to sleep. In some cultures, babies move from car to house and then back to car while seated in a molded seat. Some babies play on the floor, and some have access to stairs. Some babies have caregivers who regularly massage their limbs. The variations are many, and each baby's motor development is influenced by what the baby experiences. In the end, all these babies learn to move and to manipulate small objects with their hands in much the same way, but with variations that ensure behavior that works well within their family and culture.

Looking Back and Looking Forward

Babies master an impressive series of motor skills in the short span of 3 years. This effort captivates babies, who are highly motivated to take on the challenge of moving their bodies in increasingly more complex ways. Babies cover an amazing amount of territory in the course of a single day, estimated to be more than 9,000 steps over a distance of more than 29 football fields, covering nearly every room in their homes each day, all the while fine-tuning their locomotion and balance (Adolph & Berger, 2006). Their modes of moving transition from rolling, to crawling, to walking, to running. With their hands, they explore the shape, the texture, the size, and the resilience of objects they encounter. They spend huge amounts of energy and time practicing and refining each new skill, until they reach the point where they can do it effortlessly. The next chapter explores infants' journey within another domain of development, how infants think and organize thoughts into concepts and ideas.

CHAPTER 8

Thinking

Cognitive Development

The scientist peering into the crib, looking for answers to some of the deepest questions about how minds and the world and language work, sees the scientist peering out of the crib, who, it turns out, is doing much the same thing. (Gopnik et al., 1999, pp. 3–4)

PRIOR TO THE mid-20th century, most people considered infants to be helpless and dependent, not yet fully perceiving the surrounding world, with movements dominated by reflexes. However, pioneering scientists, like Jean Piaget, Lev Vygotsky, and Jerome Bruner, shattered this myth, with definitive observations of infants. Their work led the way in showing that infants are competent thinkers, actively organizing concepts and ideas.

Scientific study of infants took a great leap forward when researchers discovered that infants were not only very good at detecting differences between sensations they saw or heard, but also were capable of demonstrating preferences, through voluntary movements, like suck patterns, visual gaze, or turning to a sound. For example, if an infant detects a change in a sound pattern, the infant will turn in the direction of the sound, or suck faster to see a desired image. In clever experiments, scientists use the infant's gaze pattern or sucking pattern to reveal what most engages the infant's attention and whether the infant prefers one thing over another.

With this new way of inviting infants into the world of scientific study, infancy research flourished. Scientists invented a variety of experiments that helped them discover what infants were capable of perceiving and what attracted their interest. For the first time in history, they could begin to systematically study how infants form ideas and concepts and how they solve problems. Together with advances in brain imaging, these new ways of studying infants ushered in a new way of conceptualizing the infant, as a meaning-making person, and shed new light on infancy, as a period of rapid brain growth and a period rich in opportunity for learning.

Scientists who study the development of cognition in children call them "scientists in the crib" (Gopnik et al., 1999, p. viii). A large body of research provides robust evidence that infants and young children explore, investigate, experiment, and analyze. They calculate statistics on what they hear and see, as they investigate with focused attention. They gather detailed information about the objects and people they encounter and construct concepts that serve as foundations for mathematics, the sciences, and the arts. What this looks like and what it means for those caring for infants is the subject of this chapter.

CONSTRUCTING KNOWLEDGE— ADAPTING CATEGORIES OF MIND

The best way to find out how infants think, that is, how they build ideas and concepts and how these ideas and concepts get more complex over time, is to watch babies at play. As they play with objects, infants use their developing motor skills to gather information through their senses. They notice what things look like, smell like, sound like, and feel like, and within developing circuits of neurons, they hold in memory the physical features of objects and people. They organize and categorize this information, making meaning and building concepts.

Figures 8.1 chronicles an episode of spontaneous infant play, in which Severyn, a 6-month-old, discovers new objects in his play space. He is surrounded by many toys, most of them familiar to him. However, a few, including four plastic soap dishes, are recent additions to his play space. The first photo captures the moment when he first notices and picks up the small soap dish. He mouths and fingers it, peering at it intently and feeling the pattern of small bumps. When he turns it over, he sees the other side is smooth. He examines it closely, turning it over several times. This

Figure 8.1. Caught in the Act of Learning

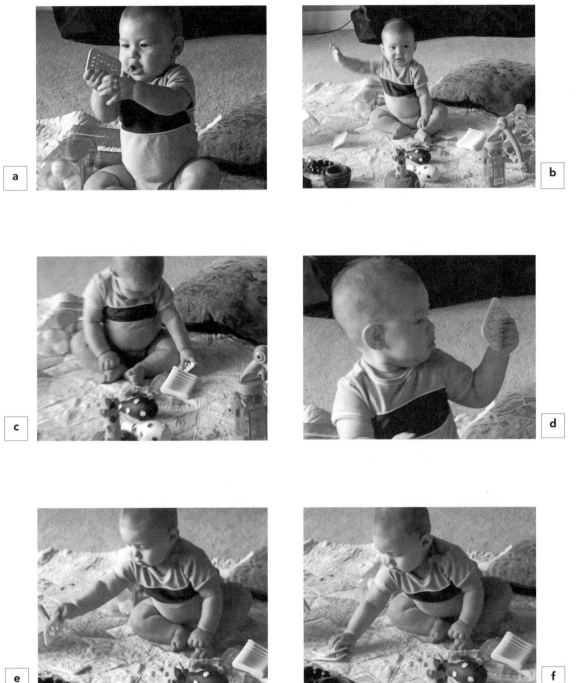

Figure 8.2. Making Sense of a Novel Object

pick up the small soap dish. In Figure 8.1d, he examines this identical soap dish, using the same strategies he used before—mouthing, fingering, and rotating it—but then he turns to his right, looks down, and sees the first soap dish. His thinking is revealed in the photos that follow. In Figure 8.1e, he leans forward with the second soap dish in hand, and in Figure 8.1f, he places one soap dish on top of the other, making an identical match.

This series of photos tells the story of how infants gather copious information about the physical features of the objects they encounter, how they hold this information in memory, and how they use it to organize and make sense of new encounters. Once Severyn had thoroughly examined the first soap dish, he literally held it in mind, within circuits of neurons within his brain. When he encountered another object with the same features, the same circuit of neurons fired in his brain. Piaget called this assimilation, fitting a new encounter into an existing category of mind.

As we assimilate a novel experience into our existing categories of mind, we build knowledge. We build knowledge in another way as well, because sometimes we encounter experiences that do not easily fit within our existing categories of mind. We may struggle a bit, looking for a fit, but in time we are forced to restructure the category in order to hold, or accommodate, the new encounter. Piaget called this accommodation, a process by which we change and make more complex and coherent our categories of mind.

Immediately following what you see in Figure 8.1f, Severyn turned his attention to the larger, ribbed white soap dish (Figure 8.2). He noticed that it was white and pliable, just like the other one, but that it had no bumps and was ribbed in a way that made it different from the others. He peered at it intently, turning it over, mouthing it, and shaking it, as if trying to figure out how to fit this new object into his existing mental category. This moment of struggle is what Piaget called disequilibrium, an intense moment of trying to make sense of something that is not yet clear.

pattern of grabbing, mouthing, and looking is one he has used many times, ever since he mastered how to successfully reach and grasp objects about a month prior. He has other ways of examining objects, and he applies these strategies to this soap dish as well. He shakes it up and down. As he shakes it, he drops it (Figure 8.1b).

To grasp what might be going on in Severyn's mind during this moment of play, it is helpful to consider his play within the theoretical framework of Jean Piaget, one of the first scientists to systematically study how infants appear to think. Piaget theorized that knowledge, from the infant's point of view, is a consequence of infants' sensory-motor experiences. From his observations of how infants examine and manipulate objects, he proposed the idea that infants build knowledge by interacting with objects and using their senses and their developing muscles to experiment with objects in order to discover what they are like. They also act on the objects in new ways to discover what they can make the objects do. This is evident in the full sequence of photos that captures Severyn's play.

When the soap dish flies out of Severyn's hand, it lands to his right, but he does not see it land, nor does he go in search of it (Figure 8.1b). Instead, he turned his attention to the toys to his left. In Figure 8.1c, he catches sight of two other soap dishes, one identical to the one he had been playing with. The other is larger, and of a different design. The identical soap dish is tucked under the edge of the larger soap dish. He reaches under the large soap dish (Figure 8.1c) to

The way children resolve disequilibrium, according to Piaget, is to modify the existing mental category to better fit the new encounter. Through his play, Severyn modified his existing category to accommodate a more expanded range of features. In so doing, he added to his knowledge, building increasingly more complex brain circuits. Piaget theorized that children build knowledge by continually adapting their mental categories, sometimes assimilating and sometimes accommodating. Through this dynamic process of adaptation, infants build increasingly more complex concepts and categories.

INFANTS' STRATEGIES FOR LEARNING

Severyn's story illustrates infants' competence in learning about the surrounding world. By around 4 months, infants discover their hands and fingers and spend a fair amount of time fingering their hands in play. This leads to reaching out and grasping objects, at first with intermittent success, but in a few weeks, with precision. From then on, they delight in picking up objects. An object in the hand becomes an object under study, as they mouth, peer at, finger, rotate, and squeeze it.

In so doing, they acquire important information about the physical properties of the object. In time, they add more complex actions—shaking, dangling, and dropping. With each new action, infants build a more detailed repertoire of knowledge about objects—what they are like. Within their developing brains, they gather, sort, and categorize details about size, shape, color, smell, taste, and sound. As they become increasingly more adept at using their hands, fingers, and even their feet for exploration, they relate one action to another and explore how objects react when they act on them. Through such investigations, they begin to build concepts about how objects fill, fit in, and move through space.

In this episode of play, Severyn demonstrates his full repertoire of learning strategies. He attends with focused attention in order to gather information about the objects he encounters. He remembers the features of what he has used before. He also invents a game, of sorts, the problem he encounters being to find an identical match. Infants imitate, they remember, they attend to one thing rather than another, and they experiment to solve problems. These are infants' learning strategies (California Department of Education, 2009), all of which are present at birth.

Attention Maintenance

Like small scientists, infants experiment with objects they encounter. Their play often looks like small experiments, driven by the question, "What can I make this do?" They fiddle around with toys in an effort to figure out the impact of their actions on an object and enjoy figuring out how simple tools work. It is not uncommon to see infants repeating and varying their actions as they experiment with toys.

Attention maintenance is the term used to describe infants' ability to exercise control over what they look at or listen to. Being able to focus on specific features and aspects of objects and events allows infants to get to know the people and objects that are most important and relevant to them. Attention maintenance makes it possible for infants to scan an object or a person for a sustained period of time in order to gather information about it and to use this information to solve problems. For example, when an infant cries with a plea for help and reaches and turns toward his or her caregiver, the infant is maintaining focus on the one most likely to provide help while at the same time filtering out the other adults in the room. Attention maintenance is present in all infants to some degree and is key to filtering information in order to learn new things.

Imitation

Through imitation, infants incorporate the ways of those who care for them. They learn patterns of speech, ways of moving, gestures, attitudes, and skills. Imitation is crucial in the acquisition of language and culture (Rogoff, 1990, 2011). Newborns are capable of imitating simple facial expressions and hand movements (Meltzoff & Moore, 1977, 1983). This innate capacity to imitate prepares infants to join in games of peekaboo and to mirror the actions, facial expressions, and vocalizations of others.

As infants age, their ability to imitate expands beyond simply imitating in the moment. Older infants imitate actions seen at a prior point in time. Imitation is especially important when it comes to learning about the social world. Infants acquire much of what Piaget described as social knowledge by simply imitating the behavior or listening to the speech of those who provide their care. Movements, words, phrases, and cadence and patterns of speech—each develops primarily through imitation.

Memory

Memory is the way the brain holds experience within new synaptic connections (Siegel & Hartzell, 2003). Two types of memory were described in Chapter 2, implicit memory and explicit memory. Implicit memory is memory of emotions, movements, sensations, and perceptions, a nonverbal form of memory that is present at birth. With implicit memory, there is no sense of recall, no sense of story of self in time. Implicit memory plays an important role in forming bonds of attachment between infant and caregiver.

Explicit memory *is* connected to a sense of recalling facts or experience of oneself in time and space. Explicit memory becomes most evident midway through the second year and develops more fully after the second birthday, when circuitry involved with longterm memory develops in higher regions of the brain. By the second birthday, toddlers are remembering and recounting events of their own recent past.

Problem Solving

A problem is a desire to reach a certain goal coupled with the need to figure out how to reach that goal. Problems present themselves in many ways for infants. Getting the attention of the one who will provide comfort presents a problem. So does being able to carry something from place to place, or making one object stay put when placed on top of another, or figuring out how things work or how to get possession of a desired toy. Each situation presents a problem to be solved. As infants mature, the problems they tackle become more complex.

INFANTS BUILD CONCEPTS

As infants explore their surroundings, they relate one thing to another, adding to their logico-mathematical knowledge. As they do so, they build concepts. They relate the physical properties of one thing to the physical properties of another, building the concept of classification. They line things in order and build the concept of seriation. They explore how things fill, fit in, and move in space, and build the concept of spatial relations. They relate cause and effect and build the concept of causality. They use actions, objects, or ideas to represent other actions, objects, or ideas and in so doing build the concept of representation.

They build these concepts as they play and interact, within the regular events of the day. For example, as they get dressed, they construct the classificatory relationship of *coat* versus *shirt*. As they enjoy water play outside, they make the classificatory relationship of *liquids* versus *solids*, build the concepts of spatial relations and number as they fill one cup and then another, and build the concept of representation as they offer the cup as a drink to a doll. The concepts infants build support a foundation for mathematics, science, social studies, language arts, and visual and performing arts.

The following discussion reviews each of these concepts with respect to what they look like in infants and toddlers and provides examples of play materials and contexts that support the development of each concept. Absent is an exhaustive list of toys or activities for learning. Instead this discussion focuses on features to look for in selecting play materials that support concept development. When teachers are prepared to look for specific features of play materials, there are endless possibilities for what the actual play materials might be.

Classification and Seriation

Classification refers to distinguishing differences and putting things into relationships. Classification underlies much of cognition and is a fundamental skill in solving problems, investigating, and experimenting. Infants build the concept of classification as they play and interact, categorizing, grouping, and sorting based on distinguishing attributes. Classification plays a key role in reading, writing, mathematics, and science.

Once infants build their skill in distinguishing differences, they pose a more complex challenge for themselves—arranging objects by degree of difference, a concept called seriation. Seriation means noticing a difference in size or degree and then applying this knowledge of size or degree to a subsequent task—physically placing objects in order, with respect to this difference. Infants build the concept of seriation as they notice how objects vary in size and line them up or stack them.

Young infants collect and categorize information about objects and people. Infants as young as 3 months old notice differences between people and objects and expect people to act differently than objects (Legerstee, 1997). Infants develop their ability to categorize through the objects and people they encounter.

When infants find objects in the play space that have like features that go together, they actively explore and compare them, relating one feature to the other. In so doing, they build the concepts of classification and seriation.

When teachers place objects that are identical in the play space, they prompt infants to discover a common feature. When they place objects that are similar but distinct in one or more features, they invite infants to notice and compare differences. Each collection provides challenges in thinking and reasoning and supports infants in noticing features that are the same and those that are different. The following is a guide to selecting toys with features that prompt classification and seriation in young infants:

- *Identical toys with the same physical features.* When teachers offer collections of identical objects, they supply infants with materials that help them construct the concept of identity, that these things are all alike. For example, three identical woven baskets might be placed together near the infant in the play space, or three identical metal bowls might be set up in a corner of the play space.
- *Similar but distinct toys, alike in most but not all features.* When teachers offer collections of toys that are similar but slightly different, they supply infants with materials to construct categories. The ability to sort and classify emerges as infants take on the challenge of figuring out how similar-looking objects actually may differ. Teachers might add to the play space objects similar in shape, but distinct in material—such as three circular bracelets, one metal, one wood, and one plastic.
- *Toys that invite comparison using all the senses.* Young infants use all their senses to gather information—sight, touch, hearing, taste, smell, proprioception (pressure response), and kinesthesia (balance). Objects in the play space should invite infants to explore using all the senses. For example, washable cloth bags filled with nontoxic dried herbs bring the textures and scents of nature to young infants; or a collection of stretchable fabric strips or cloth bags filled with sand, seeds, or cotton provide infants an opportunity to compare pressure and weight, using the senses of proprioception and kinesthesia.

In their second year, infants begin to go in search of a specific type of object, spontaneously sorting and classifying by shape, size, color, or function. When containers are available, infants begin to collect with intention (Kálló & Balog, 2005). Initially, they might add any object to their collection. In time, they get more particular and go in search of a specific kind of object. Their passion for filling and emptying containers generates much practice in sorting and classifying, foundational concepts in mathematics and science.

Teachers support such defined searches by offering collections of toys that are alike in shape, function, color, or size alongside containers. In time, infants notice similarities or distinctions that are present within a collection of otherwise quite similar objects. A mobile infant might go in search of all the blue vehicles or all the people figures. Simple objects in a variety of colors, sizes, shapes, or textures work best—baskets, boxes, cups, blocks, balls, rings, figures of people and animals, and blankets. For example, infants might find a dishpan filled with jar lids, some plastic and some metal, some blue, some green, some yellow, some white, and some clear, or a blue straw basket with a variety of swatches of blue fabric, each a different shade, pattern, or texture. This might be placed alongside a yellow basket filled with only yellow fabric swatches, each a different shade, pattern, or texture. The potential for going in search of all the blue fabric swatches or all the yellow fabric swatches is built into the collection of similar but distinct materials.

Toddlers, 18–36 months old, are mini-inventors propelled by a sense of wonder about what they can make things do or how they can make things work. They maintain their interest in collecting toys and other play materials, but they do so with a greater sense of purpose. The natural world becomes an intriguing research lab for them, so they enjoy going in search of leaves, small insects, bark, and twigs, all of which can become the focus of a collection, which in turn prompts building and pretend play.

In the 18- to 36-month phase, toddlers collect objects for their treasure value (Kálló & Balog, 2005). It is not uncommon to see a toddler give an object special value, clasping it tightly in hand, storing it away in a pocket, or entrusting it to the hands and protection of the caregiver. From an outing, toddlers often return with treasures from nature. A variety of containers, boxes, carts, and wagons support toddlers' interest in safeguarding these treasured items. Toddlers profit from props that enhance their treasure hunting, like raincoats, boots, umbrellas, hats, shoulder bags, magnifying glasses, and collection jars. Such props prompt toddlers to go in search of special items of their choice, like leaves, pinecones, seed pods, or flowers.

Toddlers enjoy the challenge of making simple patterns with objects they collect. If they select objects for collecting based on a particular physical feature, they might connect one object to the other, making a pattern relationship. This might be a relationship of identity, size, shape, or color. When collections share a common attribute, toddlers build the concept of identity. They use the concept of identity to build patterns. For example, older toddlers might gather baskets of wildflowers and spontaneously place them around the edge of the meal table, constructing a circular pattern. They might form a row in the sand with their collection of driftwood, making a straight-line pattern. They might explore a collection of cloth placemats, each a different color, with matching napkins, along with a set of plastic dishes, in corresponding colors. Such collections invite toddlers to use and arrange the items based on properties of color, shape, or design, often within simple pretend play. Collections of plastic animals, vehicles, people figures, or blocks give toddlers an open-ended array of possibilities for making patterns with objects, keeping in mind and mentally manipulating multiple attributes simultaneously.

The possibilities for infants' building the concepts of classification and seriation, using what they find in the play space, are endless. Chapter 11 explores how teachers might create a connections and construction play space, with many opportunities for infants to compare, categorize, classify, and arrange objects in series.

Causality

Everyday experiences provide opportunities for infants to learn about causality, how a specific action causes a specific reaction. For example, crying and looking in the direction of the teacher results in being picked up. Shaking a rattle causes a delightful sound. Infants as young as 2 months of age are able to predict cause-and-effect outcomes about how things move in space (Baillargeon, 1994). Understanding causality—knowing how one action causes another—not only prepares infants to predict how objects relate to each other in physical space but also prepares infants to build patterns of expectation about how people behave. Causality is an important concept in all areas of science and the arts.

Like small scientists, young infants act on an object with their hands and fingers in order to cause something interesting to happen. The question, "What can I make this do?" seems to be at the heart of their play. Play objects that offer interesting reactions when turned, shaken, or banged support infants in developing the concept of causality. Initially the actions infants perform on objects are simple. A young infant examines how an object changes and looks different when rotated in the hand. By 8 months, infants are banging and shaking objects to cause an interesting reaction. They delight in how their actions on an object result in a change or a movement in the object. They set objects upright and then knock them down, or push a small car and watch it move through space. As young toddlers, they begin to put two objects together in space. This prompts them to also connect them in terms of action, such as using one object to push another, like a simple train. Teachers support such discoveries by adding to the play space a variety of toys that offer interesting options for pushing, squeezing, banging, swinging, shaking, fingering, twisting, and throwing.

Cause-and-effect toys prompt the question, "If I do this, what happens?" Toys for exploring cause and effect might include the following:

- Objects that make noise when shaken, including not only commercial rattles but also noise-making toys made from clear plastic containers, each containing a distinct kind of safe object, selected for a distinct variation in sound.
- Play objects that cause interesting and varied reactions when dropped or banged together on the floor or against the wall. These might include metal plates, jar lids, or tins; plastic bottles and lids; wooden plates, boxes, and bracelets; and gourds and tightly strung seedpods.
- Simple and safe dials, knobs, latches, hinges, and musical instruments (e.g. wooden, metal, or plastic bells, maracas, chimes, or xylophones).
- Objects that support discoveries of tension and resistance, and things that stretch, like elasticized cloth back scrubbers, lengths of stretchy fabric, or stretchy socks stuffed with cotton fabric.

Reflection: Seeing What Makes the Sound

When rattles are made available to infants, they can explore them more effectively when they can see what causes the sound. Sound makers that give infants clear visual access to the sound-making parts give infants more visual information to work with as they explore the cause-and-effect relationship between movement and sound (Kálló & Balog, 2005). All of the objects in this photo can be used as rattles. Which of these toys will give infants the opportunity to see what causes the sound? Which would you recommend to support infants' concept development?

Older toddlers enjoy the challenge of more-complex relationships of cause and effect. Toys that have knobs that twist or levers or latches that slide to make an interesting reaction engage toddlers' interest in causality. Simple tools, like hinges, snaps, zippers, or large plastic nuts and bolts that screw together offer opportunities for exploring causality, as do lids that fit on jars or boxes of various sizes and shapes. Musical instruments like simple flutes, drums, xylophones, pianos, chimes, and bells invite cause-and-effect exploration and enhance the play space with delightful sounds when shaken, tapped, plucked, or blown. Windsocks, chimes, scarves, or sun-reflectors added to an outdoor fence invite older toddlers to explore the cause-and-effect relationships inherent in the movement of air and the properties of light. A basket of plastic mirrors, old CDs, or Plexiglas translucent colored panels placed in a sunny area of the yard or near a window invite toddlers to explore how their actions impact light and shadow.

Spatial Relations

Infants are very observant of how objects and people fill, fit in, and move in space. By acting on objects to see how they fit in containers, nest together, connect, or balance, infants construct the concept of spatial relations. By exploring how objects move in space—how they fall and how they move with speed, force, and direction—infants add to their understanding of spatial relations and build knowledge that is critical to their later understanding of mathematics and the laws of physics.

Young infants delight in exploring how objects fill, fit in, and move in space. Initially, their exploration centers on picking things up and then dropping, shaking, or flinging them aside. They repeat simple actions, like dropping toys into a container, dumping them out, and dropping them in again. These are simple investigations of how objects fall and what sounds they create upon impact. This also gives infants a sense of how containers work as tools to hold things.

Once they learn how to crawl, infants delight in flinging an object away from them and crawling after it to retrieve it. These investigations of increasingly complex ways of making things move through space provide initial experiences with gravity, weight, and velocity. When balls and small vehicles are added to the play space, infants experiment with how things roll. When tall, lightweight objects, like plastic bowling pins or bottles, cylinders, tubes, or boxes are added to the play space, infants push them over, set them upright again, and knock them over again, relating what they know about the physical property, such as, "These things are tall," to what happens when they act on the objects with force, that is, "Tall, thin objects tip over more readily than short, squat ones." These are experiences in understanding gravity. When they see that some objects stay put when knocked over, while others roll away, they build understanding of shape and weight, applying what they are learning about the physical properties of flat and curved, or heavy and light.

For decades, scientists studying infant cognition assumed that during the early months of infancy, out of sight was out of mind, and that not until about 8 months of age would an infant begin to understand that objects still exist, even when out of sight. This assumption was based on studies showing that young infants would not search for an object that disappeared from sight. For example, if an infant watched the caregiver cover a toy with a blanket, prior to about 8 months of age, the infant would simply turn away and not look for the toy, while older infants would pull back the blanket to retrieve the hidden toy. Scientists described this as object permanence and suggested that it marked a distinct advance in infants' cognition.

However, subsequent studies show that infants as young as 3.5 months appear to hold a mental image of an object, even when out of sight (Baillargeon & DeVos, 1991). Such studies make use of babies' ability to maintain their focus of attention on something of interest, a measure scientists call looking time. By timing how long a baby looks at an event, scientists measure a baby's response to an experimental situa-

---

Research Highlight:
Object Permananence Put to the Test

To test the validity of the concept of object permanence, researchers (Baillargeon & DeVos, 1991) positioned 3.5-month-old infants so that they watched a short and then a tall carrot slide along a track. The center of the track was hidden by a large screen. In the top of the screen was a window. Therefore, as the short carrot moved along the track, once it reached the center of the track and went behind the screen, it could not be seen. The tall carrot was of sufficient height such that, as it reached the center of the track and went behind the screen, the infant could still see it through the window of the screen. The researchers wanted to find out if infants this young would be surprised if the unexpected occurred. The researchers manipulated the scene so that the tall carrot, contrary to expectation, could not be seen as it passed behind the screen. The infants looked longer at the scene when the tall carrot failed to appear in the screen window. They appeared to be surprised by this event. The researchers interpreted this as evidence that infants 3.5 months and older are able to represent and reason about the existence, height, and trajectory of a hidden object, contrary to what was once believed.

---

tion. If the baby is aware of a difference or notices a change, the baby will look longer. If the baby is unaware of a change or does not notice a difference, the baby will look away. Babies will look longer at things that are unusual, surprising, and unexpected. With things they already know about or expect, they tire and look away after a short period of time.

Around 1 year of age, infants begin to show interest in connecting one thing to another. This is a prelude to connecting objects in order to build something new, often called block play. Infants' experiments in connecting and constructing are closely tied to their interest in collecting. They collect similar objects in arms and containers and then deposit them all in one place. To do this, they need access to an ample supply of containers and collections. Infants who are walking enjoy carrying around containers with their collected items. At first they collect whatever objects fit in the hand or are in easy reach, adding one item after the other to an armful of objects or to a container. Just as readily, they drop or dump them out, one by one or in one fell swoop.

Reflection: The Mathematics of Collecting, Connecting, and Constructing

Examine the objects in this photo. These are collections of ordinary objects. What opportunities might they provide for building logico-mathematical relationships? Consider relationships of

- Weight, height, shape, or volume
- Quantity, like all, some, or none
- Gravity and balance
- Order
- Pattern
- Representation through symbolic play

What possibilities do these materials offer, with respect to inviting infants to build concepts of classification, causality, spatial relations, number, or representation?

Objects collected, in time, become objects to connect, one to another. Initially, the connections might simply be lining one object next to another. By their second year, infants have begun to rest one object on top of another, experimenting with stacking and balance. The connections become more elaborate as they experiment with lining up flat-sided objects on the floor or on low raised surfaces, transforming discrete objects into a long line or a big structure. In doing so, they construct concepts of length, line, height, and pattern, building a foundation for mathematics and physics.

Once toddlers figure out that round objects roll off and that flat, angled objects stay put, they delight in balancing one thing on another. Important for such play is a floor surface that works for building up and building out. Play spaces with a variety of raised surfaces—low shelves, overturned bins, baskets, boxes, or pillows—give toddlers challenging places on which to balance and build. As they build, toddlers pose problems about weight relations and gravity: "What happens when I place the block or the ball on the edge of the box? What happens when I put it in the center of the box?" or, "What does it take to make this plastic figure stand up on the fence?" or, "What happens when I remove the box from below the block?" As they go in search of answers to these questions, their understanding of spatial relations increases.

Another variation of connections is seen when toddlers stick one object into another, using friction and pressure. For example, a toddler might stick one plastic cone into another, making a structure that grows longer. Conical plastic cups, buckets, or recycled containers, when placed one inside the other, hold the potential of becoming tall towers or long staffs. When available in different colors, such objects offer toddlers the opportunity to invent patterns, as they connect one object to the next. Toddlers manipulate ideas of space, number, size, shape, and color as they select a particular feature to appear in a certain location, at the bottom, at the top, or in the middle (Kálló & Balog, 2005).

Toddlers invent another way of constructing by nesting smaller objects inside bigger objects. Through trial and error, they discover that a slightly larger object shaped the same as a smaller object can contain the smaller object. As they explore how things nest, they build relationships of size, shape, and volume. With repeated practice, they identify, simply by looking at objects, which ones will stack or nest and which

ones will not. Nesting results in many collapsing to a few, while stacking transforms something small into something tall.

Collecting, connecting, constructing, and transforming—all are infants' ways of building the broad concept of spatial relations, a key concept in mathematics and science. Play objects that support infants' construction of spatial relations include

- Pairs of objects that can be held at the same time, one in each hand; for example, plastic cups, nesting cubes, or metal rings.
- Collections of play objects that can be used to fill and empty, and for toddlers, to line up, stack, or sequence by size or height.
- Baskets, bowls, bins, or buckets that are easy to fill, dump, move, and carry.
- Nesting objects—boxes, bowls, or cubes—that rest one inside the other.
- Collection of balls, ramps, and tubes for exploring patterns of movement.
- Cups or cones that connect with slight pressure to become taller or longer.
- Small collections of objects that vary by size and can be used for lining up or stacking.
- Large collections that satisfy the goal of gathering all, rather than some.

Number and Quantity

Infants as young as 5 months of age can discriminate among small sets of up to three objects (Starkey & Cooper, 1980; Starkey, Spelke, & Gelman, 1990). By their third birthday, most infants can quickly and accurately recognize the quantity in a small set of objects without counting, a skill called subitizing (Clements, 2004). This implicit sensitivity to number and quantity during infancy establishes a sturdy foundation for mathematics. By their toddler years, infants use language that shows an awareness of relationships of quantity and number, using phrases like "all gone" and "more" and counting aloud, although their counting is not yet accurate.

Babies as young as 5 months old show evidence of a rudimentary understanding of quantity (Wynn, 1992). Although they will not be able to count a big set of objects until several years later, they show an emerging understanding of number and quantity very early in infancy. Some scientists describe infants' awareness of quantity as an early form of calculat-

Research Highlight: Babies Calculate Statistics

Researchers (Xu & Garcia, 2008) wanted to find out whether 8-month-olds had a concept of quantity. To test this, they created an experiment in which babies watched someone pull a very unlikely amount of objects from a container that they had seen to hold very few of those objects. Their research question, "Would the babies notice that this sample of objects was illogical?"

The researcher positioned babies, one at a time, in a seat facing a box filled with small balls. The side of the box was clear plastic, so the baby could see the contents of the box, mostly red balls, with just a few white balls. The researcher lowered a screen so the baby could no longer see the box. However, the baby could still see the researcher pulling things out of the box. As the baby watched, the researcher pulled out five balls one by one. As you would expect, what the baby saw was mostly red balls, since the box contained mostly red balls. The baby watched the researcher place the balls in a line near the box. The researcher timed how long the baby looked at the sample of balls before tiring and looking away.

Then the researcher repeated the experience, but the second time, the researcher did not randomly select the balls. Instead, the researcher intentionally pulled primarily white balls from the box filled mostly with red balls. What the baby saw was a very unlikely event, but would the baby know this? Again the researcher measured the baby's looking time. A significant number of the babies looked longer at this unlikely event than they did at the likely event.

Scientists interpret this to mean that young babies notice the relative amounts of two different types of objects and use this information to make predictions about what is probable and what is not.

**Reflection:
Making Number in the Hand and the Mind**

What do these ordinary objects offer infants, with respect to possibilities for building the concept of number? What possibilities do they offer for making the concepts of classification, spatial relations, causality, or representation?

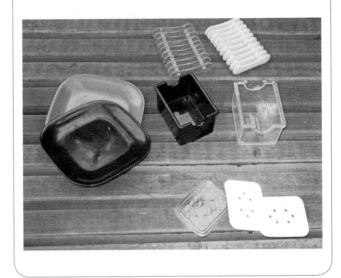

**Research Highlight:
Infants Figure Out Quantity**

Researcher Karen Wynn (1992) used the baby's looking time to find out whether infants are aware of quantity. She placed 5-month-olds in a seat facing a dollhouse, where the infant saw just one doll. She then dropped a screen between the infant and the dollhouse, so the infant could no longer see the dollhouse. As the infant watched, she placed a second doll behind the screen. She then lifted the screen, so the infant could see the two dolls in the dollhouse. She recorded the amount of time the infant spent looking at the dollhouse before getting bored and turning away. Then, to test whether infants have a concept of number, she made a change. Out of view of the infant, before lifting the screen, she removed one of the dolls. When the screen was lifted, the infant saw only one doll, where there should have been two dolls. Would the infants in the experiment look longer at the unexpected number of dolls? If so, this would show that infants are aware of the concept of quantity. Indeed, infants spent significantly more time looking at the dollhouse that had fewer dolls than expected.

ing statistics, in other words, an awareness of probable quantities. For example, babies who have not yet reached their first birthday show that something is amiss when someone pulls a sample consisting of mostly white balls from a box they have seen to contain mostly red balls (Xu & Garcia, 2008) .

Another aspect of quantity that emerges in the toddler period is cardinality. Cardinality means understanding that the last number word when counting represents the total number of objects. Toddlers begin to build understanding of cardinality as they play. For example, a toddler counts a row of three crackers by pointing and saying, "One, two, three." A moment later, when asked how many there are, the toddler responds by saying, "Three."

By their third birthday, toddlers demonstrate another mathematical concept, subitizing, which means the ability to quickly and accurately recognize a quantity in a small set of objects, without needing to count. For example, when asked how many crackers there are, an older toddler will look at a plate of two crackers and quickly respond, "Two," without having to count (Clements, 2004).

Infants build number concepts within everyday play. Once infants acquire the ability to reach out and grasp, they literally construct number as they experience and experiment with objects in hand. Over time, they notice changes in small numbers of objects, that is, how one small set compares with another. They also distinguish between large, approximate quantities, noticing "lots of" versus "some." Collections of objects, some of which are the same, and some of which are different, provide opportunities for infants to play with making number. They make number when they hold one block in one hand and another block in the other hand and bang the two together; or when they slip one metal bracelet and then another over the wrist. As they grab one object, check out its features, find another identical or similar one, and perhaps go in search of a third, they are making a relationship of one, two, and three, building the concept of number through play.

As toddlers struggle to hold onto two items while grabbing for a third, they explore quantity, experiencing more. As they fill containers and dump them, they construct concepts of more, all, some, none, little, and big. Filling and emptying containers can be messy play, but it is rich in opportunity to learn about shape, color, size, and quantity. Toddlers even try out a simple form of estimating, as they experiment with how much is just enough and how much will be too much, or decide which objects are too big and which are too small to fit in a container. These are all important ideas that build a foundation for mathematics.

Toddlers go in search of all there is of a particular type of object (Kálló & Balog, 2005). Ample collections of objects with the same or similar features and large containers that young toddlers can easily carry or push from place to place support such a search. It is important to understand that when a young toddler goes in search of and insists on having all the balls in the room, the intention is not to be greedy. It is an investigation of quantity, building the concept of all, not some.

Infants begin to respond to conversational prompts like, "Do you want more water?" When still hungry during a meal, an infant might point to the serving dish and say, "More." Having finished eating all the orange slices in a snack bowl, an infant might raise her palms in a gesture communicating, "All gone," or even say, "All gone." Older infants experience a language spurt that coincides with a developing sense of number. They begin to use relational words that indicate emerging understanding of quantity, like "more" and "all through." They love to accompany others in counting. For older toddlers, counting is an enjoyable chant, a series of numbers that begins with "one" and continues with other numbers, not necessarily in order (Gallistel & Gelman, 1992), for example, "one, two, three, six, ten." Toddlers begin to count small collections of objects. At first, as they do so, they imitate what they have seen others do. As they count, they may point to the same object twice or say a number without pointing to an object, unaware of the error and quite satisfied with their success.

Daily routines provide a rich context for toddlers to apply their emerging concept of number and quantity. A teacher might ask toddlers to put on two boots for a walk in the rain or advise that there is room for two children in the wagon. Or when a teacher asks toddlers to put all the balls inside the wagon at clean-up time, toddlers demonstrate understanding of the vocabulary of number and quantity. During family-style meal service, teachers might suggest that each toddler take one scoop of peas, or they might describe a serving as "too much" or "not enough," offering toddlers the language of number in a meaningful context.

Representation

The ability to represent, graphically or through symbolic or pretend play, shows up in the second year, when infants use one object or action to represent another in its absence. Although they might appear to be simply scribbles, toddlers' marks on a page are their attempts to "re-present" an experience. A toddler who transforms a box into a bed is using one object to represent another. Representation is a concept that is foundational for drawing, painting, sculpting, reading, and writing. It provides a critical foundation for language, literacy, and the arts. Toddlers represent as they engage in pretend play, as they explore tools of writing, and as they develop skill in using art media.

Symbolic play, commonly called pretend play, emerges during the 8–18 month period, as infants watch, listen, and attempt to make sense of the actions of others, both adults and children. Midway through the second year, when explicit memory becomes more evident, toddlers begin to act out familiar rituals in play. They can remember events from the recent past and can re-create them in pretend play. A young toddler might draw a blanket gently over a doll's body and pat the doll or pretend to feed the doll, explicit memories from the toddler's experience.

Familiar items added to the play space support toddlers' emerging ability to represent. Items commonly found in the home and used during the care routines make excellent additions to the play space. These might include sturdy dishes, hats, bags, and dolls. Toddlers enjoy simple dress-up clothes and safe accessories that they can easily pull over the head or slip arms through.

Open-ended objects, which can be used in a wide variety of ways, support toddlers' emerging ability to use symbols, that is, to transform an object, through pretend play, into something new. Boxes, bowls, tubes, and scarves are examples of open-ended objects. Toddlers apply their knowledge of the physical properties of open-ended objects to select features similar to those in the object they represent. A bowl becomes a hat, a stick becomes a broom, and a block becomes a cup.

During the 18–36 month period, infants begin to use objects creatively and spontaneously to represent an experience. As a result, pretend play blossoms. They create their own play scripts, often centered on simple re-enactments of familiar encounters. Their play reveals their ability to recall and represent prior experiences in simple pretend narratives. Pretend play initially is a solo act, but toddlers soon merge their solo pretend play with the pretend play of others. A series of cardboard boxes lined up by a team of two toddlers becomes a bedroom for two friends. A toddler might set a table with dishes, for example, and serve food to friends.

Through pretend play, toddlers consolidate understanding of the events of their everyday lives. They also try out new skills and ideas. At times, toddlers use pretend play to self-regulate, when disturbed by frustrating or unsettling events. Daily separations from family members can be emotionally wrenching, and in response, toddlers might represent separations and reunions in their play. When playing with others, toddlers have to read the intentions and feelings of others and negotiate roles, who does what, when, and how. Disagreements and conflicts arise, but negotiating an agreement is an important and central part of toddlers' pretend play.

Observing to see what toddlers are doing during pretend play can spark ideas for new possibilities for materials to add to the play space. For example, a teacher might witness a toddler patting the back of a blanket, under which lies a stuffed animal. To render this play more elaborate or more complex, a planning question might be, "What materials might we add to the play space to support pretend play around baby care?" Ideas to consider in developing pretend play spaces for toddlers include:

- Furnishings, household items, tools, and clothing that reflect toddlers' home life
- Open-ended objects, like boxes, bags, tubes, and bowls, that can be used in a wide variety of play scripts
- Toddler-height furnishings and clothes and accessories that toddlers can put on and take off independently
- Duplicates of pretend play clothing, so that a toddler can experience being the same as a friend

FROM RESEARCH TO PRACTICE: PLAY AS A CONTEXT FOR LEARNING

Infants do not build concepts through isolated instruction from adults, such as lessons designed to teach shapes or colors. Infants build these concepts when they have an opportunity to make sense of physical or social phenomena and to solve physical or social problems about objects, people, and events (Kamii, Miyakawa, & Kato, 2004). Surrounded by ordinary objects that connect and relate in some way, toddlers might select just objects that have flat sides. They might put a flat side of one object on top of a flat side of another. In doing so, the higher object stays put and does not fall. If it falls, they encounter a problem to be solved, trying to make it stay put. Applying physical knowledge and logico-mathematical knowledge, infants build concepts of spatial relations, causality, classification, number, and representation as they play.

Reflection: Naming the Learning—Concepts Revealed in Play

Reflect on Severyn's play with the soap dishes, introduced in the photos at the beginning of the chapter. Did you see him gathering information about the features of these objects and thereby adding to his physical knowledge? What about logico-mathematical knowledge? Was this in evidence? What concepts were revealed in his play? Did you see evidence of classification, causality, spatial relations, number, or representation? Is learning happening in this moment of play? Is it curriculum? (Keep in mind the broad definition of curriculum introduced in Chapter 3.)

As outlined in Chapter 4, planning curriculum when working with infants originates in observing, watching to see what infants use in play, and how they use it. As we observe, infants reveal to us the concepts they are building in the moment. This guides what we offer next, that is, what new possibilities to present, what new contexts they might enjoy, to support infants as they deepen their investigation and build increasingly complex and coherent concepts and ideas.

Teaching and learning with infants is a dynamic, interactive process. Teachers prepare the contexts for learning and invite infants to explore those contexts. As they do, infants reveal their thinking and their ideas. The concepts described in this chapter provide teachers with a vocabulary for naming those ideas and, in so doing, provide an authentic means for assessing infants' learning. Through documentation of infants' play, teachers capture evidence of infants in the act of building these concepts as they relate one thing to another, investigate, invent, and create, all in the act of play.

Looking Back and Looking Forward

Just as scientists research the unknown in order to discover what it holds, infants do the same with the world they encounter. As infants explore objects and people, they think, compare, interpret, reason, and solve problems, all aspects of cognitive development. They build foundations for thinking and reasoning that will influence their understanding for a lifetime. Within the play spaces, during the routines of care, and in simple moments of conversation and interaction, infants reveal how they are making sense of number; how they are sorting and categorizing in order to classify; how they are representing an event from a prior day in symbolic play; or how they are experimenting with cause and effect and exploring spatial relations. In the next chapter, we turn to another aspect of infants' thinking and discover what scientists are learning about how infants construct the complex code of language.

CHAPTER 9

Communicating
Language Development

Action, communication, and social interaction are the indisputable sources of thought refinement, cognitive development, cooperative learning, and also the source of the powerful tool that is language, even before it becomes verbal. The more we are convinced of this, the more our educational theories and attitudes toward the world of young children will express . . . greater respect. And seeing the way the world is going, we greatly need to develop a . . . higher quality dialogue with children, and offer them broader opportunities in which to seek each other, to talk together, to make friends. (Malaguzzi, 1996, p. 19)

FOR MANY YEARS, scientists assumed that newborns and young infants were oblivious to the sounds around them, incapable of distinguishing speech from surrounding sound. However, clever ways of measuring what newborns distinguish and pay attention to reveal that they are born actively listening to the sounds of language. They notice and hold in memory the various tones, rhythms, and inflections of speech. They organize these variations within developing brain structures. These brain structures give them the capacity to construct understanding of the complex language code. This work begins in the months prior to birth and, by the first birthday, babies reap the fruits of their labor and begin to utter their first words.

Many studies document newborns' exquisite sensitivity to language sounds and expressive gestures. Newborns easily distinguish speech from nonspeech sounds (Vouloumanos & Werker, 2007). Their innate sensitivity to language sounds is so precise that they can distinguish sounds that are very similar, like /dah/ and /tah/, or /bah/ and /pah/ (Golinkoff & Hirsh-Pasek, 2000). They prefer their mother's voice to the voice of another woman (DeCasper & Fifer, 1980). As newborns, they prefer listening to stories that their mothers had read aloud during the prenatal

Research Highlight: Newborns as Language Detectives

One way scientists test whether newborns can distinguish between patterns of sound is to connect a pacifier to a machine that detects the pressure of sucking. Instead of producing milk, the baby's sucking produces language sounds from speakers near the baby. Through these speakers, a newborn hears alternating minutes of different speech sounds. After each hard suck, the baby hears a sound, for example, the sound of the letter *b*. Babies appear to love the novel sound and keep sucking in order to keep generating the sound. In time, however, the baby tires of the same sound and stops sucking.

Then the sound is switched to another sound, like the sound of the letter *d*. When babies hear the new and different sound, they begin sucking again in earnest. This renewed bout of sucking reveals that babies can clearly hear and distinguish the discrete sounds of speech, even those that are acoustically quite similar, like /bah/ and /pah/.

Researchers also track newborn sucking in response to a recording of the mother's native language. Then they switch the recording to another language. Newborns suck harder in response to the mother's native language, having grown accustomed to it in the womb (Moon, Lagercrantz, & Kuhl, 2013).

period (DeCasper & Spence, 1986). This demonstrates a sensitivity that begins long before birth. The brain systems that organize sound patterns are functioning in the womb. As the mother speaks, the vibrations of speech conducted through skeletal bones are encoded in the sensory neurons of the fetal brain.

BABIES SEEK PATTERNS IN LANGUAGE

Babies have an acute sensitivity to the rhythm and inflections of speech. Newborns are hooked on the music of the voice, especially the biological mother's voice, the voice experienced in the womb.

Protoconversations

Within the early months, even though they cannot yet produce speech of their own, young babies seek to join in the rhythm of the human voice. They partake in conversation with others through an early form of conversation that researchers call protoconversations. Protoconversations are babies' attempts to try out the role of conversation partner, without yet knowing how to speak. Using slow-motion cameras, scientists capture such conversations as a contingent exchange of expressions, movements, gestures, and vocalizations between baby and engaged caregiver. "I do this and in turn you do that, which prompts me to do this and await what you do next." A largely nonverbal dialogue, these early conversations are marked by rhythmic flows and pauses, by upward and downward turns of the voice, of the hands, and of the eyebrows. Such conversations have all the elements of a verbal dialogue, yet only one partner, the adult, knows how to speak.

Parentese, Lullabies, and Rhymes

Adults who care for infants have a special way of intuitively and subconsciously helping infants track the reciprocal back and forth of conversation. They use a unique form of child-directed speech called parentese. Parentese is marked by cadenced rhythm, contrasts in intonation, and exaggerated vowels. In parentese, adults exaggerate stress patterns, for example, "There's the baaabiee!" They also exaggerate inflections, in this case, the two syllables of *ba-by* might be spoken with a sharp drop in pitch. This practice has the effect of helping infants discriminate among distinct speech sounds. A distinct speech sound is called a phoneme. As we stretch out the vowels in words, we make it easier for infants to hear the distinct phonemes and, as a result, to become familiar with each small part of the speech code.

The unique structure of parentese also gives babies verbal cues about what the sounds mean. For example, in the parentese phrase, "There's the happy baaabieeeee," the stretched out vowels, the order of sounds, and the drop in pitch provide the infant with verbal signals. Over time, babies figure out that the sound pattern at the end of the word most likely indicates a noun, a word with special importance to the

---

Research Highlight: Babies Get in the Groove

Researchers Condon and Sander (1974) used a high-speed camera to film infants lying in a crib while two people talked nearby. Analysis of the film record showed a distinct pattern. Infants were moving in synchrony with the adults' speech. Not apparent to the naked eye, the infants made slight movements of the head, eyes, shoulders, arms, hips, legs, fingers, and toes in synchrony with changes in the vocal patterns of the adults' speech. The infants' movements started, changed, or stopped in perfect concurrence with the patterns of speech they were hearing.

In another study, researcher Colwyn Trevarthen (2005) recorded the play of baby Maria as her mother sang to her. Maria had been blind since birth. As her mother began to sing a familiar song, Maria laughed and began to move arms and legs. She moved her arms up, down, and sideways as her mother continued the song. When Trevarthen did a slow-motion analysis of Maria's finger, hand, and arm movements in relation to her mother's singing, he saw Maria moving her arm just before the start of each stanza in the song, leading her mother by about one-third of a second. He also found that in some cases, Maria moved her hand up or down with the rise and fall of her mother's voice. Maria also synchronized the movement of her fingers with the sharp consonant sounds that appeared in words at the end of a line. Maria was "in synch" with her mother's singing. In a way, Maria, having learned the cadence of this familiar lullaby, was conducting her mother's singing.

---

context. They also figure out that a downward inflection followed by a short pause signals that a pattern of thought, that is, a phrase or sentence, is coming to an end. Parentese happens without the speaker's conscious awareness. Studies show that babies prefer the musical quality of parentese to regular speech, and that it is the variation of pitch, not the words themselves, that seems to excite babies' interest (Fernald, 1985).

Another way caregivers serve as unconscious language tutors is in their use of lullabies and traditional chants and rhymes. Lullabies and traditional nursery rhymes exist in similar form across cultures and throughout history. Lullabies and nursery rhymes follow a distinct pattern. Each line of a typical lullaby or nursery rhyme lasts about 4 seconds, and each stanza lasts about 20 to 40 seconds before a distinct pause. Trevarthen's (2005) analysis shows that these intervals coincide with the rhythmic cycles of the human body. For example, in the traditional lullaby "Rockabye Baby," each stanza lasts about 30 seconds. This corresponds to the time it takes for the human body to cycle through a rhythmic pattern of heartbeat and breathing, a pattern that also is linked to bursts of neural activity in the brain, believed to be evidence of memories being consolidated.

Lullabies and nursery rhymes, across cultures, appear to have this same rhythmic cadence. Scientists suggest that the sound pattern universally recognized as a lullaby or a nursery rhyme is the result of attunement between the biological rhythms of the human body and the signs and sounds that give meaning to communication. Through speech, chant, and lullaby, matched to bodily rhythms, caregiver and baby literally get in tune with each other.

HOW THE BRAIN ORGANIZES LANGUAGE

A baby's brain expects to experience language. Incoming sounds, images, and movements enter the brain through sensory and motor neurons. It is the social exchange that happens within everyday conversations that enables babies to learn language. Studies show that simply hearing language sounds through audio or video recordings will not result in language learning (Kuhl, Tsao, & Liu, 2003). Babies need interactive language partners in order to learn language.

Scientists once thought that language was an innate package of skills encoded in the genes. Current studies suggest otherwise. Babies play an active role in building language structures in the brain. However, they rely on those who care for them as language partners in building these brain structures. When babies hear or see others talking, they closely attend to the rhythmic patterns of sound, and they hold these in memory in various parts of the brain. In essence, they knit together circuits of neurons into language maps (Kuhl, 2000). These language maps allow them to organize the sounds they hear and the communicative gestures they see. Once these language maps form, they influence the processing of all later language encounters. In this way, the language maps formed during infancy either constrain or expand potential for language learning. The language maps formed in infancy influence all future processing of language. This makes language exposure during infancy extremely critical.

Of concern is what happens when babies do not hear sufficient language. If the language maps babies build early in life are compromised, these compromised maps limit all later language learning. Denied conversational experiences with others early in life, babies, because of their compromised language maps, may lack the capacity to speak coherently and clearly. Children who experience neglectful isolation during infancy will rarely progress to a point of language proficiency, even with intense rehabilitative therapy later in life (Eliot, 1999).

Language Experience Warps Perception

Within everyday moments of care and interaction with others, babies are bathed in the sounds and gestures of language. By 6 months of age, they have gathered a great deal of information about the sounds spoken around them. They detect the fine sound shift between the sounds made by the letters *m* and *n* or *s* and *f*. They have begun to sort these sounds into categories of alike and different. Consonants produced nasally, like *m* and *n*, go in one category and those produced by stopping the flow of sound with lips, tongue, or throat, like *s* or *f*, go in a different category (Kuhl, 2000).

Clever experiments reveal babies' amazing competence in hearing speech sounds. In fact, babies in the first 6 months following birth outshine adults when it comes to hearing language sounds, a finding that helps explain how babies build language maps. Until a few months prior to the first birthday, young babies, no matter where they are born, can detect practically every sound spoken in every language around the world. Scientist Patricia Kuhl (Gopnik, Meltzoff, & Kuhl, 1999), who studies language development in infants, explains that babies, at birth, are like citizens of the world. They have the capacity to detect the nuanced sounds used in every language, even those they have never heard. Somewhere between 6 and 9 months of age, however, babies lose this ability, and they can detect only the language sounds spoken around them.

To understand this change, it is important to note that not every language uses the same sounds. Some sounds show up in some languages and are absent in others. For example, the Japanese language does not use the *r* and *l* sounds, whereas English does. A native Japanese-speaking person who is trying to learn English as an adult will find it exceedingly hard to hear and consequently to pronounce the *r* sound as used in English. However, this is not the case for very young Japanese babies. They can hear the *r* sound with ease until about 6 months of age. In fact, they respond to the *r* sound just as readily as do babies of the same age who are raised in English-speaking homes and who hear the *r* sound spoken frequently. By the baby's first birthday, however, this has changed. They will no longer be able to detect the *r* sound. Somewhere between 6 and 9 months of age, babies raised in Japanese-speaking homes, and who do not hear the *r* sound spoken around them, will lose the ability to hear it.

Kuhl explains this narrowing of language capacity as experience warping perception (Kuhl, 2000). What she means by this is that for the first 6 months, babies listen to people talk. This experience allows them to get very good at hearing and grouping sounds within the neural circuits of the brain. They construct a language map of the commonly heard sounds. To make this map efficient, they collapse some sounds. For example, babies who hear English spoken daily will hear many *r* sounds, so they develop a marker that represents the *r* sound. Babies who hear Japanese spoken daily will hear many sounds, but they will not hear the *r* sound and consequently will not develop a marker that represents the *r* sound. One-year-olds who have heard only Japanese and not English, when played a recording of sounds that include the *r* sound, will not respond to the *r* sound, indicating that they can no longer distinguish it from other sounds.

Once babies build markers into their language maps, what they hear is warped by these markers. In the example cited, the 1-year-olds who heard only Japanese have no marker for the *r* sound, so they will ignore the *r* sound and variations of that sound that may exist in other languages. Prior to this point, these babies would have heard and responded to each of those variations. By their first birthday, babies have a fairly good working language map and will slot variations in sound into the slots they have constructed on their experience-based map. For 1-year-olds, a sound from a nonnative language, easily heard when they were younger, gets morphed and perceived as a sound more commonly heard in the baby's native language. What babies experience in language distorts what they are able to perceive in language.

Multilingual Babies

Babies who hear conversations in different languages have the capacity to map multiple languages within their developing brains. Born with an ample supply of neurons, more than they will ever use, babies build

Research Highlight: The Multilingual Baby Brain

Researchers (Garcia-Sierra et al., 2011) studied what goes on inside the brain of a baby hearing just one language at home as compared with a baby exposed to two languages. The researchers outfitted babies, 6–12 months of age, with special caps that measure electrical activity in the brain. In the background, the babies heard a sound used in both Spanish and English. Periodically, a sound used only in Spanish, a Spanish /da/, or a sound used only in English, the English /ta/, randomly occurred in this background flow of sound. If the baby detected the contrasting sound, the researchers would see a noticeable change in the pattern of electrical activity. At 6 months, test results for each group of babies were the same. Whether hearing just one language at home or hearing more than one language at home, the 6-month-old babies noticed all of the sounds, those unique to English and those unique to Spanish.

However, when the babies were tested at 10–12 months of age, the findings were quite different. The babies who heard only one language at home could detect only the language sounds heard at home. At 10–12 months, they showed no response to language sounds not present in their home language. In contrast, the bilingual babies retained the ability to hear the contrasting sounds in English as well as those in Spanish. Researchers interpret this to be an advantage in terms of keeping open and flexible the neural circuits that process language in the developing brain.

their brains to fit the unique language context in which they live. Babies who grow up in homes where two languages are spoken attend to the speech of each language and build a language map in the brain for each language heard (Kuhl, 2000). If provided regular conversation partners, babies efficiently map multiple languages in the brain. Bilingualism and multilingualism are easy for babies, as long as they have the opportunity to engage socially with a speaker of each language (Kuhl, 2000).

Studies suggest that learning more than one language as a baby may be advantageous, because the brains of multilingual infants may retain for a longer time the capacity to process language sounds (Garcia-Sierra et al., 2011). In addition, studies suggest that this flexibility may confer an advantage in toddlers' ability to switch between two contrasting situations with two distinct sets of rules (Poulin-Dubois, Blaye, Coutya, & Bialystok, 2011). Irrespective of how many languages a baby is exposed to in natural conversational settings, learning one language well is critical, because learning a first language provides a template for more readily learning a second language (Garcia, 2005).

Babies Calculate Language Statistics

Before infants are a year old, they have begun to organize the chaotic world of sound into a complicated but coherent structure unique to their particular language environment. Babies actively search for language patterns. They notice sounds that are familiar and sounds that are not. They look for regularities in the sounds they hear. For example, they notice that some sounds regularly appear together when people talk. Since most babies spend their days in familiar surroundings with fairly ordered experiences, they hear phrases repeated in predictable contexts throughout the day. They use these predictable contexts to decipher the language code. Babies rely on caregivers to be generous in their use of language, that is, to give them plenty of material with which to work. Caregivers do so by bathing babies in the sounds of language during everyday moments of conversation and care.

Over time, babies construct expectations about what sounds they will hear when. They hold in memory the sound patterns that occur on a regular basis. They make hypotheses, like, "If I hear *this* sound first, it probably will be followed by *that* sound." Scientists conclude that much of babies' prowess in learning language is due to their ability to calculate statistics. For babies, this means that they appear to pay close attention to the patterns that recur in language. They remember, in a systematic way, how often sounds occur, in what order, with what intervals, and with what changes of pitch. This memory store allows them to track, within the neural circuits of their brains, the frequency of sound patterns and to use this knowledge to make predictions about the meaning in patterns of sound.

Frequency of Linked Sounds. Babies learn very early on that some sounds are used frequently, that some sounds are rarely or never used, that some sounds often occur together, and that some sounds never occur together. Adults rarely need to consider such details, but babies are busy listening for these patterns and building their language maps. For exam-

---

Research Highlight: Babies Calculate Statistics—What's Possible or Not

Dr. Peter Jusczyk (2000) tested babies to see whether they could tell the difference between two languages—Dutch and English. He chose these languages because the cadence, that is, the rhythm of speaking, is quite similar in English and Dutch, but the sound combinations are quite distinct. For example, the *r* sound in Dutch is like a trill akin to the sound made when gargling. This sound is not heard in English. Also, some Dutch words start with sound sequences never used as initial sounds for words in English, like /vl/, /kn/ and /zw/. The babies in the study were seated in an infant seat and to their side heard words through a speaker. The words spoken were either English or Dutch. The baby's head turn was used as an indication of what the baby preferred to listen to. These babies, when tested between 6 and 9 months of age, revealed that they had no preference, that is, they were just as likely to turn to listen to the Dutch words as they were to the English words. However, by 9 months of age, things had changed. Nine-month-olds began to show a preference, turning more frequently toward the speaker emitting words in their native language. The researchers concluded that by 9 months, babies were noticing sound patterns that were familiar and turning preferentially to these patterns.

---

ple, a baby in an English-speaking environment never hears the sound combination "kto," whereas a baby in a Polish-speaking environment hears this combination frequently. In the everyday course of hearing and seeing language spoken around them, babies figure out which sounds predictably occur together and which sounds do not. By 9 months old, babies categorize sound combinations that occur frequently as "familiar" and "preferred," and sound combinations that rarely or never occur as "unfamiliar" or "not preferred" (Jusczyk, 2000).

By 9 months old, babies are calculating the possible as distinct from the impossible in language. This gives them considerable advantage when it comes to finding words in the flow of speech sounds. They figure out that some sound combinations occur together frequently whereas other sounds never occur together. As they listen, babies log frequencies of occurrence. This body of data helps them know where one word might begin and another end. For example, a baby raised hearing English will never hear the sounds /zb/

or /gb/ together. Therefore, if /gb/ occur together in a stream of sounds, like *youaresuchabigbaby*, the baby would perceive two words, *big* and *baby* rather than three words, /bi/, /gba/, and /by/. Researchers suggest that by knowing the possible sound sequences, babies make sense of where words begin and end (Golinkoff & Hirsh-Pasek, 2000).

Stress Patterns. By their first birthday, babies also figure out stress patterns in words and use these as a clue to finding words in the stream of sounds (Golinkoff & Hirsh-Pasek, 2000). In most languages, there is a pattern as to how syllables in words are stressed. In English, there is often a strong–weak pattern of stress, with emphasis on the first syllable, for example, in the pronunciation of *baby*, *mommy*, and *doggie*. In other languages, this pattern is reversed. When tested at 6 months of age, babies raised in English-speaking homes show no preference for either a strong–weak or a weak–strong stress pattern. However, test these same babies at 9 months old, and they show a strong preference for words with the strong–weak pattern. For babies raised in language environments where the stress pattern is reversed. Similar findings occur with respect to the timing of pauses typically used as boundaries between clauses of speech. At 6 months, babies cannot detect differences, whereas at 9 months they prefer to listen to the pauses that typify what they hear in their native language.

After 9 months of listening to spoken language, babies prefer to listen to words and speech patterns typical of their own language, even though they do not yet understand the meanings of these words. They also are gathering clues that will help them figure out meaning. By 9 months of age, babies raised in English-speaking families have begun to expect that the significant object most often is placed at the end of the phrase, as "ball" is in the phrase, "Give me the ball." Studies show that caregivers speaking with infants tend to use recurring sentence frames that highlight new words at the end of the sentence, like, "Where's the . . . ," "See the . . . ," and "That's a . . . " (Kuhl, 2000). Through these subconscious patterns of speech, adults caring for babies support them in constructing systematic rules for finding words within the language stream.

By their first birthday, babies, who still have no clue as to what many words and clauses mean, have constructed a framework for understanding the regularities and rules of language. They listen and watch, and by virtue of what they attend to, construct networks of neurons that form language structures within their developing brains. These structures become language maps for how they expect speech to sound. At 12 months, babies have constructed a language map that will serve them well as they venture into the next phase of language development, trying out their first words.

LANGUAGE LEARNING: A SHARED SOCIAL EXPERIENCE

The gaze, how we intentionally shift what we look at, helps infants decipher the meaning of words and connect words with objects. The message in the gaze is, "I want you to pay attention to what I am paying attention to." At around 3 months of age, babies turn to follow the gaze of the caregiver, the first sign of joint attention, a concept introduced in Chapter 6. At first the pattern of joint attention is simple. The adult looks at an object. The baby looks at the adult's face and then turns to look at the object the adult is looking at. The bonus with joint attention is that when babies turn to look at what the caregiver is looking at, a delighted caregiver usually names the object. In a short time, babies reverse the action and use the power of their gaze to lead the attention of the caregiver to a desired object, with the caregiver naming and possibly retrieving the desired object.

Gesture and Language

Around 9 months of age, babies also begin to point as a way to relay intention, often accompanied by vocalizations like, "eh, eh, eh." By their first birthday, babies have figured out that pointing is a gesture that connects them to other people's thinking. For example, when they see someone point at an object and follow the direction of the pointed finger, they surmise that the object being pointed at is important to or desired by the person pointing. Pointing is a clue to understanding another person's intention. It is also a powerful catalyst for vocabulary development, because the object to which babies point becomes an object to be named. Pointing can be a request for help, an offer of help, or a sharing of useful or interesting information.

Gestures, like pointing, allow preverbal infants to communicate with others, but they also support infants in building a vocabulary. Gestures serve as a way for infants to call attention to things that con-

---

Research Highlight: Baby Signs

Researchers (Acredolo & Goodwyn, 1996) designed a study in which they asked parents to intentionally and systematically use simple signs and gestures with their infants and to study the vocabulary development that ensued. This study was prompted by an observation made by one of the researchers, who had noticed her 12-month-old making a blowing gesture with her lips and pointing with excitement at a fish in an aquarium. The baby appeared to be remembering a nightly ritual of watching with delight as her mother blew on a fish mobile near the baby's bed. The daughter appeared to be connecting the gesture of blowing to a fish, although in a different context. Building on this observation, the researchers asked parents to use simple signs with their infants, for example, touching the index finger to the palm to communicate "more" and twisting the wrist in a circular motion to request "open the door and go outside." Babies who were taught to use the baby signs knew about 50 more words at the age of 2 when compared with peers who had not been systematically taught baby signs.

---

cern them, with the added benefit of prompting immediate translation into words and phrases. Acredelo and Goodwyn (1996) demonstrated that babies who were taught to use simple hand signs for desired objects or actions had a larger vocabulary at the age of 2.

When using baby signs with babies who are not yet speaking, the key is to speak naturally with the babies while using the signs. Speech and language specialists emphasize that gestures and signs used to teach communication strategies to hearing children are not a substitute for conversing with them naturally, but serve to scaffold language during the transition between babbling and words.

Negative Impact of Media

Babies respond to more than just acoustic sounds or symbolic gestures. It takes a human being, a shared social context, for infants to learn language. When infants hear or see someone speaking to them, they expect a responsive social partner, a person-to-person connection, in real time, complete with a synchrony of gesture, shared rhythm, and inflection. It is this social context that supports infants' language learning, a fact that must be emphasized as the commercial market for infant acoustic and visual media flourishes. Experts recommend that visual media not be used with infants under the age of 2. Despite the

research demonstrating the importance of social context for learning language and recommendations to avoid using visual media with infants, visual media are marketed heavily for children, including infants under 2 years of age. This poses a critical risk to infants' language development.

To build language competence, babies need contingent, shared, social interaction and conversation. When the language a baby hears comes through a screen, there is no reciprocal interaction. The baby tries to engage with the speaker on the screen, yet gets no response. Television running in the background and in the same room with the baby can interfere with language learning, as well. A young child at play in the same room while the television is on will glance frequently in the direction of the television, a distraction that reduces sustained attention in play and consequently impacts learning.

A strong message emerges from studies of the impact of media on infants. Time spent tuned into media translates to reduced time spent in shared, contingent person-to-person interaction. A study of the amount of time infants spend watching media revealed startling statistics (Zimmerman, Christakis, & Meltzoff, 2007b). By 3 months of age, 40% of babies are regularly watching media; by the time they are 2 years old, almost 90% are spending 2 to 3 hours each day in front of a screen. A policy statement from the American Academy of Pediatrics (2011) explains that media, whether playing in the background or designed as an educational tool for babies, "have potentially negative effects and no known positive effects for children younger than 2 years. . . . Although infant–toddler programming might be entertaining, it should not be marketed as or presumed by parents to be educational" (p. 1).

Research Highlight:
Infant Exposure to Media—A Language Liability

Exposing babies to visual media appears to do more harm than good (Zimmerman, Christakis, & Meltzoff, 2007a). In comparison studies of babies exposed to visual media, for every hour spent watching some form of visual media, infants learned six to eight fewer vocabulary words. The strongest detrimental effect is seen in babies 8–16 months old, a period of rapid vocabulary development. Researchers surmise that when the television is on, those near the baby converse less, with a consequent reduction in conversation between baby and caregiver.

THE EMERGENCE OF SPEECH

Infants' receptive speech, what they understand when others speak, is an important measure of their language development in the first year. Babies show that they understand the meaning of words long before they are able to produce those words themselves. As a general pattern, expressive speech, what infants can say through either words or gesture, lags behind receptive speech by about 5 months (Eliot, 1999).

Cooing and Babbling

Cooing, which is a pattern of vowels, marks babies' first attempt to enter the stream of conversation. Cooing appears to be a universal language that shows up in all babies in an identical fashion, even in babies born deaf. Cooing requires fairly simple motor actions of the mouth, whereas what comes next, babbling, requires more motor control. When babies babble, they repeat syllables made up of vowel sounds and consonants, like, "dadada" or "mamama" or "gagaga." Babbling provides excellent practice for the vocal cords. As they babble, babies figure out the relationship between the movement of their mouths, throat, and tongue and the nuanced changes in the sounds they produce. Babbling gives babies practice in producing sounds. Deaf babies not only babble with their voices, but they also babble with their hands (Golinkoff & Hirsh-Pasek, 2000). With no sound feedback, their oral babbling soon decreases, while their signed babbling, rich in visual feedback, increases. Babbling gets more complex as babies begin to mix syllables, producing variegated babbling, for example, "madamada" or "gabagaba."

Babies appear to put all they are learning about sounds, pauses, and inflections into their babbling. They babble in accordance with the sounds, the pauses, and the inflections of their native language. For example, babies hearing English tend to drop the intonation at the end of a string of babbles, whereas babies learning French tend to do just the opposite, each group of babies reflecting the intonation pattern common to the native language they hear. With respect to the actual sounds used in strings of babbles, babies use those heard around them, which will vary with each language.

First Words

First words are often names of family members or items used or seen regularly, like *shoe* or *bird*. From 9–12 months, babies show clear signs of comprehension of many word meanings. By the first birthday, babies understand on average around 70 words. There is wide variation in the types of words learned first. Some children learn more nouns, that is, words for people and objects, while other children learn more words geared to social interaction, like *goodbye* or *more*.

The number of words a baby comprehends, receptive language, far outpaces the number of words or phrases a baby can say, expressive language. The median number of words spoken by 12-month-olds is six. The range is broad, with some infants speaking

Research Highlight: Detecting Language Delays

Large studies have looked at the age at which children achieve language milestones. Such studies help determine signs of language delay. Expressive speech emerges across a wide spectrum of time. However, the point when babies comprehend what others are saying is less variable, so speech comprehension is useful as a potential indicator of language delay (Golinkoff & Hirsh-Pasek, 2000). If a baby neither comprehends nor produces words by 18 months of age, experts suggest, this may be cause for concern. If babies comprehend speech, but do not yet speak at 18 months, there is less cause for concern. Serious ear infections are sometimes the cause of language delay, because they prevent sound from reaching sensory neurons. Therefore, regular medical checkups in the first year and diligent monitoring of ear infections are important.

upward of 50 words by the first birthday and others not yet doing so until well after the first birthday.

Toddlers' Language Explosion

On average, about halfway through the second year, infants reach a point where they can speak about 50 words. This marks the beginning of what some describe as a vocabulary explosion. At around 18 months, infants enter a period when they are like word sponges, learning up to nine words a day. This coincides with the period when there is a peak in the number of synapses in the vocabulary region of the brain (Eliot, 1999). A peak in synapse formation indicates the start of a period of rapid brain growth. By around 18 months of age, babies are on a mission to learn and produce new words, and once they do so, they begin to figure out how to string them together. Their experience in hearing language, or in seeing sign language, prepares them to figure out the basic rules of syntax—that is, how to string together words with the right inflections to make sense to others.

It appears that infants figure out the rules of word order prior to the point when they actually apply the rules in speech (Golinkoff & Hirsh-Pasek, 2000). They do this by detecting patterns and exploiting those patterns to make predictions about what is "legal" in speech and what is not (Kuhl, 2000). They also figure out the meaning and use of small words like *the*, *a*, and *with*. They will respond to a request like, "Give me the ball," but appear confused if the

request is phrased as, "Give me gub ball." Although infants may not yet be saying *the*, or *a*, they expect them to be there as they listen. They have a similar reaction if the *-ing* ending to a word is tampered with, for example, changing *walking* to *walkly*. Babies are sensitive to the fact that *-ing* and not just any syllable belongs at the end of the word. Such is the power of babies' ability to calculate language statistics. Goodsitt, Morgan, and Kuhl (1993) demonstrated this in 7-month-old babies' ability to distinguish an artificial word from an actual word. By the time babies begin to use their first words and phrases, they have accumulated much useful information about the way speech should sound.

When infants first begin to speak, they use an efficient strategy called telegraphic speech. As infants string together words, they often select just the key words, like the name of the object or person to which they are referring, and leave out short words that simply modify or connect the key words, like *of*, *to*, *the*, *am*, *do*, or *in*. Examples of telegraphic speech are, "Where juice?" or "Mommy go work."

Infants employ another, quite efficient strategy

Research Highlight:
Big Bird Tickles Cookie Monster

Researchers (Hirsh-Pasek & Golinkoff, 1991) seated babies 16–18 months old in front of two television monitors. They wanted to test the point at which infants could tell the difference between these two spoken sentences: "Cookie Monster is tickling Big Bird" and "Big Bird is tickling Cookie Monster."

The test babies were familiar with Cookie Monster and Big Bird, two popular characters from the children's television show Sesame Street. On one monitor the infants saw a scene in which Big Bird tickled Cookie Monster, who shook a big box of toys in response. On the other monitor, the infants saw a scene in which the roles were reversed, Cookie Monster tickled Big Bird, and Big Bird shook a box of toys in response. Up to this point there was no sound, but then a voice from a speaker placed between the two monitors said, "Where's Big Bird tickling Cookie Monster? Find Big Bird tickling Cookie Monster." The infants consistently looked at the monitor showing Big Bird tickling Cookie Monster. When the speaker said, "Where's Cookie Monster tickling Big Bird?" the babies looked at the other screen. It was clear that these babies used word order to find the correct event.

Figure 9.1. Plan of Possibilities: Books in the Play Space

Context: Add collection of cat puppets in basket along with books about cats to the book and story area. Add collection of books about trains adjacent to train in connections and construction area. (11/4–8)

Planning Question: What play and conversation will these books and related materials prompt when toddlers find them in the play space?

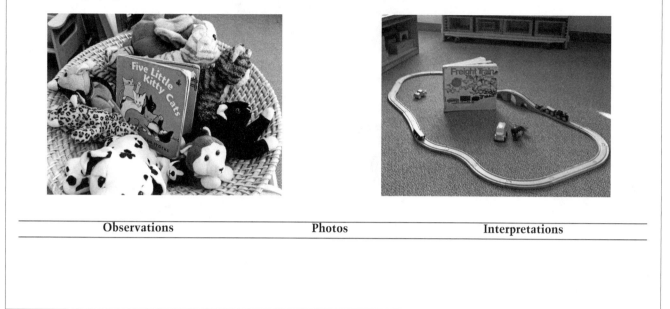

Observations	Photos	Interpretations

when they begin to hammer out the rules of language. They overgeneralize, meaning they appear to apply a rule of speech all the time, even when not needed. For example, in the early months of speech, a toddler might repeat exactly what the caregiver says, in a sentence like, "Jessie ate the cracker." However, months later, this same toddler might say, "Jessie ated the cracker." It may sound like a language mistake, but in reality it is a common pattern that reflects toddlers' attempt to actively experiment with language in order to hammer out the rules of speech.

REFLECTIVE PLANNING: INVITATIONS TO USE LANGUAGE

Infants are ready and willing to learn new expressions and phrases, and caregivers are ready and willing to accompany them as helpful tour guides on their journey into the world of language. A primary way young children learn language is through observing, listening in on conversations, and pitching in to help with ongoing activities (Rogoff, 2003, 2011). This section describes how language learning can be supported within a broad definition of infant curriculum—within materials made available in the play spaces, within

the care routines, and within the everyday conversations and interactions.

Play Spaces as Context for Language

Within thoughtfully stocked play spaces, infants encounter novel objects and experiences that they can independently access and explore, all of which have potential for building vocabulary. Chapter 11 describes how play spaces can be designed with distinct identities, like a book and story area or a connections and construction area. For example, a book and story area can be stocked with books, but also finger puppets, small stuffed figures, and laminated photos of some of the objects and characters that appear in the books. When one item holds potential to relate to another, there is tremendous possibility for infants to hear conversation and story laced within many repetitions of the same words (Figure 9.1). Redundancy, hearing a phrase in more than one context, supports language learning.

As they observe the play, teachers support language development by narrating the play or describing what appears to be the baby's intention; for example: "It looks like you know how that book works, Samson. You lifted the flap so you could see the baby!

Figure 9.2. Plan of Possibilities: Sign-In Area at Entry

Context: Create a space near entry where toddlers can write in imitation of what their families do at arrival. (12/12–16)

Planning Question: What will the toddlers do if we create a place for them to sign in adjacent to where their families sign in?

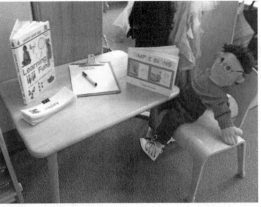

OBSERVATIONS	INTERPRETATIONS

And now you're going to do it again." Just the right dose of narration is important, because too much talk can overwhelm and distract an infant.

In the toddler years, infants begin to experiment with written language. Although it will be years before they are skilled in writing words, infants are intently curious about tools of writing and other tools that make marks. As toddlers, they love to experiment with how pens and pencils work and will seek out a flat surface at their height to explore how these objects make marks. Writing is part of the surrounding culture, a phenomenon that does not go unnoticed by observant toddlers. Figure 9.2 provides an example of how teachers modified the entry area to create a sign-in area for use by toddlers, who had begun to show an interest in making marks.

Routines as Context for Speech

Diapering, putting down to rest, and mealtimes provide natural opportunities for infants to hear descriptive language and for them to participate in one-on-one language exchange. During routines of care, adults can bathe infants in language within a meaningful context, for example, when the caregiver invites the infant, "Would you like me to change your diaper?" or when the caregiver narrates what occurs during the diapering. Two types of narration occur—self-talk and parallel talk (Davidson, 1979; Mangione, 2011). Self-talk is when caregivers narrate what they are doing during the care. The value of self-talk is that it gives infants words and phrases in the context in which they hold meaning. An example of self-talk is, "And now I'm going to pull the shirt over your head." With self-talk, even though only the adult is talking, the infant is actively listening and watching, gathering the sounds, holding them in memory within the context of the experience and, over time, learning to predict what is about to occur simply by hearing the familiar language sounds. This can be seen when an infant, upon hearing, "And now I'm going to wipe your face," shifts his head in anticipation of what is about to occur.

Parallel talk is when the adult narrates what the infant is doing as the infant plays. The following is an example of parallel talk: "You see the bird outside on the tree branch. Yes, that's a bird! I think you like seeing that bird, because you're smiling." Adults support infants' language development when they stay alert to what captures an infant's interest and take time to describe and narrate for the infant what occurs in the moment.

Other routines of care also present opportunities for language learning. For example, a helper chart can be added to the play space, inviting toddlers to participate in various daily routines. With a helper chart,

Figure 9.3. Plan of Possibilities: Helper Chart

Context: Create a helper chart. Add to group gathering space. (1/10–14)

Planning Question: In what ways might the helper chart offer new opportunities for toddlers to apply emerging skills and elicit more conversation?

OBSERVATIONS	INTERPRETATIONS

toddlers see and handle print during routines that occur throughout the day (Figure 9.3). A helper chart is made using a simple frame and laminated strips of paper, each printed with a child's photo and name. A second set of laminated strips depict the helper jobs, with each strip printed with a photo or drawing of a special activity for which a designated toddler takes the lead. When placed at toddlers' eye level, a helper chart becomes a point for daily conversation for children and families. From this and other experiences with print, toddlers over time learn the significance of printed letters, as they pitch in to help with the everyday tasks.

Conversation and Story as Context for Comprehension

Conversation is key to language development. Whether reading or telling a story or enjoying a moment of play together, infants use the experience to add to their language repertoire. Infants are often the ones to initiate a conversation and, when they do, the conversation tends to be longer than one initiated by the adult (Bloom, Margulis, Tinker, & Fujita, 1996). Adults who are responsive language partners nourish infants' language development.

Story Reading—Questions to Prompt Dialogue. Reading a book or telling a story to an infant is a mutual endeavor, one enhanced by a strategy called dialogic reading (Whitehurst & Lonigan, 1998). Infants enjoy listening, but they also enjoy helping to tell the story, applying their emerging language skills. When adults read or tell stories with infants, they facilitate language learning by pausing periodically to pose leading questions, like:

- What do you think he is trying to do?
- Where do you think he went?
- I wonder what comes next. What do you think?

Young infants help to tell a story in simple ways, through their gaze, movements, expressions, vocalizations, and words. Very young infants may respond with brightened eyes, lifted eyebrows, smiles, arm motions, leg kicks, or imitative sounds. Older infants may add their own words to the story. Infants join in the story by turning the page, pointing to pictures, or flipping through the book in somewhat random order. When adults frame book reading as an interactive dialogue, they support infants' language learning, pointing out objects, naming them, and narrating what catches children's interest.

Fingerplays, Songs, and Chants. Songs, chants, and fingerplays support infants' oral language development and simultaneously help them fall in love with the experience of reading and telling stories. Ritualized games, like peekaboo, offer infants some of their first opportunities to use language systematically, as adults accompany words with gestures within predictable frames, one partner acting, and the other reacting, spawning many pleasurable repetitions of the same predictable sequence of words and gestures. The gestures, moves, and expressions of fingerplays are easy for infants to imitate. They have a predictable, ritualized format, often marked by the appearance and disappearance of an object or a person. Ritualized games establish a shared social context (Tomasello, 2009), often involving turn-taking back and forth and switching of roles. Through traditional games and songs, babies make sense of words and gestures long before they begin to utter their first words.

Features to Look for in Selecting Stories, Songs, and Fingerplays. Features to look for in selecting books, stories, songs, chants, ritualized games, or fingerplays include:

- Opportunity to play with sounds
- Predictable rhyme and rhythm
- Themes that reflect infants' lives
- Predictable elements mixed with elements of surprise
- For books, sturdy construction that invites infant exploration

Many popular books, songs, chants, or fingerplays invite babies to play with phonemes, the distinct sounds of language. A phoneme can be thought of as the sound made by a single move of the mouth. For example, the word hop has three phonemes, /h/, /o/, /p/, and the word chop also has three phonemes, /ch/, /o/, /p/. Infancy is a time for noticing these distinct phonemes and exploring how to make them over the course of many repetitions of a sound. When babies coo and babble, they are playing with phonemes. When they enjoy the repetitive sound patterns in chants, rhymes, stories, and songs, they are playing with phonemes.

Other features to listen for when selecting books and songs are rhyme, rhythm, and repetition. Recall from earlier in this chapter how infants show evidence of being particularly sensitive to the rhythm and the inflections in speech. They are primed to listen to patterns of sound and track the cadence of speech. Many popular infant books, stories, fingerplays, and chants are rich in rhyme, rhythm, and repetition, with patterns of sound that engage infants. This feature is a useful guide when selecting books, songs, chants, and stories for infants. A good test, when selecting books for infants, is to read the book aloud and listen as you read, for repetition of the same or similar sounds. If you detect such a pattern, chances are you have found a book worth using with infants.

A story line that gives infants a chance to predict what will come next is another feature to look for in selecting infant books, stories, fingerplays, and chants. Infants quickly learn that an expected element leads to a culminating event, like a clap, a sudden move of the arm, or a special word or phrase tied to an action. When songs, games, books, and chants combine the expected with an element of surprise, toddlers sometimes take the lead on the parts they expect will come next. Such stories are rich in ritual and invite infants to become language detectives, listening for a particular word or phrase that serves as a clue for them to chime in with the next action, word, or phrase.

A final consideration when selecting books for babies is to look for how the story theme corresponds to events that occur in the everyday experiences of a baby. Babies' relationship with members of their families is a prominent theme. Stories that relate to everyday routines and common events that occur within the lives of infants are also popular. Stories about going down to sleep and missing favorite people help babies make sense of these tender moments.

Books for infants must be able to withstand intense manipulation. For young infants, books serve as an interesting object of play, one with an engaging hinge-like motion. In the hands of an 8-month-old, who is mastering the pincer grasp, a board book, with its fan-like structure, in addition to offering a story, is an engaging cause-and-effect toy.

FROM RESEARCH TO PRACTICE: LITERACY BEGINS IN INFANCY

Infants gather information about how language works, they experiment with speech sounds, and in the short span of 3 years, they become fluent speakers. If all goes well, they fall in love with stories, songs, poems, and books, and by 3 years of age, build a firm foundation for literacy. Studies of oral language competence show a direct relationship between children's spoken language vocabulary and their later success as readers (Hart & Risley, 1995). One of the best predictors of a child's learning to read and write is the size of his or her vocabulary at age 3 (Whitehurst & Lonigan, 2002). Both vocabulary development and literacy have roots in infancy.

The kind of talk and the amount of talk infants hear relate directly to their progress in language development. Socioeconomic pressures on a family tend to negatively impact how much language a child hears. This puts the child at risk of having a smaller vocabulary at the age of 3 (Hart & Risley, 1995). Researcher Anne Fernald (Fernald, Marchman, & Weisleder, 2013) traced this gap to infancy. She found that toddlers from low-income families were significantly slower in identifying objects based on simple verbal cues, an indication that socioeconomic factors may begin to depress vocabulary learning in infancy. Poverty depresses the language environment, which has the effect of reducing infants' exposure to language within everyday contexts. This in turn reduces the words that are familiar and increases the challenge of learning to read and write. Children who are faster at recognizing familiar, spoken words at 18 months have larger vocabularies at age 2 years and score higher on standardized tests of language and cognition in kindergarten and elementary school. This finding is cause for concern, with respect to giving every infant a strong start in learning.

Research Highlight:
Language Gap Begins in Infancy

Researcher Anne Fernald (Fernald et al., 2013) used a simple experiment to detect the speed with which toddlers could identify an object by hearing the name of the object spoken. As the toddler sat on the parent's lap, Fernald showed the toddler two images, each a familiar object, like a ball or a dog. Then the toddler heard a recording, like, "Look at the ball." A camera recorded the moment when the child shifted his or her gaze to the image of the object described. At 18 months, toddlers from a higher income group could identify the correct object in about 750 milliseconds, while toddlers from a lower income group were 200 milliseconds slower to respond.

Since toddlers learn new words from context, the faster they can process the spoken words, the sooner they are ready to make sense of the next word in context. The more familiar a word, the faster the infant's processing time, freeing the infant to attend to the next word in context. The less familiar a word, the slower the infant's processing time, causing the infant to miss other words in context.

Looking Back and Looking Forward

Infants are actively engaged in learning language from the moment of birth. They detect, analyze, and organize language as patterns. They store it within circuits of neurons that serve as language maps. What these maps look like is largely a function of the everyday language and conversation to which they are exposed. Therefore, they rely on those who care for them to be generous in their conversations. Infants experiment with the sounds of language. Much language learning happens through stories, books, songs, fingerplays, and chants, rich in rituals that invite infants to use language. By the close of infancy, infants are competent communicators and use their language foundation to support all other aspects of learning, including making and keeping friends, solving problems, understanding and expressing feelings, and sharing stories and conversation.

Part III

INFANT CARE IN PRACTICE

T HE CHAPTERS THAT follow complete the final part of this book, an application of the research on how infants learn and what they learn. Caring for infants outside the family home requires a thoughtful system for organizing who cares for whom. Chapter 10 addresses policics that build strong relationships among infants, their families, and teachers. Caring for infants in groups requires thoughtful organization of the play spaces and the care routines so that both optimize possibilities for infant learning. Chapter 11 describes how to plan play spaces as contexts for learning. Chapter 12 describes how to design care routines that invite infants as active participants. Chapter 13 explores how to use respectful conversation to help infants negotiate conflicts and experience the joy of making friends and keeping friends. The book concludes with Chapter 14, which describes visual narrative as a tool for sharing with others the story of infants' meaning-making.

CHAPTER 10

Policies That Support Relationships

How babies are treated . . . while being cared for by people other than their family member . . . affects the development of their brains, their functioning in school, and their productivity as citizens. (Lally, 2013, pp. xv–xvi)

Aɴ ɪɴꜰᴀɴᴛ-ᴄᴀʀᴇ program is more than a building with furnishings, staff, and schedule. It is a dynamic system of relationships among families, their infants, and the infant-care professionals who work in the infant center. Carlina Rinaldi, who has helped shape exemplary schools for infants and young children in the Italian city of Reggio Emilia, suggests that a sense of "we" is created in quality early childhood programs, not just a sense of "I" (Rinaldi, 2001). Three organizational policies—primary care, continuity of care, and small group size—generate this sense of "we" and are the focus of this chapter. These policies support infants, families, and teachers in a triangle of relationship and guide decisions about the design and operation of group care.

RELATIONSHIPS: THROUGH THE EYES OF INFANT, FAMILY, AND TEACHER

Developmental psychologist Jeree Pawl (1990) compares the relationship infants form with their teacher with the relationship they form with an occasionally visiting relative.

The 15 minutes shared with Uncle Al cannot compete in the moment, and is a different category of experience, from 8 hours, 5 days a week with Martha, even though Uncle Al may be around for the next 40 years. It is true that Uncle Al will be a part of one's ongoing life, but the Martha or Ann or Bess who cares for an infant or toddler over long periods of time and then disappears will be tucked away inside, shaping the child's expectations and coloring what he imagines relationships can

give him and what he can give them. Those expectations should be as hopeful and as promising as we can devise. (p. 6)

Pawl refers to the important role of the teacher, who cares daily for an infant while the parent is away. She emphasizes that the infant-care teacher, during a significant portion of the day, influences the experiences of the child and consequently influences the way that child expects others to be.

Those who provide daily care for an infant can be thought of as architects of the child's day, with profound influence over what the child experiences and how the child comes to know the world. Parents hold this role most of the time, for most infants, but many parents, willingly or at times unwillingly, must find others with whom to share this influential role, an experience captured poignantly by author Tillie Olsen (1961) in the story of a single mother.

She was a beautiful baby. She blew shining bubbles of sound. She loved motion, loved light, loved color and music and textures. She would lie on the floor in her blue overalls patting the surface so hard in ecstasy her hands and feet would blur. She was a miracle to me, but when she was eight months old I had to leave her daytimes with the woman downstairs to whom she was no miracle at all. . . . [And then] she was two. Old enough for nursery school, they said, and I did not know then what I know now—the fatigue of the long day, and the lacerations of group life in the kinds of nurseries that are only parking places for children. (p. 2)

Pawl (1990) references Olsen's narrative of a mother's plight and cautions that infant care "must not be a 'parking place for children,' but a viable, rich place for safely learning more about the very complicated but very worthwhile things in the remarkable world of human relationships" (p. 6).

The decision to place a young infant in the care of others can generate feelings of ambivalence and

---

Figure 10.1. First Day at the Infant Center, Vignette #1

Joanna's maternity leave is coming to an end, and today Joanna is taking Maria, her 6-month-old baby, for her first day at the infant center. As Joanna enters with Maria in arms, Carol, one of the teachers, greets them, "Welcome! We're glad to see you again. Maria, do you remember being here last week for the orientation?" Maria buries her face in the folds of her mother's sweater. Carol sees this and steps back, as she motions to a nearby couch. "Would you like to sit with her on the couch? We have a basket of books you might enjoy reading with her, and I can join you in a minute. We like to hear how she slept and what she ate prior to arriving, so I'll need you to fill out this card, but it looks like Maria wants to stay in your arms. I'll fill it in for you as we talk." On her way to the couch, Joanna notices on the wall a cluster of photos of teachers and infants under the words "Primary Care Groups" and sees Maria's photo near Carol's. Carol records Joanna's responses to the questions and finishes with, "Do you think Maria is ready to join the others in the play space?" Joanna looks down at Maria, whose head is turned away, "I don't know. It seems like she doesn't want to be here." Carol responds, "She probably needs a bit more time to just watch, so I'll leave you be."

Carol greets a toddler who has just arrived and is peeking at her from behind his father's legs. He runs into the play area, turning to wave as his father bids him goodbye and leaves. Carol follows the toddler to the play area and beckons to Joanna and Maria to join her on a rug in the play area. Joanna lays Maria on the rug and sits near her. Carol places a toy between herself and Maria, saying, "There are a lot of things to explore here, Maria. While you do that, I'll let your Mom tell me a bit about how you like to nap."

Figure 10.2. First Day at the Infant Center, Vignette #2

Joanna's maternity leave is coming to an end, and today Joanna is taking Maria, her 6-month-old, for her first day at the infant center. She joins several other families with babies in the tiny entry area of the room to which Maria has been assigned. A counter and a gate separate the entry from the rest of the room. A teacher named Sue Ellen approaches the counter from the opposite side and says to the families, "Good morning. Make sure you fill out all the information on this card." Joanna balances Maria in arms as she writes in information on the card. She hands the card to Sue Ellen, who slots it in a binder before reaching for Maria.

Maria turns away from Sue Ellen and buries her face in her mother's sweater. Sue Ellen motions to Joanna to enter through the gate and says, "We don't allow street shoes inside, so you need to take off your shoes." Joanna looks around for a chair, so she can sit down and remove her shoes. Seeing none, she balances tentatively on one leg, but Maria pitches backwards in her arms and starts to cry. Joanna looks pleadingly over the counter at teacher Sue Ellen, who takes crying Maria from her mother's arms and says, "Probably easiest if you leave quickly so she doesn't see you exit. As soon as you leave, she'll be fine. She'll stop crying. When parents stick around, it makes the babies just cry even more." Joanna turns to leave and tears well up in her eyes. She waves at her daughter before she exits, but her daughter, still crying, does not see her.

Sue Ellen hands Maria to co-teacher Jake, points to a printed schedule on the wall, and says, "She's an angry one! We are way behind schedule. See if you can calm her and keep the others happy while I set up an art activity." Jake shakes a doll in front of Maria and says, "It's OK. No need to cry. This dolly wants to play with you." Maria's cry gets louder, as she arches back and turns toward the door, struggling against Jake's hold.

---

uncertainty. Families have many questions, among them:

- Will this be a safe place for my baby?
- Will the adults there know how to care for my baby?
- How will they respond when my baby cries?
- Will my baby have to compete with the other babies for attention and care?
- Will my baby feel comfortable in their care or fearful and sad?

When parents place their infants in care outside the home, they often place their trust in someone they barely know. This makes the arrival ritual that takes place upon entry into an infant center a rich time for building acquaintances among infants, their families, and teachers. Teachers get a glimpse of the infants' relationships with their families, and infants

and their families get a glimpse of what the care will feel like for the baby. Within the first minutes and hours in the infant center, relationships begin to form among families, infants, and teacher. Figures 10.1 and 10.2 recount two vignettes, each a story of an infant's first day in an infant center.

The experiences of infant, parent, and teacher in the vignettes in Figures 10.1 and 10.2 present a stark contrast. In the first, the teachers view the arrival time as a delicate period of separation and transition. The questions that most concern the teachers are:

- How does this infant respond to me?
- How does this infant respond to the environment?
- How do the infant's family members relate to me?

- Are my efforts to try to put this family at ease successful?
- What might I discover about how to best care for this baby by watching the interactions between baby and the family member?

The teachers in vignette #1 (Figure 10.1) greet each child and family, and, as they do so, they read each encounter for clues that will help them best care for the child. Their goal is to make the families comfortable and at ease. The teacher shows genuine interest in the mother's description of her baby's morning. The mother, in turn, relaxes, knowing that what she says or feels matters to the teacher. The teacher watches how the mother handles and talks to the baby. She knows that the baby is used to these patterns of care and that later, after the mother departs, if she can hold or talk to the baby in ways reminiscent of the mother, she might be able to ease the baby's sadness.

In vignette #2 (Figure 10.2), the teachers view the arrival as a task to move through as quickly and efficiently as possible. Babies are signed in and dropped off, forms are filled in and filed, and activities are set up according to schedule. The teachers keep their focus on getting through the administrative tasks within the required schedule.

The disparity between these two vignettes can be traced to differences in philosophy and policy with respect to how people are expected to carry out their roles, how the environment is arranged, and how time is used. Who cares for whom, where, when, and how—these are the questions framed by infant-care policies. The internationally acclaimed WestEd Program for Infant/Toddler Care, along with prominent agencies and organizations serving infants and families (California Department of Education, 2006; Provence, Pawl, & Fenichel, 1992), recommends three policies for group care of infants—primary care, continuity of care, and small group size. Together these policies provide a framework for respectful, responsive, relationship-based care.

PRIMARY CARE

Primary care is a system for organizing who cares for whom. With primary care, infants are assigned to a specific teacher. An infant's primary care teacher develops a close relationship with the infant and the infant's family, provides most of the care, and assumes the primary responsibility for the infant's physical and emotional needs. Each teacher has primary care

---

> ### Reflection: Through the Eyes of the Infant, the Parent, and the Teacher
>
> Figures 10.1 and 10.2 recount two vignettes, each a story of an infant's first day in an infant center. As you read and reflect on each story, consider the experience through the eyes of the infant, the infant's parent, and the teacher. For each vignette:
>
> - Describe your feelings.
> - What conditions were present that generated these feelings? (For example, what provoked comfort, discomfort, calm, anxiety, satisfaction, or worry?)
> - What information did you gather about the people you were with?
> - What expectations do you have as a result of this experience?

responsibility for a group of 3–4 infants. If there were 12 infants assigned to a room, there would be three primary care groups of four infants, or four primary care groups of three infants, depending on the ages of the children in the group. A typical ratio of adult to infants would be one adult for every three infants and one adult for every four toddlers.

Within each primary care group, enduring relationships are built. Each infant and each family builds a unique relationship with the primary care teacher to whom the infant is assigned. In addition, each infant builds a relationship with the other infants assigned to the same primary care group. Without a policy of primary care, there is no system in place to promote strong relationships, and who cares for whom is left to chance, creating uncertainty for baby, teacher, and family.

Pawl (2011) uses dance as a metaphor for primary care. She points out that each caregiver must learn the preferred rhythm and dance style of each infant, and each infant must do so for each caregiver. When there is no primary care assignment, the baby experiences a changing array of dance partners. Each infant must learn to dance with each partner, which consumes a great deal of energy and time. With primary care, each baby has one or two dance partners, with whom the baby learns to dance well. This takes less time and energy, opening more opportunities for babies to explore and learn.

Within a system of primary care, the infant learns what it takes to attract the attention and read the cues of his primary care teacher, and to anticipate

Reflection—When Primary Care Is Absent

Observation:

Infant Talia is one of 12 babies in the room. There are three teachers, but there is no policy of primary care. The teachers respond as needed to all the babies. Talia is hungry and begins to cry. No one comes, so she cries louder. Teacher Patricia is diapering another baby and glances up to see Talia crying, but she sees co-teacher Benjamin a short distance from Talia. In the meantime, Benjamin does not respond to Talia, because he was the last one to feed a baby and thinks one of the others should take a turn. A third teacher, Kathy, is near the entry talking with a parent, and she assumes her co-workers are taking care of Talia.

Reflection:

Reflect on this experience from the perspective of the baby and the teachers involved. What does Talia learn in this situation? What does she learn about her ability to communicate her needs to others? Why do you think this program has chosen not to adopt a policy of primary care? Why do you think a program might resist implementing a policy of primary care and at what cost to the baby, to the family, and to the teacher?

how that person will pick him up, hold his bottle, or respond to his cry or gestures. Likewise, the primary care teacher learns the unique patterns of each of four babies, a more manageable task than trying to do so for a group of 12 or more babies. Primary care also ensures that each family has someone dedicated to their unique concerns.

A primary care system provides predictability without rigidity. Primary care does not mean that a teacher never cares for a child who is not a member of the primary care group. It means that most of the care experiences that occur during the day and most of the conversations with family members will involve the primary care teacher, but not exclusively. There will be times during the day when other teachers diaper, offer meals, settle an infant down for a nap, or talk with an infant or the infant's family. For example, others may provide the care when an infant's primary care teacher is taking a break, or at the beginning or end of the day when the primary care teacher has not arrived or has left, or when one toddler remains inside, still enjoying lunch, while his primary care teacher takes the other toddlers outside to the yard. At the beginning and the end of the day, there is often just one teacher on duty, greeting and talking with all arriving families, irrespective of the primary care assignment. Such flexibility is built into primary care and ensures a system in which, for most of the day, the infant's primary care teacher is the one providing the care.

Each primary care teacher also serves as secondary teacher to other infants in the room. When the primary care teacher is absent, on break, or busy with another child, the other primary care teachers in the room assume the role of secondary teacher for the infants in this teacher's primary care group. This ensures that infants will always have a familiar person responding to their needs.

If the group-care setting is a family child-care home, where services are provided within the home of the infant-care provider, primary care happens naturally, if the program is small. For example, if the family

Reflection—Primary Care That Fuels Babies with Attention

Consider this experience, from the perspective of baby and teacher, when a policy of primary care is in place.

Observation:

Patricia, Talia's primary care teacher, is busy diapering another infant, Adrienne. Talia, lying in the play space on a blanket, begins to whimper and cry. Patricia looks over at Talia and then turns back to baby Adrienne and says, "Talia is crying. Do you hear her? I think she is hungry. I'll let her know that it will be just a moment and then I can get her bottle." Patricia turns and says to Talia in the play space, "I hear you, Talia. You're calling me. I think you're telling me you are hungry. As soon as I finish with Adrienne, I'll bring you your bottle. It will be very soon." Hearing her voice, Talia turns toward Patricia. Her cry subsides.

Interpretation:

The teacher does not leave what she is doing to attend immediately to Talia. However, as Talia's primary care teacher, she acknowledges Talia's cry with words of comfort. She lets Talia know that help is on the way. Her words calm Talia a bit, even though Talia is still eager to be picked up. Talia feels heard. She can distinguish the voice of her primary care teacher from other voices. Although Talia does not comprehend the meaning of Patricia's words, she notices Patricia's expression and the tone, pitch, and rhythm of her voice. She associates this pattern with a good feeling and anticipates that in a moment she will be picked up.

child-care program has a capacity of six children, there is typically just one person caring for the children. With a group size of six, the expectation would be that no more than two of the six would be infants. A family child-care home serving more than six would require a second caregiver. When there are two adults who provide service in a large family child-care home, primary care for the infants can be achieved by assigning one of the adults as teacher for the infants and the other adult as teacher for the older children.

CONTINUITY OF CARE

A second essential policy for infant programs is continuity of care. Whereas primary care ensures that a strong relationship of trust and affection develops between teacher and infant, continuity of care ensures that these relationships will last over time. The concept of continuity of care means that a primary care teacher stays with the same group of children from the time of enrollment until 3 years of age, or the point when the child departs the program. It also means that the children's peers remain the same over the course of stay in the program. Families exit a program, and new families enroll, so the composition of a primary care group may not remain the same. However within a system of continuity of care, program administrators commit to doing all they can to keep primary care groups together over the course of the program.

There will be times when administrators need to adjust the composition of the primary care groups, to ensure efficient staffing. This happens when infants transfer into preschool rooms, when families move or change programs, or when one teacher leaves and a new teacher is hired. Such changes require an adjustment in the composition of primary care groups. When doing so, an administrator can preserve the primary care relationships as much as possible, even when adjusting staffing assignments. For example, a primary care teacher leaves to take another job, so for the children and families, primary care and continuity of care are lost. However, by keeping the primary care group of children together in the same room, with the same secondary teachers, the administrator maintains some continuity of relationships.

When a family departs, leaving a vacancy in a primary care group, ideally a new infant of similar age is enrolled to take that child's place. However, this may not be possible, especially when children are grouped by similarity of age. Sometimes, enrolling a new infant may require transferring a child from one primary care group to another, in order to fully enroll the program. An attempt should be made to transfer the infant to a primary care group in the same room, if possible, to maintain continuity of peers. The new primary care teacher would be familiar to the child, having been in the same room. If it is necessary to move an infant from one room to another, effort should be made to have the infant move with either a primary care or secondary care teacher, and, ideally, with other infants from the same room.

SMALL GROUP SIZE

Primary care and continuity of care work best when coupled with a third program policy, small group size. Small group size refers to the recommended maximum number of infants assigned to a room. Group size influences whether an infant feels safe and secure or whether an infant feels lost, overwhelmed, or afraid. When the size of the group is sufficiently small, infants readily come to know those with whom they share the space. When the size of the group is too large, infants feel overwhelmed by the number of people—adults and other infants—with whom they must share space, toys, and attention. The result is reduced exploration, less-complex play, and fewer possibilities for learning.

Recommended Group Size

The number of infants cared for in a room, relative to the number of caregivers, should facilitate, rather than compromise, infants' learning. The Program for Infant/Toddler Care recommends a maximum group size of six to eight for infants and a maximum group size of eight to twelve for toddlers, the actual number dependent on the age range of infants served (Torelli, 2006). The younger the infant, the smaller the recommended number of children per room.

Infants are most at ease in small groups. Infants cared for in a large group may feel anxious, confused, or fearful. They may cope by withdrawing, disengaging from play, wandering aimlessly, or restricting themselves to rigid, repetitive play with the same toys. All such means of coping limit children's exploration and learning.

Reflection: Transitions—At What Cost?

Consider this observation from the perspective of the baby, the baby's family, and the teachers involved.

Observation:

Antonio is 12 months old, and he has just started to walk. He has been in the crawler room since he began to crawl, about 5 months ago. The policy of this infant center is to move infants, when they learn to walk, into a young toddler room, which is staffed by another group of teachers. The center director advises one of the teachers who works in the crawler room to notify Antonio's family that the transfer will occur the next morning. She asks his teacher to deliver his extra clothes, his file, and the name on his storage bin to the toddler room, so that they will be ready for him the next morning.

Interpretation:

Do you see any evidence of primary care? Do you see any evidence of a policy of continuity of care? Reflect on what this experience will be like for Antonio, his family, and the teachers who have cared for him for the past 5 months. Will it feel abrupt? Will there be sadness? Consider what you feel like when you have to leave behind those who are familiar and loved. What will it feel like for Antonio and his family when they enter a new room, with new faces, new routines of care, and a host of other unfamiliar and unpredictable sights, smells, and sounds?

In group-care settings, a small group of infants, their families, and their teachers form a community. An infant-care center usually has multiple infant communities, the number dependent on the overall size and capacity of the facility. The number of staff assigned to each infant community will depend on the age group served in each room. The number of adults available to care for a group of infants is referred to as the adult-to-child ratio. A 1:3 ratio means one adult for every three infants in attendance. Likewise, 1:4 means one adult for every four infants. The ratio typically is set by government regulatory agencies, but the Program for Infant/Toddler Care recommends primary care ratios of 1:3 or 1:4 in groups of six to twelve children, depending on the age (Lally, Stewart, & Greenwald, 2009).

When the groups are kept small, infants, their families, and the primary care teachers develop a web of friendship and a bond of expectation and trust.

Teachers more effectively tune in to infants' cues, and infants more easily focus on that which interests them, creating a comfortable climate for learning. Small group size also reduces the risk of illness, with fewer points of exposure to infectious disease.

Group Composition

There are two ways to think about composition of groups in infant-care programs. One way is to assign infants to a room serving a mixed range of ages. The other is to assign infants to a room with children of similar age. When the group is composed of mixed ages, children might range in age from 2–36 months. When grouped by similarity of age, children span a smaller range of ages, typically a young group, that is, those not crawling; crawlers and young toddlers; and older toddlers.

With similar-age groups, as each group matures and requires more complex furnishings and materials, there are two options. One is to transform the furnishings and layout of the room. The other is for infants and teachers to move together to another room. The goal is to maintain continuity of relationships, children remaining with the same teachers and friends.

There are both advantages and disadvantages to mixed-age and similar-age groups. In mixed-age groups, it is easy to enroll new children when there is a vacancy, as a new child can be assigned to any room. However, creating a strong learning environment is more difficult in mixed-age settings. In an infant room of typical size, it is hard to set up play spaces that meet the diverse interests of the broad age range inherent in a mixed-age group. Infants not yet crawling require a protected play space; whereas crawlers need more space where they can master the crawl and practice pulling to standing and walking; and toddlers need places to climb and jump. Each group also has distinct needs with respect to play materials, with complexity increasing with age. Furnishings for meals vary, as well, across the ages.

The risk in mixed-age rooms is that older infants may lack access to play materials that challenge them, and younger infants may lack protection from more active toddlers. Some teachers in mixed-age rooms divide the play space into three discrete areas, one for each age group, but unless the floor space is ample, this often results in cramped play that fails to serve the interests of any of the age groups.

Figure 10.3. Floor Plan, Infant Center

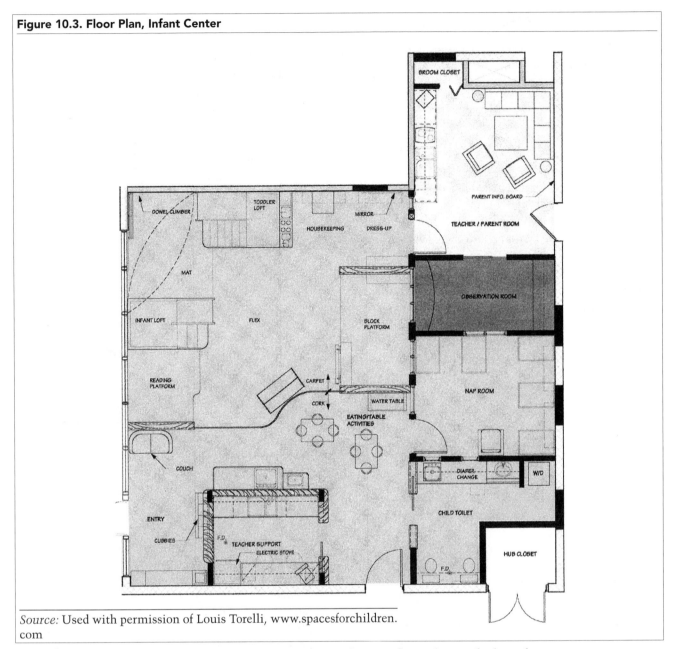

Source: Used with permission of Louis Torelli, www.spacesforchildren.com

Self-Contained Communities

The space allocated to each infant community includes floor space used for care routines—like the diapering, eating, and napping areas—as well as floor space used for infants' play. Ideally, the small group of infants in the infant community play, rest, eat, and are diapered within a distinct, self-contained space. This means that each infant community has what is needed for napping, diapering, meals, and play and teachers do not need to exit the room in order to accomplish these tasks. This is important, because many infants become anxious and fearful if they see their primary care teacher leave the room. Figure 10.3

shows a floor plan with these features.

Ideally, a facility has a separate room for each infant community. However, this is not always the case. Sometimes a large room has sufficient floor space to serve 20 or more children, yet to do so would mean a group size that is too large. One way to reduce the group size, yet still maintain cost-effective use of space, is to divide the large room to create two separate infant communities. The obvious solution is to construct a wall to create two smaller rooms; however, a less costly solution is to use portable, sturdy partitions to divide the space. The advantage of a partition is that it divides the space, but still allows visual access by adults from one side to the other.

Partitions also provide flexibility. They can be moved as the space requirements of the group change. When separate infant communities are created using partitions, each community should have service areas for meals, diapering, and naps; ample activity space for play; and a distinct entry.

When small group size is a policy, relationships flourish, as captured in the following comments from teachers who transformed a large classroom of 24 infants and toddlers into two distinct infant communities (C. Grivette, personal communication, 2004):

> We realized that frenzy and chaos had become the norm for us. It was particularly bad at mid-day, when all the children were present. By dividing the room into two distinct communities, we reduced the group size. It was amazing how much this calmed the climate of the room. The change was remarkable in that it gave us time to observe and notice what was going on with our babies. We could relax and enjoy their play, rather than having to focus solely on "supervising" the play to keep them safe.

Looking Back and Looking Forward

Program policies that support secure, enduring, and predictable relationships must be at the heart of infant care. Small group size is a policy that ensures each infant the opportunity to develop a sense of belonging within a predictable group of friends. When primary care and continuity of care are adopted as policies, a primary care teacher works with the same group of infants and families over time and learns to read the cries, expressions, and gestures of each infant in the group; to appreciate each infant's unique personality; and to anticipate and to understand the values, beliefs, and expectations of each infant's family. In the next chapter, we will build on the foundation of relationships made possible by these essential organizational policies and explore how to design play spaces as contexts for learning.

CHAPTER 11

Play Spaces
Contexts for Wonder and Learning

We value space because of its power to organize, promote pleasant relationships among people of different ages, create a handsome environment . . . and its potential for sparking all kinds of social, affective, and cognitive learning. All of this contributes to a sense of well-being and security in children. . . . The space has to be a sort of aquarium that mirrors the ideas, values, attitudes, and cultures of the people who live within it. (Malaguzzi, as quoted in Gandini, 2012, p. 339)

S PACES SPEAK TO us in ways beyond words. Have you ever entered a room or a yard for the first time and felt an immediate sense of calm or, in contrast, a sense of tension, or even boredom or threat? Spaces speak through both the objects encountered and their arrangement. A space can invite or a space can turn away, simply by virtue of the objects, smells, and sights encountered there.

Through our senses, we gather information when we enter and inhabit a room. We read it for clues as

---

Reflection: Spaces Speak

Imagine walking into a living space for the first time. Daylight, the chirping of birds, and a fresh breeze filter through a window near a couch draped with a quilt of muted colors. On a low table nearby is a short stack of books and a vase filled with fresh flowers. Consider each element, texture, smell, sight, and sound. Does this space beckon you to settle in or does it prompt you to move away? Now imagine another living room. As you enter, you are forced to step over and around objects left behind by others who have used this space before. You approach the sofa, but you are forced to push aside papers, empty food containers, crumbs, and clothing strewn randomly. The faint smell of dust rises and mingles with stale, heavy air trapped by walls and closed windows. Is your urge to settle in or to move away?

Reflection: Looking for Something Lost

Have you ever gone in search of a particular object that you recalled being stored amid a pile of other objects in a box or an overstuffed drawer? Recall what this experience felt like. What was it like to sort through many objects in search of a particular item? Did you find yourself getting frustrated? Did you succeed, or did you give up the search? What relevance does this example have to the experience of an infant at play?

---

to how to behave. A room can generate a feeling of calm, excitement, curiosity, fear, or tension. For families seeking infant care, the first hint of how their infants will be cared for comes from the environment that greets them upon entry. How the environment is prepared as a context for learning and how the space speaks to those who inhabit it are essential elements of infant program development. This chapter explores how to design play spaces as engaging contexts that inspire thinking and support learning.

A SYSTEM FOR ORGANIZING PLAY MATERIALS

Infants use their senses and their developing muscle systems to gather information and make sense of it. In the short span of a few years, they build increasingly more complex knowledge, much of it within simple moments of play. What they encounter in the play spaces will either limit or expand their learning. How teachers organize the play spaces and offer materials for infants' ease of access is a critical aspect of teaching and learning when working with infants and toddlers.

When groups of infants use a play space, toys get heavy use. The more children, the more play materials needed. An ample supply of play materials requires ample space for storage and use. Selecting and organizing toys and materials for a group of infants requires a clear system that works for both infants and teachers. A system for organizing play materials includes layout of the play space, as well as means of storing and giving infants free access to play materials. Without a clear system for organizing the play materials, toys are haphazardly dropped in boxes or bins, or piled onto shelves to get them off the floor. Some may be visible and accessible to infants, but most remain out of sight, out of reach, or buried deep within the recesses of box or shelf.

A system for organizing the play materials within a well-designed space requires a plan that ensures infants and adults can find play materials in predictable locations. The goal is not to impose a strict order on how and where toys get used. The goal is to organize the play environment so that it invites, rather than discourages, the delightful messiness and creativity inherent in play. This means tolerating a delicate tension between order and disorder. Order promotes ease of access by infants and makes the play space predictable, but disorder is the natural consequence of a well-used infant play space. Although infants may mess up the order of a prepared play space, in doing so, they transform the materials into an order of their own. Toys in use mean toys that may be carried and dropped in spots throughout the room. Infants' active

meaning-making relies on their being free to handle objects, move objects, relate one to another, experiment with them, and transform them in an endless variety of ways. Teachers working with infants, therefore, inevitably spend time returning toys to storage containers. This ongoing task maintains order, yet the order will change, an open invitation to infants to build an order of their own.

Play Space with Distinct Identity

One way to preserve order within the messiness of infant play is to adopt a predictable layout, with distinct play spaces, each having a unique identity. A large floor space allocated for infants' play can be divided to make multiple play spaces, each with a distinct identity. This design principle applies equally well to center-based care and home-based care, irrespective of the size of the room.

A play space with a unique identity means that the space is stocked with materials that invite a particular type of play. To establish a distinct identity for a play space, teachers select and arrange together materials that share a common attribute or function. For example, a space designed for connecting and constructing has an ample supply of objects that infants can nest inside one another, stack on top of one another, or easily connect one to another. This might include a collection of flat-sided boxes that invite stacking or

> **Reflection: Play Spaces That Inspire New Ideas**
>
> In many ways, giving play spaces a distinct identity reflects the same thought that store managers put into the display of store merchandise. Consider how a store manager plans the display space within the store, so that customers readily find exactly what they are looking for. Also, consider how a store manager looks for ways to beckon the customer to try new things.
>
> - What planning goes into the arrangement of displays and the store layout? How are items organized and displayed?
> - How does the arrangement of items ensure that customers will stumble upon new items they had not anticipated buying?
> - How does the display impact the customer's experience, that is, comfortable and easy or frustrating and confusing?
>
> Now switch your thoughts to the layout and design of an infant play space. Compare your reflections on organizing merchandise in a store with organizing materials for infant play. When a play space has a distinct identity, with materials that relate to one another, how does it influence the play? How might distinct play spaces inspire new materials to add to the play? How do distinct play spaces impact maintenance and care?

lining up. It also might include lightweight cardboard or plastic blocks and recycled plastic jars with lids, all of which have flat surfaces for stacking or openings for nesting one object inside another.

Another example of a play space with a distinct identity is a book and story area, which can be stocked with sturdy cardboard books alongside baskets that hold puppets and pretend animals, similar to those featured in some of the books in the play space. When located within a somewhat secluded area, bordered with a low partition that holds pictures of children enjoying favorite books, this play space communicates a clear message: "Come and enjoy a story with the materials assembled here." For toddlers, a book and story space also might include a place where they can initiate telling and retelling favorite stories, selecting from a basket of laminated figures that easily stick to a felt-covered surface. A book and story area makes it possible for stories to extend beyond the pages of a book.

When the materials housed in a play space share a common identity and when the layout of the play space is somewhat predictable, infants easily make

sense of the space. They become familiar with it and can reliably find what they need when they need it. When infants know where to find a favorite object or a particular kind of object, their attention can turn to creative play, rather than be lost in a frustrating search. Such spaces also make sense to teachers, making it easy to organize materials for productive play. When the materials in a play space share a common identity, they relay to child and adult a clear message of the kinds of things found there. This feature also makes clean-up easy for adult and child, both of whom can predict what goes where.

Time spent preparing and maintaining the play environment has a direct return for teachers in time available to observe from the sidelines or to carry out the care experiences. They can watch to see how the infants use the play materials. This prompts ideas for creating new contexts for learning to expand the play. In well-organized and thoughtfully stocked play spaces, infants readily explore on their own, providing an important balance of time spent together with the teacher and time spent apart. Infants and teachers profit from this exchange. When infants explore independently in the play spaces, teachers are able to spend time with individual babies during the care routines, in essence, refueling each infant with attention. Fueled by the quality time spent together during diapering or a meal, infants are ready to explore on their own in a well-provisioned and well-organized play space.

A Space That Communicates

A play space that has a unique identity communicates to the infants what might be experienced there. In other words, simply by storing materials together in the same play area, teachers invite infants to use objects together, but they do not tell them to do so. This takes teaching out of the realm of telling knowledge and into the realm of constructing knowledge. What infants find in the play space motivates them to build new ideas and to explore new possibilities for relating one thing to another.

For example, in a play space organized around connections and constructions, toddlers might explore the assembled materials and discover that they can stack one item on top of another and have it balance. Nearby, they find other flat-surfaced items that hold this same potential. This might inspire them to create something bigger, longer, or higher, that is, "If I put one of these on top of the other, I make something taller than I had before!" Or, "If I put one inside the other, I get something small, and now I can carry them all together."

Reflection: Figure–Ground Relationship as Provocation in Play

Study this photo taken in a toddler play space. What do you think was the teacher's intention in the selection of play materials? Do the materials have a distinct identity? How would you name that identity? Is there a specific intention in how the materials are arranged? Can you explain this in terms of a figure–ground relationship? How does the arrangement of the materials in the play space impact the play?

The "something more" that gets created makes this play space an important area for infants' building relationships of size, shape, weight, and order, all important concepts in mathematics and science.

The walls and dividers that border the play space also communicate. To a visitor, the walls convey a story about the play that occurs there. This is more than just a sign to identify an area. It is a simple panel of photos accompanied by brief text to illustrate the learning that occurs within the play. For example, in a connections and constructions play space, the documentation on the wall communicates the identity of the space as one where concepts of spatial relations and number are built. A photo might show an infant at play, connecting a series of conical cups to make a long staff, with a caption that says, "Infants make number." Another photo might show a toddler collecting all the blue blocks from a multicolored assortment of blocks, with a caption that says, "Infants sort and classify." A third photo might show a toddler lining up a string of blocks, with a caption that says,

"Infants explore line and shape, a foundation for geometry." A brief note near the photos connects play and learning, "Playing with line, number, and shape to build a foundation for math and science."

Familiarity and Surprise

Infants, even those very young, get to know well the play spaces within the infant center. Each play space serves as a predictable home to a set of known objects, while at the same time a place to encounter new items of interest. A predictable inventory of known objects ensures that when infants enter a play space, they find what they remember having used before. They anticipate familiar things, return to use them in familiar ways, and invent new ways to use them. In a pretend play area, for example, toddlers find familiar objects used in the home, like empty cardboard or plastic containers from the kitchen, pots with lids, bowls, and cups. Such a predictable supply of props gives toddlers the opportunity to represent

Reflection: How Do Environments Support Relationships?

Reflect on how indoor and outdoor spaces support the development of relationships of care and trust. Imagine the impact of each of these recommendations on how infants experience themselves in relationship to others they care for and trust.

- Arrange furnishings and equipment so that adults can comfortably observe infants while they play.
- Create somewhat secluded play spaces where infants can play without distraction from the sights and sounds of people entering, leaving, or moving through the room.
- Provide spaces and comfortable seating within or near play spaces where infants and adults can sit together and enjoy play materials or books.
- Create play spaces where infants can be alone as well as together in small groups.
- Include furnishings, visual arts, and pretend play materials that reflect the cultures of the families in the program, like hammocks, baskets, cooking implements, or scarves.
- Modify spaces and furnishings to support full participation of all children, including those with disabilities and special needs (e.g., pathways wide enough for a wheelchair or a hammock-style swing that provides an option of a high-sensory experience).

Reflection: Play Space as Inviting Nook

Loris Malaguzzi, the founding director of the system of early childhood schools in Reggio Emilia, Italy, suggested that effective play spaces are like "'market stalls,' where customers look for the wares that interest them, make selections, and engage in lively interactions" (Gandini, 2012, p. 336). Examine the design depicted here, from a toddler room. How have the teachers attempted to create a sense of seclusion? What is required to create seclusion, without compromising visual access and supervision?

their everyday experiences, in increasingly complex ways.

A basic inventory of play materials anchors a play space. On a regular basis, teachers add novel materials to provoke new directions. Novel items bring an element of surprise and wonder and prompt new investigations. Teachers in the schools in Reggio Emilia describe these as provocations, things that provoke new possibilities for exploration and play and new possibilities for learning. They also speak in terms of problematizing (Rinaldi, 2006b) the play. By this, they mean intentionally adding objects that prompt infants with a new problem to solve; for example, adding materials that may not respond in predictable ways. Provocations suggest new problems and challenges, with endless possibilities for building new relationships of thought.

Sometimes simply rearranging the layout of furnishings in a play space provokes new exploration

and learning. For example, low, hollow rectangular benches are a common structure used as a divider in infant programs. They provide surfaces where infants can find toys. They also serve as ready supports for pulling to standing. When inverted, however, they prompt a different kind of play. Inverting them invites climbing in and climbing out, suggesting a wide variety of new play scripts. When teachers make slight changes in the play environment, so that infants see the play materials from a new and expanded perspective, they adopt a teaching strategy that Jones and Reynolds (2011) describe as changing the figure–ground relationship. In other words, by rearranging

---

Reflection: Secluded Space

Consider the times and places where you do your best learning. Does it happen more readily when you are relaxed and can focus with calm and clarity? Does it become harder when distracted by sounds or sights? Most people require a certain level of quiet and focus in order to truly engage with and learn from an experience. Infants are no different, with respect to the conditions that make it easy to pay attention and learn.

---

furnishings and materials in the play space, teachers draw attention to uses, features, or relationships previously unseen. What was once in the background is now in the foreground, with the possibility of being used in new and different ways.

DESIGNING THE PLAY SPACE

For a play space to work well, it must speak to infants in ways that beckon and invite. Several design elements make this possible. These design elements include division of play space to provide a degree of seclusion; clear pathways that do not compete with play spaces; and accessible storage.

The space used for group infant care is allocated to two different uses—space to carry out the daily routines of care and space dedicated to play. Where these spaces lie within a facility is determined, in part, by existing plumbing, entries, and walls. However, to the extent possible, it also should be planned with social-emotional relationships in mind. Relationships are influenced by the layout of space. Infants expect the teacher to be close at hand, whether during a daily care routine like meals or when they are engaged in play with toys. Therefore, the play spaces in an infant program should be contiguous to the care spaces.

To investigate requires focused attention. An infant play space should make it possible for infants to focus on small things, like the contrasting colors in a toy or the reverberating sound that a sharp tap draws from a hollow wood block or metal tin. For infants in group care, the distractions are many—people entering and leaving, people talking, and other children playing. The sights and sounds can be overwhelming, making it hard for infants to maintain their focus of attention. Dividers are useful in this regard. They not only create distinct play spaces, but they also reduce visual and auditory distractions, so that infants can pay attention to the sight, sound, smell, or feel of objects they encounter in play. Teachers can reduce the

sensory stimulation by designing spaces that create a sense of seclusion.

A variety of furnishings and materials can be used as dividers to separate the play spaces, without isolating infants from adults' visual supervision. Shelves are a common divider, sufficiently high to give infants a sense of seclusion, yet sufficiently low to allow adults to supervise the space from a distance. A visual divider also can be created with a length of fire-retardant fabric, hung like a canopy from the ceiling. A large, comfortable chair, small sofa, or low bench also can divide the space, as can a panel of wood or Plexiglas secured to the wall or to a sturdy shelf.

The size of a play space is determined by the placement of dividers. Some play spaces are designed to accommodate a group of five or six infants, while others are designed for the play of just one child or as few as two or three, like a small alcove underneath a counter or below a loft or climber. Such small, intimate spaces are important in group care, because they offer infants the option of retreating to a somewhat quiet space to escape the busy atmosphere of the larger room. In contrast, it is helpful to have one play space sufficiently large to hold the entire group of children, like a toddler area designed for active movement that also can serve as a gathering place for storytelling, dancing, and singing songs.

The identity of the play space, that is, the focus of play around which the area is designed, influences the amount of floor space allocated to a particular type of play. A book and story area stocked with baskets of books, puppets, and laminated photos should be large enough to accommodate some type of comfortable seating for adult and child together. This might be a soft, low mattress or a small couch where several people might sit together and read a book. Other play spaces might require a raised work surface, like a table or a low counter or bench for doing small puzzles or playing matching games with toddlers. Not every infant play space needs shelves, nor does every play space need a table. For infants, the most appropriate play surface is often the floor, especially for very young babies and crawlers. For these younger babies, storage baskets that are low, wide, and placed in the play space at the infant's level of gaze are more appropriate than traditional storage shelves (Figure 11.1).

Pathways to, Not Through, the Play

A critical design consideration relates to the proximity of pathways to play areas. People move through the room throughout the day, entering and leaving and walking from place to place. Since the ideal is to create play spaces as free of distraction as possible, traffic patterns matter, because the movement of people from place to place is a major distraction for infants. The location of doorways, including entries and closets, will influence traffic patterns and define pathways. To limit distractions for infants at play, pathways should lead *to* a play space and, if possible, should not cross *through* the play space. It is important to identify the pathways before dividing the space into smaller nooks. If not, pathways will compete with floor space designated for play.

Pathways and play spaces should be sufficiently wide and uncluttered. This ensures safe passage and access for all. If children or adults using the room have special needs related to mobility, a pathway or a workspace may need to accommodate a mobility device. For example, a wheelchair will require clear pathways and access to usable work surfaces. A child with visual impairment needs a clear path as well, one marked with tactile cues, like raised symbols on the edge of a low bench to mark the entry to a play space.

An efficient floor plan for an infant room dedicates the minimum space necessary to pathways, leaving the majority of the usable activity space for infants' play. Figure 10.3 shows a floor plan for an infant room. Notice the relationship between pathways and activity space for play. A variety of partitions break the large room into distinct play nooks. The partitions extend perpendicular from the walls, creating two sides that enclose each play nook. This leaves one side open, as an entry, providing a sense of seclusion and minimizing distractions. The primary pathways move through the middle of the room. They do not cross through the middle of the small play spaces. In addition, the entry doors are positioned so that the flow of traffic moves through the center of the room, rather than through the small play nooks. Because the pathways lead to, rather than through, the small play spaces, infants' primary areas for play remain somewhat protected.

Accessible Storage

Storage of play materials should be convenient for both infants and adults, with attention to the type of containers used to store materials as well as their location. Infants should be able to readily see and find play materials in the play space. Storage may be on shelves, in baskets, or, for large items, simply on the floor. Baskets often work better than shelves for storing toys and materials, especially for crawlers and for

Figure 11.1. Baskets Ease Access to Toys

babies not yet crawling. Storage baskets woven from natural materials (see Figure 11.1) provide an aesthetically appealing texture and smell. Woven baskets must be sturdy and durable and pose no risk of having small pieces break off to become choking hazards.

Clear storage containers make it easy for children to see the contents. Clear containers serve as an invitation to infants to go in search of what is inside. When placed on a low shelf, clear containers attract the attention of a crawler as well as a toddler. When placed somewhat higher, they invite crawlers to pull to standing in order to explore enticing objects placed slightly beyond reach. Size and weight are important. Containers too large mean toys get buried and remain unseen and unused. Containers too heavy relay a clear message, "Leave me put." Some teachers add labels, with pictures, photos, and/or words, to give children clues as to what is found inside. Labels are helpful when returning items during clean-up. They also expose toddlers to meaningful print, photos, and symbols, an experience in early literacy. Storage shelves accessible only to adults are best situated high on a wall near the play space. This keeps back-up supplies close at hand, out of children's reach.

Figure 11.2. Ordinary Objects as Toys

Ordinary Objects in the Play Space

Many educators in recent years have begun to think beyond commercial and traditional children's toys and have begun to use ordinary objects, repurposed and recycled materials, and natural materials in the play spaces. Ordinary objects and natural materials are delightful additions to play. Most are open-ended, with features that invite infants to use them in a wide variety of ways.

Ordinary objects are simple things like pots, boxes, bowls, cups, tubes, utensils, or swatches of fabric. When offered as an infant toy, the original purpose or function of such objects may change. In the mind of an infant, an object like a basket becomes a car or a cup. A rich variety of safe infant play materials can

be found in kitchen cupboards, like storage containers, food tins, or empty paper rolls. Figure 11.2 shows examples of ordinary objects that might be offered in infant play spaces.

When ordinary objects and repurposed objects are offered as collections, they prompt many possibilities for creating, engineering, and transforming. Described by Nicholson (1971) as loose parts, such collections can be thought of as objects that do not have a prescribed identity and are available in quantity. Offered an ample supply of loose parts in the play space, infants assemble, invent, and create patterns and structures, making something new and distinct. They transform a single item into something different or something more—bigger, taller, fuller, or longer.

Reflection: Invitation for Infants to Explore Nature—Proposing Possibilities

Explore the following questions to generate ideas for planning contexts that invite infants to explore nature:

- How might we add opportunities for infants to experience the effect of wind?
- How might we create a context for toddlers to explore creatures that live in the yard, like snails, worms, or ladybugs, and for experiencing their habitat?
- How might we offer opportunities for infants to explore the physical properties of water and what they can make it do?
- How will toddlers explore variations in rocks, and what patterns might emerge in their play as they explore them?
- What materials might we use to offer infants a context for experiencing the textures, smell, and feel of wood?
- What context might we offer toddlers to experience plants as they come from the garden?
- What context might we offer infants for getting to know all the small parts that flowers are made of, dissecting them, squeezing them, and smelling them?

When collections of loose parts are found in the play space, infants sift through them, to get to know their features. This prepares them with the physical knowledge they need with respect to how the loose parts might be used, that is, for potential logico-mathematical relationships. They might go in search of a particular kind of loose part, with features that correspond to an idea held in mind. A recycled metal food tin makes a perfect pot, and metal lids make perfect food items to drop into the perfect pot. A nearby box becomes a stove for cooking.

Loose parts make it possible for infants to engage in shared symbolic and social play. They optimize the possibility that an idea held in mind becomes an idea that can be touched, seen, and shared with others. The benefit of loose parts is that they typically are recycled, found, or repurposed objects, available at little or no cost. They have rich potential when it comes to infant learning, because they can be transformed, arranged, and used in an endless variety of ways.

Natural Materials in the Play Space

One of the most exciting areas for curriculum planning with infants and young children relates to exploration of the natural world. As infants explore materials from nature, they nurture understanding of biology, chemistry, earth sciences, and physics. Experiences with the elements of water, earth, and air and experiences with plants and small creatures that live nearby offer infants the opportunity to get to know the world of nature.

Richard Louv (2008) argues for the importance of preserving children's relationship with nature. His research documents the effects of decreased exposure of children to nature and presents a compelling argument for how isolation from nature harms society. A critical question for early childhood teachers, as they plan curriculum, is, "How might we bring natural materials into the play spaces indoors and outdoors, so that infants and young children have opportunity to build a relationship with nature?"

Outdoors as a Learning Environment

The outdoor space holds as much possibility for both the care routines and play as does the interior. Meals, diapering, and naps can happen as comfortably outside as they do inside, when thoughtful furnishings are provided. The same principles used in designing the indoor play space apply to the design of the outdoor play space—seclusion, proximity of storage space to workspace, predictability of materials within the play spaces, and attention to traffic areas.

Active Movement Challenges. Places to crawl onto, over, and through, as well as places to pull up and to cruise along, are outdoor spots that appeal to the crawler and young toddler. Toddlers delight in challenging places to climb, to slide, to roll, to swing, to balance, and to meander. Infants mastering how to walk enjoy pathways through tall grasses, along stepping stones, onto raised surfaces, under low arches, and through hinged gates. Pathways also invite toddlers to maneuver small wagons, tricycles, and carts through turns, up and down low hills, and through short tunnels. Slopes, raised surfaces, and ramps to climb up or slide down can be created using simple, natural materials, rather than relying on expensive commercial play structures. Figure 11.3 illustrates a simple active movement space created for an infant yard, using recycled tree logs.

Reflection: Natural Materials—Maximizing Opportunity, Minimizing Risk

What might these materials from nature offer infants, with respect to learning about the natural world? What safety issues should be considered when adding natural materials to the infant play spaces? What tension might exist between the opportunity to offer infants experiences with natural materials and concerns about safety and liability? How do you suggest teachers address this tension and safeguard infants' opportunity to build a relationship with the natural world?

Figure 11.3. Outdoor Active Movement Space

Insects in Their Natural Habitat. Toddlers are fascinated by insects that live in the yard. To support this interest, teachers and parents can introduce toddlers to respectful ways to investigate insects in their natural habitat. Insects' natural habitat is often the yard they share with toddlers. The natural habitat of common insects, like ladybugs, pill bugs, snails, or worms, might be the bushes, leaves, or soil in the yard. These habitats are quite accessible to infants and toddlers. Bushes, shrubs, and grasses can be planted, with the expectation that they will provide natural habitat for safe and nonthreatening insects. This builds into the infant play yard opportunities for science investigation.

A simple way to make a new context for exploring insects is to rest a planter over a moist patch of dirt. Wait a day or two, and return with toddlers to discover what insects might be living in the moist soil below. Another way to build habitats that toddlers can freely explore is to create a terrarium for snails, where they can watch the snails eat leaves and live in a prepared habitat. With teachers' help, they can examine how snails move on a clear sheet of Plexiglas suspended over low platforms, offering two points of view. With eye droppers and water, they learn how to keep snails moist and protected, and with a choice of options, they discover what snails like to eat (Figure 11.4).

Such opportunities give toddlers a chance to examine what insects look like, how they move, and what they need to survive. In so doing, toddlers build a relationship with living creatures and a respect for their habitat. Over time, they come to recognize, respect, and care for the places where insects live. They become champions for keeping safe those insects that are beneficial to the environment. When toddlers have respectful experiences with worms, ladybugs, and snails, they know how to go in search of where they might live in the yard, aware of where to find them and mindful of how to keep them safe (Figure 11.5).

Figure 11.4. Getting to Know a Snail

Figure 11.5. Finding Insects in Their Natural Habitat

Figure 11.6. Discovering Vegetables from the Garden

Plants in Their Natural Habitat. Many plants that are nontoxic are quite hardy and survive well when subjected to investigation by inquisitive toddlers. Nontoxic herbs are an easy option. Many are hardy and grow profusely once established, like mint, lavender, sage, and lemon balm. Toddlers can regularly pick them, with no harm to the plant and no harm to themselves. Raised gardening beds put herbs and hardy vegetable plants at eye level for toddlers. Fruit trees, pruned so that some branches remain at toddler level, invite toddlers to pick ripe fruit. Small vegetable gardens also attract insects, providing an enchanting place to go in search of insects in their natural habitat. Natural materials, like bamboo stalks or long, thin tree branches secured together at the top, support vegetable plants that vine, like peas and beans, but also, when covered by vines, provide small play nooks for toddlers.

In a plant-rich yard, as seasons change, toddlers experience leaves drying, seedpods forming, blossoms emerging, fruit popping out, vines twisting and drying, and roots tangling, all of which invite toddlers to experience biology in action. Tree branches with blossoms, sheets of bark, branches with leaves, fruit drying, vegetables to peel (Figure 11.6), and uprooted plants provide contexts for toddlers to discover what is inside or underneath the outer layers of a plant and expose them to how things change with time.

Places to Explore the Elements. Water in puddles, water sprayed on plants, water transformed into ice—each is an invitation for toddlers to get to know the properties of water. The outdoor environment is a natural laboratory for infants to build physical knowledge about water, a basic element of the natural world (Figure 11.7). The outdoors is also a natural laboratory for infants to build physical knowledge and logico-mathematical knowledge about light and shadow. Toddlers can experience the rainbow of reflected light that bounces off recycled CDs hanging in the sunlight. They can watch the shadows of objects hung in the window move steadily across the ground, as the angle of the sun changes. They gather physical knowledge about color as they arrange sheets of translucent colored plastic, hung from a clothesline on a sunny day, making colored shadows on the concrete below. Wind exploration happens in the outdoors when infants encounter mobiles, pinwheels, chimes, windsocks, or scarves tied to a sturdy chain link fence. The outdoors is the ideal place for sound exploration, so gongs and chimes can be placed low and fastened securely at toddler level (Figure 11.8). Good items to stock in the yard, to facilitate outdoor investigations include rubber boots, collecting baskets, insect boxes, magnifying glasses, recycled CDs, Plexiglas mirrors, and rolls of colored cellophane.

Figure 11.7. Place to Explore Water

Figure 11.8. Place to Explore Sound

PLAY SPACES FOR INFANTS

The play of a 4-month-old is different from that of a 12-month-old, which differs from that of a 24-month-old, so the focus of the play changes as infants develop, as do the types of play spaces. The sections that follow provide recommendations for designing play spaces for infants, birth to 18 months of age, and for toddlers, 18–36 months of age. The intent is to inspire thinking about what might go into the play spaces. The recommendations should not be interpreted as definitive or exhaustive with respect to materials to offer.

In addition, consideration must be given to the cultural context of the children, families, and teachers. In group settings, the play materials should reflect and respect the concerns and interests of the infants, families, and communities served. Each infant program is unique, shaped by the dynamic forces of culture, geography, time, space, climate, and life experiences. Teachers should select play objects that respect and fit with the values and expectations of the community served. For example, a toddler program located in a coastal area might have a selection of natural science play materials that include large, sturdy shells, plastic figures of various types of sea life, and dried pods from nontoxic marine plants, alongside books with photos of the ocean and sea life. In contrast, a toddler classroom in a high mountain area might have a selection of natural science play materials that include pinecones, tree bark, and plastic figures of squirrels and raccoons, alongside books with photos of forests, lakes, and woodland creatures.

Active Movement Play: Infants

At about 3 months of age, infants are at ease lying on their back in a protected floor-level play space. On their back, they are free to kick their legs, flex their arms, stretch, and reach, all movements that help them organize their muscle systems in preparation for what comes next, rolling over, crawling, grasping objects, and pushing into a seated position. Not until neck and shoulder muscles mature to the point of the infant's being able to look up and around comfortably, will babies enjoy spending much time on their stomach.

To accommodate infants' innate push to kick, flex, and stretch in preparation for independently moving from place to place, play spaces for young babies should ensure they can move freely. This means unrestricted floor space for babies to move, once the ability to roll from place to place develops. Seats or circular pillows intended to prop very young babies into a seated position restrict a baby's ability to move freely and should not be used in the play space.

Although they need a place to move freely, young infants also need a sense of emotional protection and seclusion when placed in a play space on the floor. A simple divider, made with low rails or panels, provides a sense of seclusion as well as physical protection for babies not yet crawling. They can play without interruption from infants who are crawling or walking. In family child-care settings and mixed-age infant centers, there might be just one or two infants not yet mobile, so a section of the room can be partitioned to create a clearly defined, sufficiently large play space for these nonmobile infants.

Equipment that traps infants in positions that restrict their movement—like walkers, bouncers, and swings—should not be used in the play space. Just like learning to ride a bike, a smooth, effortless crawl requires time and space for practice. As infants learn to roll over, pull to a seated position, and pull to standing, they flex and stretch their bodies, refine their movements, and master each move with confidence and grace. Therefore, they need an active movement area that includes ample space to roll and crawl, as well as low raised platforms to crawl onto, slightly graduated stairs or ramps, and big floor cushions, all of which invite crawling at varied elevations.

Low platforms and surfaces invite crawlers to pull to new heights. When interesting objects are placed on a raised surface, crawlers reach to grasp them, eventually pulling themselves up, using the raised surface for support. An active movement play space can accommodate infants who are pulling to standing, by offering low ramps with sides, low bars or handles secured to the wall, or low, stable benches or boxes. These structures double as dividers, secluding the play area for nonmobile infants.

Connecting and Constructing Play: Infants

Once infants master the skill of grasping objects, they begin to explore the physical features of the objects and to relate them, one to the other, building physical and logico-mathematical knowledge. A play space stocked with objects to explore, relate, and investigate may be thought of as a connections and construction play space. For the youngest infants, around 4 months of age, this play space should contain, within sight and within easy reach, a variety of safe, nontoxic objects that are easy to grasp. Features to look for in selecting such toys are reviewed in Chapter 7, in discussions of fine motor development. Infants who have mastered the grasp are no longer content to just pick up an object. They investigate what they can make objects do, shoving or shaking them to see how they move. A connections and constructions play space for infants includes a variety of objects that provide a range of physical features to explore—metal, wood, fabric, durable cardboard, as well as plastic. When free to explore such collections, infants learn about the physical features of objects, but they also put them into relationships of similarity and difference, causality, and number. For example, they learn that tall, thin things tip over, that curved things roll, that flat, compact things stay put, and that smaller things nest inside larger things (Kálló & Balog, 2005). They inspect with their hands and mouth, poking, tasting, smelling, and moving objects in a variety of ways, gathering information about texture, size, color, shape, smell, and taste, as well as how the physical attributes relate one to the other.

Infants are intrepid investigators, repeating an action over and over, trying to duplicate what they once achieved. Older infants enjoy researching material from nature. They delight in exploring the sights, sounds, and smells of plants. A handful of rose petals squeezed in the hand or the scent that greets them as they squeeze a mesh bag filled with lavender or mint—these are opportunities for infants to experience the scents and the texture of natural materials. When they bang on a metal tin and then on the wooden floor using a piece of driftwood, they hear two very different sounds, generated by natural materials. Their experiments are many and varied. They apply force to an object and cause it to move. They lift large, lightweight objects, like dishpans or baskets, and throw items from here to there, exploring how objects fill, fit in, and move in space. These are experiments in spatial relations, a key concept in math and science. As they fill and empty containers or hold one and then two objects, they construct ideas about number and quantity and build a foundation for mathematics.

Once infants learn how to balance and to sit or stand with ease, they begin to explore how one object can be made to connect with another, constructing something taller, longer, or bigger. Over time, these connections turn into structures. Older infants take the features they have come to know, like flat surfaces and sharp corners, or cups and cones that have openings, and they relate these features by lining things up, stacking them, and nesting smaller things into larger things. The following types of objects work well in an infant connections and construction play space, where the floor surface is firm, flat, and open:

- A few large, wooden hollow blocks or a low platform on which to build
- Blocks, boxes, cans, or bins with at least two flat, smooth surfaces
- Objects that stack and line up and offer opportunities to play with balance
- Containers or cups that fit into or onto each other, that is, connect, nest, or stack to make longer or taller extensions
- Objects that come apart and fit back together, like single-piece puzzles, Velcro-stripped blocks, large Lego cubes, links, or interlocking beads or pegs
- Simple play vehicles and figures to use as props in constructions

Pretend Play: Infants

Infants 8–18 months of age begin to imitate prior actions they have seen or experienced, which gives rise to pretend play. A play space stocked with familiar household objects accommodates this interest. The play materials can be simple. Infants might use a box as a bed or a bucket as a hat. Their choice of materials for pretend play depends on what they find in the play space, but it will also reflect their own life experiences. Most infants will engage in pretend play related to meals, bedtime rituals, dressing, and going places. Stocking the pretend play space with items that reflect these common rituals provides infants with materials to work with as they recollect and represent familiar events. Blankets, scarves, and dolls; baskets, boxes, and carts to fill and push from here to there; and utensils from which to eat or drink are basic, open-ended materials that support their pretend play. A pretend play area can be furnished at little cost when repurposed or recycled objects are used. When infants' families are invited to help stock the pretend play space, infants find familiar items, a good fit when representing familiar ideas and actions. A pretend play area for mobile infants and toddlers might include as a basic inventory:

- Furnishings that reflect toddlers' lives
- Objects that reflect what toddlers see adults use at home or at the infant program
- Clothes and articles that toddlers can put on and take off independently, like hats, necklaces, vests, bracelets, purses, scarves, or bags

Figure 11.9. Infant Book and Story Play Space

- Containers and collections of open-ended items that can be transformed in a wide variety of ways

Book and Story Play: Infants

A book and story play space gives infants access to sturdy cardboard books, along with simple props for making stories (Figure 11.9). The space should provide a comfortable place for an adult to sit along with several infants, in order to share stories, songs, chants, and books. A basic inventory of materials for a book and story play space for infants includes

- Baskets, shelves, and/or wall pockets with cardboard books that have pages that turn easily, using the pincer grasp
- Baskets with familiar hand puppets and small figures and dolls
- Books with familiar themes and objects
- Books rich in rhyme, rhythm, and repetition
- Laminated photos or cardboard books of animals or plants, assembled in baskets with matching figures, puppets, or objects
- Books made of sturdy cardboard with photos of the babies themselves
- Wall posters with favorite book illustrations

Crawlers have easy access to books when they are offered in low, wide baskets. Baskets of books also can be left at other points around the room, with special consideration given to a basket in the nap area as well as one near the entry where children enter and leave with their families.

PLAY SPACES FOR TODDLERS

The play spaces described for infants 18 months or younger continue to work well for toddlers 18–36 months old, with the addition of more complex materials. Toddlers 18–36 months will enjoy additional play spaces focused on art media and tools of writing.

Active Movement Play: Toddlers

By 18 months, most toddlers have mastered the ability to walk, so they take on new motor challenges that include climbing, jumping, running, and balancing. They push and pull wagons and scoot themselves along in toy vehicles. They haul heavy items from here to there. And they begin to enjoy tossing and catching. Ideally, they have opportunities to pursue these activities both indoors and outdoors. Since active movement is a major interest, it is wise to identify a specific interior play space sufficiently large for climbing and jumping.

An active movement area indoors for toddlers would include the furnishings and materials described for infants, with these additional challenges:

- Elevated surfaces and structures on which

toddlers can climb and balance, including steps, inclines (slides), rungs, and balance beams

- Lightweight objects for rolling, tossing, and catching
- Objects that have some heft and that can be carried from place to place, like a sturdy 10-pound bag filled with sand or rice
- Carts or wagons to push, pull, and ride in

Connecting and Constructing Play: Toddlers

Collections still hold strong interest for older toddlers and form the basic inventory of a toddler play space focused on connecting and constructing. Collections provide raw material to work with as toddlers engage in logico-mathematical thinking and build the concepts of classification, seriation, spatial relations, causality, and number. When collections provide some materials that are identical and some that vary in one or two attributes, they prompt toddlers to classify in increasingly complex ways. For example, a basket might hold a collection of objects, some of which share a common feature and others that are similar yet distinct. This serves as an invitation to toddlers to spontaneously select only those with a particular feature. For example, older toddlers might search for all the cars of a certain color or type, leaving the others in the storage bin. They might then drop them in a wagon and push them around the room. Or they might drop all the metal lids into a metal container, dump them out, and proceed to refill the container again, repeating this action again and again. We can interpret such self-initiated play as toddlers' building the math skill of classification, making sets and subsets as they create *some but not all*.

Baskets and containers that hold a large amount of a particular type of object give toddlers a chance to construct, on their own, concepts of quantity, including *more, a lot, some, all*, and *none*. Collections also prompt toddlers to engage in patterning and sequencing. A toddler might select just the plastic horses stored in a bin of small animal figures, notice that they vary in size, and, with no prompt from the teacher, line these up in order, a pattern of size and sequence. Toddlers classify and pattern as they try to fit pieces into simple wooden puzzles, noticing how the contour of one piece is the same as or different from another and how one side aligns with another.

As toddlers play with collections of objects, they also explore the concept of number. Toddlers build number concepts as they use multiples of identical or similar objects. In their play with collections of objects, toddlers literally make number, as they place one box next to another, and then reach for another, making a line of three. This act of lining up three objects sequentially—first one, and then two, and then three—is where the concept of addition first begins. When such play gets narrated as, "one, two, three," by an observant adult, toddlers begin to learn number names and their sequence.

Toddlers build and balance with increasing skill. They delight in a play space where they can stack things and knock them down. A variety of raised surfaces—low shelves, overturned bins, boxes, and low, wide cushions—provide places for toddlers to balance and build. By 18 months, toddlers have learned a lot about object shape, weight, density, and size, the beginnings of geometry. They also have had many experiences filling and emptying containers and dropping objects, all of which prepare them to explore how to balance one object on another to make a tall structure.

Blocks can be anything with at least two flat, parallel surfaces, including cardboard boxes, cylinders, and tubes. Many found and recycled objects can be called into service as stackable blocks, including cardboard or wooden boxes, cans, jars, cylinders, tubes, or storage bins, all of which have at least two flat, smooth surfaces.

In addition to the materials suggested for an infant connections and construction area, the following items add more-complex challenges for older toddlers:

- Simple puzzles and other frames or containers that can be filled up or filled in
- Objects that nest or connect together, like large-headed pegs, boxes, cups, bowls, rings, or links
- Toys and tools that create an interesting reaction when acted upon, for example, knobs that twist and open or make a sound; hinges that open and close; lids that screw on or push down; plastic nuts and bolts that screw together; musical instruments that create interesting sounds; small plastic mirrors; small frames holding clear and translucent colored Plexiglas
- At least three types of flat-surfaced blocks and objects that hold the possibility of experimenting with balance and building
- Collections of objects from nature, like shells, dry wood, large leaves, and pinecones
- Props that add pattern and story to simple scenes, like small vehicles and figures that

- Purses, backpacks, and bags
- Shoes, hats, scarves, and ties

Pretend play materials for toddlers do not have to be expensive or complex. In the mind of the toddler, a cardboard box transforms readily into an oven, a car, or a place to hide; and a paper bag with a handle becomes a purse, a hat, or a place to hold treasures. Simple objects that can be used in multiple ways have the advantage of letting toddlers give identity to the object. Many commercial toys marketed for pretend play fail in this regard, as they are detailed with such specific features that toddlers use them in only one way. Too often, the only pretend play materials offered toddlers are plastic imitations of real items, when in fact the real objects can be safely included in a toddler pretend play area (Figure 11.10).

Book and Story Play: Toddlers

Conversations become more elaborate as toddlers add new vocabulary words daily. They delight in being read to, engage actively in songs and chants, and begin to make their own simple stories using puppets, stuffed animals, and dolls. They begin to take an active role in helping to tell or read stories and become more adept at singing songs and participating in fingerplays. In addition to the materials described for the book and story area for infants, a book and story play space for toddlers might include a simple felt board and a basket of Velcro-backed laminated cardboard story characters. Furnishings like small benches or couches can be added, an invitation for two or more toddlers to sit together as they share a book or story with a friend (Figure 11.11).

Art and Writing Play: Toddlers

Toddlers are ready for two new play spaces—an art area and a writing–marking area. Toddlers are fascinated with exploring the physical properties of art media and tools—clay, water, paint, brushes, wire, and paper. They are intrigued with how marks are made, how paper crumples, and how wire coils. Toddlers are also fascinated with tools of writing and will seek out pens and pencils to explore how they work. This coincides with more-focused interest in the illustrations and the print in books. An art-media play space might be created in addition to a writing tools play space, or the materials could be combined as one play space. A stand-alone writing play space for toddlers works well when placed near the entry area where families complete the daily sign-in register (Figure 11.12).

Reflection: Exploring the World of Nature

The natural world is an intriguing research lab for toddlers. They explore leaves, rocks, bark, twigs, herbs, flowers, fruit, seedpods, and insects. They transform these ideas and invent with them. They pick blossoms from a tree branch. They enjoy digging a hole to plant the tree branch in the sandbox. They enjoy amassing a collection of round cross-sections cut from a tree limb and carting them to the pretend play area to use as food. How common do you think it is for teachers to offer activities that use materials from nature, like leaves, sticks, or water? How common do you think it is for teachers to give infants and toddlers access to rocks, bark, pinecones, sturdy vegetables pulled from the garden, or tree branches with blossoms ready to pick? What safety issues should be considered when adding ordinary objects or natural materials to the infant play spaces? What tension might exist between the opportunity to offer infants experiences with ordinary objects and natural materials, and concerns about safety and liability? What thoughts do you have about how teachers should address this tension, so that children have the opportunity to build a relationship with the natural world?

represent familiar people, animals, and objects

- Photos, books, and puppets that relate to the collections of figures and objects
- Low, raised surfaces for balancing and building
- Collections of recycled and repurposed objects

Pretend Play: Toddlers

Older toddlers represent their everyday experiences in pretend play, so a pretend play area expands to include an ample supply of familiar items that reflect their daily lives. Their pretend play elaborates to include invented "scripts" that imitate remembered events and that begin to include friends. Toddlers enjoy "becoming" someone else, by donning pretend play clothes and accessories. Pretend play clothing that toddlers can don independent of adult help includes:

- Smocks that pull over the head
- Capes that attach at the neck with Velcro
- Vests with no buttons
- Accessories like large plastic glasses, with no lenses

Figure 11.10. Pretend Play Space

Figure 11.11. Toddler Book and Story Area

Figure 11.12. Toddler Writing Area

and liquid work together as a print tool and medium. When teachers find safe, easy ways to give toddlers experiences with marking, writing, and painting implements, they nourish the roots of writing. Possibilities include:

- Baskets with tools for writing, for example, plain and colored pencils, crayons, chalk (for toddlers 24 months and older)
- Baskets of paper in a variety of colors, thicknesses, sizes, and shapes
- Message-making props, like envelopes, mailboxes, and pads of paper
- Laminated cards on a ring, with the name of each child printed in large letters
- A binder of pages, with each page holding one child's name in large letters at the top, to serve as a pretend sign-in book
- Collection of magnetic alphabet letters adjacent to a metal surface for sticking
- Stencils for outlining shapes and letters
- Flannel surface near entry, with headings "Home" and "School," alongside basket of Velcro-backed cards, each printed with a child's name and photo

SAFE PLAY SPACES

Play spaces need to be safe and comfortable for infants and for teachers. They also should be easy for teachers to supervise. Every space to which infants have free access needs to be reviewed for safety.

Safety in Mixed-Age Settings

For mixed-age groups and particularly for infant play spaces set up in home settings, teachers tailor the play spaces to the ages represented within the group. In a typical mixed-age setting, this means smaller play spaces and fewer play spaces, yet still organized such that each space has a distinct identity. If a group consists of six toddlers and three infants not yet walking, an area for crawler play can be sectioned off, providing the remaining space for toddlers. This ensures a protected, well-defined play space where children will be safe and have access to engaging materials matched to their interests. Without such clear boundaries, toddlers hear frequent admonitions to stay away from the infants, or they experience disturbing interruptions as infants interfere in their play.

Leaving pens and pencils out for infants to freely access and explore presents a safety hazard for infants younger than 24 months, who still routinely explore objects by mouth. When children this age are present, no object should be left out in the play space that could cause choking if lodged in the throat. Pencils, pens, crayons, chalk, and long-handled paintbrushes are small enough to be choking hazards, so only when the toddlers are 24 months old, and beyond the point of routinely exploring things by mouth, should these art tools be left out in the play space.

One way to make drawing tools available to toddlers in the play space, yet prevent them from being carried around the room and posing a choking risk, is to drill a small hole in the end of a wooden carpenter pencil, loop strong twine through the hole and tie it securely to a sturdy support, like a low easel covered with paper and positioned an appropriate distance from the wall. A supply of recycled paper or a large sheet of paper taped to the tabletop or easel gives toddlers a safe place to experiment with how pencils work.

An art area for toddlers is as much an area for exploring art tools as it is a place for exploring art media. An art area for young toddlers can include short-handled brushes sufficiently wide in girth as to not fit in the mouth. These include shaving brushes and scrub brushes. For older toddlers, buckets of water near the brushes invite exploration of how brushes

Reflection: Challenge or Risk?

The loft in this photo has wide stairs as well as a wide slide. Imagine being a toddler in this room. Would the idea of climbing up the slide be just as enticing as the idea of climbing up the stairs? How about sliding down the slide head first, or crawling down the stairs head first, as the toddlers in this photo are doing? Imagine yourself as the teacher in this toddler room. How would you respond?

Some adults are reluctant to let toddlers climb up a slide, and they restrict toddlers to using slides only for sliding down. Some are nervous when a toddler decides to try descending head first, so they restrict this as well. What would be your response?

If a ramp or slide is sufficiently wide to accommodate two or three toddlers, if it has raised sides of sufficient height, and if it is not too steep, is it possible for a slide or ramp to safely accommodate toddlers who want to experiment with challenging ways to ascend and descend?

Safe Furnishings

Furnishings should be arranged so that infants and adults can move safely from place to place without confronting hazards. Crawlers and toddlers need safe places, both indoors and outdoors, to crawl up and crawl down and to climb up and jump down. Changes in elevation, like raised surfaces, steps, or low barriers, are important in the design of infant play spaces, but they should be easily seen and well marked. Sharp corners on furnishings should be padded. Pathways should be kept free of clutter.

These safety precautions are especially important when those who use the program have a visual impairment or a motor planning challenge. Tactile or auditory cues can be added to the furnishings and pathways to assist infants with visual or motor planning challenges. For example, a small bell hung from the lower rung of the wall climber in an active movement space provides a clear marker to guide a child with impaired vision. Or a child with a visual impairment or a motor planning challenge might find helpful a strip of Velcro, sandpaper, or satin cloth to mark the place where an inclined slope begins on a climbing structure (Gould & Sullivan, 1999).

Various kinds of exercisers, walkers, swings, and jumpers, although marketed for infant use, pose a risk in group care, as they can be toppled by other children or propelled down stairs. Chapter 7 provides a more in-depth discussion of this concern. Play equipment that confines infants and restricts their ability to get in and out on their own and their ability to move freely should not be used in a group-care setting. There is a risk, that, in the name of supervision, infants will be left in such devices for long periods of time, unable to get out on their own.

Active movement areas, like stairs, slides, rungs, platforms, and ramps, are essential to both the indoor and outdoor play environment. Although they harbor an element of risk, active movement experiences open a world of challenges that bring delight, joy, and mastery of new skills. When climbing platforms are too high, ramps too steep, or floors too slick, however, adults worry about risks and consequently limit and discourage children's natural inclination to climb, jump, and run. When adults know that climbing and running spaces are safe, they can enjoy rather than limit the active play.

Safety assurances with respect to climbing structures include attention to the surface below the climbing structure, the area called the fall zone. It should be sufficiently resilient to prevent injury. Teachers should keep the fall zone clear of objects, thereby reducing risk of injury if a child were to fall. For infants who are mobile, but not yet walking independently, recommended height for climbing equipment is no more than 2 feet. For toddlers, this height is no more than 3 feet (Lally et al., 2009). Flights of stairs that are higher should be blocked with a gate, to prevent falls.

Some general safety precautions apply when equipping and maintaining infant play spaces. Adults caring for infants should stay current on consumer product safety standards and keep abreast of any alerts or recalls of infant play materials. Especially when stocking a room with used furniture, updates are important. For example, the gaps between slats or sides of cribs and other equipment should be no larger than 2-3/8 inches (Cryer, Harms, & Riley, 2004). Before purchasing new or used equipment, it is wise to check for whether the item meets consumer safety standards. Other considerations include ensuring that childproof covers are secured on open electrical wall outlets; ensuring that there are guards around radiators, hot pipes, and other hot surfaces; removing broken items or repairing surfaces that pose tripping hazards; and safely securing, out of infants' reach, loose cords, like those used for window shades, as these pose risk of asphyxiation (Lally et al., 2009).

Safe Materials

Infants and toddlers frequently will put objects in their mouths in order to explore them. This is a natural way of getting to know what things are like in terms of their physical properties, like size, shape, and texture. With respect to the kinds of play materials left in the play spaces, objects that are too small in diameter might cause choking if accidentally lodged in the throat. As a general guide, toys for infants under 2 years of age should be sufficiently large so that, along any one dimension, they cannot fit inside the cardboard tube used for rolls of toilet paper.

If the play space is used by infants or toddlers younger than 24 months, who may still be putting play materials into their mouths, only items that are sufficiently large in size so as not to present a choking hazard should be left out in the open play space. For example, small rounds of wood cut from a 4-inch diameter tree branch can be safely left out in the play space, but twigs could not, as they fit inside a toilet paper roll. For toddlers 24–36 months, mouthing toys is rare, reducing risk of choking on small parts, so, in most circumstances, smaller items like a tree branch with blossoms could be safely left out for exploration.

Some commonly used art materials pose a risk of choking or are toxic if ingested, so teachers should carefully review the ingredients and safety warnings on packaging. Glitter, for example, could pose a choking hazard if ingested or could easily scratch the eye (Cryer et al., 2004). Shaving cream, used by some teachers as an art medium, is not recommended for infants, as the label warns of its toxicity if ingested. Teachers who use sensory exploration trays should fill them with material that is sufficiently large in diameter and will not present a choking hazard. This caution does not mean that objects like rocks and shells cannot be used with infants. They make delightful materials to explore during supervised small-group experiences. Rocks or shells or other items from nature that are small enough to pose a choking hazard should be offered only within well-supervised encounters and not left out and available to infants on a continual basis.

The outdoor play area must be fenced, with hinged gates secured with locking mechanisms that children cannot open. Toxic fertilizers or pesticides should be avoided. When working with young children, it is important to know how to find out which plants are toxic and to ensure that there are no toxic plants in the yard. Research into plant properties also can reveal which plants attract bees, a potential hazard. Local health departments are a good source for lists of toxic plants and plants associated with allergies. In some communities, cats or other small animals might access the yard after hours, so having a secure cover for the sandbox promotes sanitation and safety.

CLEAN AND COMFORTABLE PLAY SPACES

Since an infant who mouths a toy may expose others in the group to unwanted germs, regular procedures for sanitizing toys will limit the risk of passing infections from child to child.

Sanitation

A system for once a day gathering all the toys offered in the young infants' play space and sanitizing them reduces the spread of infections. Throughout the day, if a teacher sees an infant mouthing a toy, it may make sense in the moment to pop the toy into a sanitation solution. However, it is unreasonable to expect

> **Reflection:**
> **A Space Through the Eyes of Infants**
>
> A good way to see whether a room or yard is safe for infants is to get down and look at the entire room or yard from the infant's level, looking for the safety hazards noted, as well as other situations that pose safety risk, among them:
>
> - Places a small hand or head could get caught
> - Door hinges, rocking chair glides, or other equipment that could pinch or trap small fingers or toes
> - Standing water, which can harbor mosquito larvae or pose risk of drowning, if the water level rises high
> - Small objects that could cause choking or other hazardous items tossed into the yard by passersby

teachers to do this every time an infant mouths a toy.

Washing and rinsing toys with soap and water is the first step in sanitation, followed by disinfecting with a sanitation solution, and then laying them on a rack to air dry. Another option for sanitizing toys is to place them in a dishwasher where water temperature is set at 140 degrees Fahrenheit, the recommended temperature for sanitizing.

A regular schedule for cleaning and sanitizing the walls and partitions of the play spaces, pillow or cushion covers, as well as carpets or rugs is also important. Hardwood floors, linoleum, or tiles should be washed daily. Carpets can hide small objects, inadvertently dropped, that might cause infants to choke. Carpets also harbor dust, so they should be vacuumed daily. As part of a daily safety inspection, carpets should be checked for frayed edges.

Air Quality

A well-maintained ventilation system is important in maintaining a healthy environment, as it will filter dust and residue that cause odor and stale air. Ideally, the room is equipped with screened windows that open to provide natural air flow.

Infant centers are smoke-free environments. Those caring for babies should eliminate exposure to second-hand smoke. Exposure to second-hand smoke is related to significant health concerns in infants, including middle ear infections, asthma, bronchitis, pneumonia, and sudden infant death syndrome (Centers for Disease Control and Prevention, n.d.). Even if a caregiver elects to smoke away from an infant, in a different room, the infant will likely be exposed to secondhand smoke through residue that settles on the adult's clothes and gets inhaled by the infant. Cigarette smoke also contaminates dust that settles on the floor, putting infants at risk as they crawl on the floor; contaminates toys, which later get mouthed by the infants; and settles on furnishings. Sharing these concerns with infants' families is important, as it is sharing them with infant program staff. Program policies should clearly describe a safe location for smoking that is a sufficient distance from the building and the play yard.

Lighting and Visual Stimulation

Natural light supports emotional well-being, so a room lit by natural light promotes a healthy environment for infants (Mead, 2008). This has the added advantage of reducing reliance on costly artificial light. Light bulbs should be covered to eliminate access by children, and also to soften lighting placed above the area where infants sleep. Since infants often gaze up as they lie down to rest, exposure to bare lights can cause eye strain (Lally et al., 2009).

Keeping the visual environment comfortable for infants means keeping it calm and relaxing, rather than visually busy and distracting. Wall decorations, brightly patterned wallpaper, or murals hung over infants' heads can be visually overwhelming for infants and cause them to withdraw, reducing engagement in play. Low-intensity colors for walls, floors, and furnishings offer a calm, soothing visual environment.

Ambient Sound

Background music or television competes with infants' attempts to pay attention to what people around them are saying. This undermines language learning. Infants work hard to figure out language and rely on conversations to make sense of it. A good rule of thumb is to keep the infant center free from the distractions of background music or TV and to use recorded music only when dancing or intentionally listening to music together. Ambient noise can be lowered with sound-absorbing materials, such as acoustic tiles, fabric wall hangings, and floor rugs and pads.

Comfortable Surfaces

Infants in their first year transition from rolling to crawling to sitting to standing and, in each phase, they need surfaces that are firm and flat to support their efforts. Soft, cushiony carpets make it hard to control balance and to get traction. Floor surfaces should be kept clean, but they should not be highly polished, as this poses a risk of slipping and falling.

Comfortable seating for adults near the play spaces makes it easy to observe infants as they play and interact. What constitutes a comfortable seat may vary by culture and by individual. Some adults find it comfortable to sit with children on the floor, while others do not, preferring an appropriately sized chair, bench, or sofa. Some seating near play spaces indoors and outdoors, sized to fit an adult alongside a child or two, invites adults and infants to enjoy quiet moments together. Low platforms or risers serve multiple purposes in a play space—as dividers, as elevated play spaces for infants, and as seating for adults.

Looking Back and Looking Forward

For infants and toddlers, their play spaces are their first laboratories, their first studios, and their first libraries—their first environments for learning. Those caring for infants are responsible for what goes into these play spaces, so their job is to offer infants materials that can be used to investigate, to create, to relate, and to represent, since play spaces are contexts for learning. Sometimes the learning materials are toys, but more often they are ordinary materials that have features that attract the inquisitive mind or the emerging skills of the infant. Each phase of infancy requires a different inventory of materials, matched to skills and concepts under construction during that period of development. When teachers understand how infants are building concepts and mastering skills within each domain of development, they can match desired features of play materials to infants' emerging pursuits. The next chapter addresses a second context for curriculum, the daily routines. In the same spirit of creating play spaces that support infant learning, teachers create care spaces that invite infants to apply emerging skills and concepts.

CHAPTER 12

Care Routines

Contexts for Joy and Learning

> Hands constitute the infant's first connection to the world. . . . Hands pick her up, lay her down, wash and dress and maybe even feed her. How different it can be, what a different picture of the world an infant receives when quiet, patient, careful yet secure and resolute hands take care of her—and how different the world seems when these hands are impatient, rough or hasty, unquiet and nervous.
> (Pikler, 1994, p. 20)

A GROUP INFANT PROGRAM is like a carefully tuned machine, with many moving parts, each connected systematically to another. This chapter explores how routines like meals, diapering, and napping transpire within a context of respectful relationships. In the same spirit that play spaces are designed to invite infants to explore, investigate, and learn, the rituals of care are designed to invite infants to actively participate and thereby use their emerging skills and concepts.

In the introductory quote for this chapter, Pikler draws our attention to the way we handle babies during moments of care. For newborns, the rituals of care can be unsettling. Pikler (1994) suggests that if we handle infants peacefully and patiently, they discover increasingly more joy in these activities, learn to trust the person providing the care, and in time play a larger role in the experience. As example, she offers the following:

> When we wash a child's hair . . . he will lift his head a little so we can get our hand under it. He already knows the order in which things will happen in the care situation. He gives us a hand as we dress him, and gives us one foot to dry after the other. Later on, when he sees that we are getting ready to diaper or feed him, he will approach the side of the crib and reach up with both arms, getting ready all over to be picked up. He is looking forward to something pleasant happening. (pp. 20–21)

WELCOMING, PEACEFUL SPACES FOR CARE

The first ritual of care is the moment of arrival. It is important to look at this ritual from the perspective of the baby, the family, and the teacher. The arrival marks an important, tender ritual—a ritual of hello and good-bye. The entry speaks to those who enter by virtue of the arrangement of space and furnishings and the selection of materials found there. A thoughtfully arranged entry can ease the transition from home to the infant program, offering a welcoming space and a welcoming ritual. The entry is generally where procedural tasks occur, like recording the time of arrival and departure. The entry is also the place for a simple health check and an exchange of clothing, meal supplies, and information about the infant, both at the beginning and the end of the day.

Aside from accommodating these procedural tasks, the entry marks the transition between home and school. Furnishings in the entry should invite families to spend as much time as they need to support infants in making the transition. The walls and shelves welcome and invite, with photos of familiar people from home and from school. Examples of what might be placed in the entry include

- Photos of the children at home and in the first days in the program
- A row of clear boxes, in each a child's photo, along with a piece of yarn, cut to the child's height on the first day in the program
- Photos of each child at home and at school
- Photos of the primary care teachers on a movable cardboard disc, mounted on the wall and surrounded by photos of all the children in the room
- Two-way journals that families and teachers use to record notes about the child

The entry is a portal to the greater expanse of the infant room. The floor space of the infant room can be thought of as play space surrounded by space for diapering, toileting, meals, and naps. Ideally, there are no more than 12 infants served in each room, with easy access for adults to all the areas dedicated to the care routines. Proximity of play space to care space is important, but equally important is to protect a degree of quiet and intimacy during one-on-one care routines, like diapering and feeding. This will happen when the diapering area, the bottle-feeding area, and a quiet area for settling an infant to sleep are somewhat secluded, situated away from busy walkways, yet still within sight of the play space. Half doors, low partitions, or low counters can be used to divide a service area from a play area. This makes it possible for infants to still see the primary care teacher, even when involved in one-on-one diapering or feeding.

CARE THAT INVITES PARTICIPATION

During meals, diapering, and napping, teachers meet infants' physical needs, but they also meet their emotional needs. Caregiving routines are precious opportunities for one-on-one time between an infant and the primary care teacher. The undivided attention that an infant receives from the primary care teacher during such moments fuels the infant emotionally and builds an enduring bond of affection and trust.

Caregiving routines are also opportunities to invite infants to be active participants in the care, in which they can use emerging concepts and skills. In conversations that occur while being diapered, dressed, or fed, infants learn about themselves, about others, and about meaningful events. They also build language skills as they hear speech in meaningful contexts; learn to anticipate that one experience will lead to the next; and learn the give-and-take of social exchange as they share in the task at hand.

Gerber and Pikler (Gerber, 1979; Gonzalez-Mena & Eyer, 2012; Pikler, 1994) urged those caring for babies to treat them with respect, as subjects with feelings, expectations, and desires, and to invite them to participate in things that concern them, like diapering, dressing, and meals. An invitation to participate in the care begins by simply observing, to see what the baby is doing or appears to be feeling or wanting. Sometimes it is hard to know with certainty what this might be. In such moments, it helps to say to the baby, "I don't know what you are feeling or want from me, but keep trying to tell me and I will keep trying to

> ### Reflection: An Invitation to Participate
>
> Listen to how each phrase invites. Imagine what gesture the caregiver might use to signal what is about to happen. What might you expect will happen, in the pause that follows?
>
> - Come, I'm going to take you to the table to change your diaper.
> - I'm going to wash your face with this cloth. It is wet. I'll let you touch it first with your finger. Here.
> - Now it's time to put your diaper on. Are you ready? Here it is. You can help me lift your legs.
> - You like being here with me. You're smiling. What else do you have to tell me?

figure it out." In so doing, we acknowledge the baby, and we ask for her help (Lally, 2011a), encouraging the baby to communicate at the same time that we improve our ability to read her cues.

The invitation continues by touching the baby gently, establishing eye contact with the baby, then describing what you are wanting or what you are about to do, gesturing to communicate this request, and then waiting for a response. By pausing after making a request, we give the infant time to respond with a movement, expression, or gesture. For example, when offering a young baby liquid from a cup, the caregiver holds the cup where the baby can see it, moves it near the baby, and then pauses, giving the baby a chance to grasp the cup. The caregiver does not simply put the cup in the baby's mouth.

Each of the care routines presents opportunities for infants to participate. When putting a shirt on an infant, for example, the adult can use one hand to gather the fabric from the wrist side of the sleeve and insert the fingers of her other hand into the sleeve at the wrist opening. Then, holding the sleeve where the baby can see it, the adult makes eye contact with the baby and says, "It's time to put on your shirt. Can you put your hand in the sleeve?" The adult pauses to give the baby a chance to move his arm to the sleeve and then pulls the sleeve over the baby's arm, instead of pulling the baby's arm through the sleeve.

When we rush through the care, we deny infants a chance to actively participate. Although this is done with the intention of completing the task quickly and efficiently, without interruption from the baby, the baby has little opportunity to notice, anticipate, and respond using emerging skills. When we engage *with* babies, rather than act *on* them, we give them the chance to build skills and concepts and to make sense of language.

MEALS AS INVITATION TO PARTICIPATE

Mealtimes with infants have immense potential for learning. Mealtime changes over the course of infancy. In the short span of 12 months, newborns transition from being fed breast milk or formula to drinking and eating on their own. Changes in what, when, and how babies are fed are determined largely by developmental advances during the first year, although they are also influenced by prevailing practices and beliefs within the culture. Babies are born with a repertoire of reflexes related to sucking and swallowing. Within the first 6 months, these reflexes drop out and babies develop the ability to chew, sip, and swallow solid food, abilities not present at birth.

Around the same time that babies begin to coordinate their jaw and facial muscles to chew and to sip, their teeth emerge through the gums, and they master two very important motor skills—reaching and grasping, and getting into a seated position on their own. This confluence of developmental changes can be viewed as an indication of infants' readiness for solid food. Once infants can independently sit, grasp, sip, and chew, they transition gradually from being largely dependent on others for feeding to eating independently.

Infant Meal Patterns

In the early months, infants rely on reflexes to get food into their bodies. The newborn rooting reflex causes the infant to turn toward the source of a touch on the cheek. When the newborn's cheek is touched, the newborn reflexively turns and begins to root in the direction of the touch, in search of the nipple. The sucking reflex is triggered when the newborn's lips are stimulated. Milk that hits the back of the tongue triggers the swallowing reflex. The extrusion reflex is triggered by a touch to the front of the tongue, and the infant will thrust out the tongue, repelling anything that is not liquid. Together these infantile reflexes ensure that newborns get the right type of nourishment, admitting liquids and rejecting solids. The digestive system of the newborn is prepared for breast milk and is not yet mature enough for solids. Between 2 and 4 months of age, these reflexes begin to subside, and control of the mouth becomes voluntary.

Breast milk is perfectly matched to the newborn's nutritional needs and rich in antibodies that combat infection. Commercial formula closely approximates the chemical components of mother's milk, and for families who prefer this option, formula satisfies infants' early nutritional needs. However, formula does not carry the longterm health benefits of breastmilk and breastfeeding, notably reduced risk of gastrointestinal disease, lower respiratory tract infection, sudden infant death syndrome, childhood cancer, and maternal breast cancer. Not breastfeeding is also likely to increase risks of illnesses, including Type 2 diabetes, celiac disease, otitis media, obesity, and indicators of futre cardiac disease in the child and ovarian cancer in the mother (Renfrew, 2012).

Cow's milk, which has a different composition from the milk of human mothers, should not be used as a substitute for breast milk or formula, not until the infant's stomach has matured to the point of being able to process the more complex protein molecule in cow's milk. Most pediatricians recommend waiting until around the first birthday to transition from formula or breast milk to cow's milk, or a suitable substitute. Infants who transition to cow's milk should be offered whole milk, rather than reduced-fat or skim milk, because reduced-fat or skim milk is too low in calories and too high in protein in relation to what infants need. In contrast, whole milk has desirable fat, cholesterol, and vitamin E, providing critical nourishment for the developing brain.

Caregivers of babies being bottle-fed or breast-fed need comfortable seating, where they can hold babies in their arms for feeding. This can be a chair or a sofa, or, for some, a comfortable place to sit on the floor. Infants enjoy this close physical contact during feeding, whether the nourishment comes from the mother's breast or the bottle. To eliminate distractions, the meal area for babies fed by bottle or breast should be away from busy pathways and set aside from busy play spaces. For mothers who are breast-feeding, the infant program should create space and schedules that make it possible for infants to continue to receive breast milk. Some mothers who are breast-feeding prefer a completely private space, while others feel comfortable nursing in a chair situated in the infant room. Some parents bring prebottled breast milk, making it possible for teachers to keep the infant on breast milk during times when the mother is absent.

When babies are held in arms for bottle- or breast-feeding, they are nourished emotionally and physically, as they are talked to, sung to, and enjoyed. As a consequence, they are more likely to play or rest contentedly on their own after the meal is over. As much as possible, the infant's primary care teacher should be the one to offer the baby the bottle. A well-provisioned play space keeps babies engaged in play, while the primary care teacher devotes individual attention to each baby being fed.

With a system of primary care in place, each teacher has the support of the others, so that one teacher can enjoy time with one infant being diapered or fed, knowing that other teachers are supervising the infants at play. If an infant at play begins to fuss and cry out for the primary care teacher, words of acknowledgment often will suffice, like, "I hear you, Yulisa. I think you are hungry. I will be there soon." With words of acknowledgment, infants feel heard and learn to manage a short wait. Never should a baby be propped with a bottle, in a crib or play space. This poses a risk of choking and a risk of tooth decay, because the sugar content of formula, juice, or milk is sufficiently high that, when pooled around the teeth, will promote decay in existing and erupting teeth. An infant lying down with a bottle also is put at risk of ear infection, as the sweet liquid not only pools around the teeth but also flows into the ear canal and into the middle ear.

Experts suggest waiting until around 6 months of age before introducing solid food (French et al., 2012). Introducing solids prior to 4 months of age is associated with an increased risk of obesity. An iron-fortified baby cereal, prepared with a tablespoon of breast milk or formula, is the perfect first solid food. An infant, by the age of 5–7 months, has begun to deplete essential stores of iron available at birth. Children absorb only about 10% of the iron they consume, so most children need to receive an iron supplement. Breast-fed babies need less, because iron is absorbed at three times the rate when it is in breast milk. An iron-fortified baby cereal mixed with a small amount of formula or breast milk also ensures the proper balance of protein, fat, and carbohydrates (Satter, 2000).

Gradually increasing the consistency of infant cereal allows the baby to get used to the texture of solid food. As is true for all aspects of infant learning, some babies are temperamentally cautious in trying new things, while others take to new experiences with glee. It is important to respect the way an infant gathers information about each new food. Some babies may be more sensitive to texture and taste, requiring more time to get used to each new food. Never force a child to eat. Doing so will frighten and

overwhelm the infant and cause the infant to resist the food being offered.

A respectful way to invite the infant to participate in the experience is to hold the spoon so the infant sees it, before moving it close to the baby's mouth. Babies will see this and open the mouth, taking an active role in the ritual of care. When babies are first introduced to solid food, a gentle touch of the spoon to the baby's lip, followed by a pause, is an invitation to the baby to open the mouth and scrape food from the spoon with the lip. This requires attention and intention on the part of the caregiver, watching and waiting for cues to establish the rhythm of the meal.

Between 6 and 8 months of age, pureed fruits and vegetables are introduced, one by one, over the course of weeks, to expose infants to a variety of flavors and textures. Portions are small, just 2–4 tablespoons once a day. It is easy to prepare purees from scratch, using fresh fruits and vegetables and a hand masher or an electric food processor or blender. This allows babies to experience the appealing, natural taste and reap the nutritional benefit of fresh fruits and vegetables. Experts caution against substituting juice for fresh fruits and vegetables, as the sugar content per serving is much higher in juice and could lead to obesity (French et al., 2012).

The newborn bite reflex restricts movement of the jaw to an up and down motion. As the newborn reflexes subside, the muscles of the jaw come under voluntary control. At this point, the infant starts to chew in a rotary pattern. This coincides with the ability to reach and grasp. Somewhere between about 7 and 10 months of age, babies' teeth begin to emerge from the gums. Muscles of the tongue strengthen and get better at moving food in the mouth. The ability to swallow comes under voluntary control, and infants are able to hold food in their mouths longer in order to chew it. These changes signal the point when the infant is ready to try more than simple purees. They can be introduced to strained or pureed meats or chicken, chopped or mashed fruits, cooked vegetables, beans, or cheese, as well as strips of bread or crackers.

As the grasp improves, babies start to grasp at the spoon in the caregiver's hand during feeding. By 8 months, infants are starting to use the pincer grasp to pick up small pieces of food. Steamed vegetables and soft tofu are appealing finger foods that are free of sugar, preservatives, and additives. Small, circular food, like grapes, should be sliced first. Popcorn or slices of sausage should be avoided, because if not chewed sufficiently, they pose a choking hazard. From 9–12

Reflection: Furnishings for Face-to-Face Feeding

This low table and attached seat is a design of the Pikler Institute. The baby is comfortably seated in front of the low table. The adult offering the food sits on the small stool facing the baby. How might this set-up facilitate a partnership between baby and caregiver during the meal?

months, small bits of soft foods, including tender chopped meats and casseroles, or eggs, can be added; by 12 months, babies are eating a full range of soft foods from the family table (Satter, 2000).

Infant Meal Furnishings

Mealtime furnishings for infants should take into account comfort for the baby as well as comfort for the caregiver. Around 6 months of age, infants begin to push themselves into a seated position, where they can balance easily on their own. Infants not yet able to get into a seated position on their own are most comfortable when fed in arms, rather than in a seat or carrier.

Infants who are able to get into a seated position on their own are ready to eat meals in low chairs with sides. Ideally, the adult and infant are seated at the same level, so the adult can offer a spoon of food to the infant, and the infant can easily see it and signal readiness by opening the mouth. Infants this age still deserve to have their meal offered as a one-on-one experience, fueling them with the smiles, voice, and attention of the caregiver.

An infant room serving crawlers and young toddlers requires at least one adult chair where a caregiv-

Figure 12.1. Inviting Infant Participation in Meals

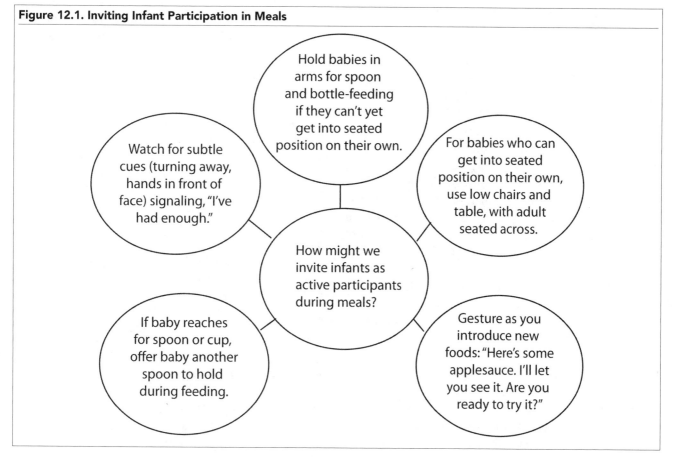

er can comfortably feed an infant in arms. High chairs are a safety risk in group infant care, as they can be toppled by a child who pushes from below. Infants seated in high chairs, unless they are closely supervised, may attempt to climb out, risking a fall. This risk is also inherent in portable infant seats attached to the table edge and in infant feeding tables that have multiple seats built into the surface. There is also a risk that infants will be confined in these chairs for long periods of time, unnecessarily restricted and unable to get out on their own. Many feeding chairs and tables position infants so high above the floor that their legs dangle, a posture that compromises motor development.

As dexterity improves, infants show interest in spoons and forks. Offering infants a spoon to hold, while still being fed, gives them a chance to explore what this simple tool feels like and, in time, how it works. Once the biting reflex subsides and they can form a seal around the edge of the cup, infants can begin to drink liquids from a cup, instead of a bottle.

Toddler Meal Patterns

The first birthday marks an important milestone with respect to the division of responsibility between adult and child. Toddlers who have passed their first birthday are ready to take responsibility for what they eat and how much they eat (Satter, 2000). For infants older than 1 year, caregivers assume responsibility for preparing and offering nutritious food, and infants assume responsibility for deciding what and how much to eat. For some adults, this can be hard. They may worry when they see a toddler suddenly begin to eat less than before. They may be concerned about whether the child is eating enough. However, there is a natural decline in growth rate in children 1.5–3 years of age. This decline in growth rate and food consumption can be seen as a touchpoint (Brazelton, 2006), a normal part of the growth cycle, but one that is potentially alarming to caregivers, who may worry when the child suddenly eats less than before.

A caregiver should never force or bribe a child to eat, but instead find ways to encourage a child's interest in trying each food item available at a meal. Research shows that children this age, when offered a balanced diet and allowed to choose how much food they eat at each meal, will, in a day's time, consume a balanced diet (Satter, 2000). One way to encourage reluctant eaters is to phrase a request as a simple choice, as in, "Do you want to try the potato first or the pear?

Reflection: Mealtime Conversation with Toddlers

Observation

A primary care teacher sits at the meal table with her group of toddlers, Alexia, Jason, Yuri, and Olivia. As she passes the serving dish, she says, "Alexia is serving the pears. And now Jason is next. Do you want one spoon of pears or two, Jason?" "Two!" shouts Jason, serving himself a second scoop. The teacher sees Yuri reach toward Jason's bowl. "That is Jason's bowl, Yuri. Your bowl is this one, in front of you. Please do not take food from Jason's bowl, because that's Jason's food to eat. Who is ready for milk, anyone?" Olivia reaches, as she says, "Milk!" The teacher takes two translucent glasses, one blue and one yellow, from the nearby serving cart. "Which one do you want, Olivia, blue or yellow?" Olivia points to the yellow glass, and the teacher sets the yellow glass to Olivia's right, along with a transparent measuring cup into which she has poured ¼ cup of milk. Olivia slowly pours the milk, and as she does so, the teacher says, "There it goes. You poured all the milk into your cup, Olivia. Who is next?"

Relate this observation and interpretation to your understanding of curriculum for infants and toddlers. Is this curriculum? What kind of planning goes into this experience?

Interpretation

In this scene the teacher has chosen to offer the milk after the children had served themselves each of the other food items. She is mindful of the tendency of some toddlers to fill up on milk at mealtime, and she wants to make sure they have time to enjoy the other foods offered. She wait s to offer milk until later in the meal. She makes the task of pouring easier by pouring only ¼ cup of milk from the larger milk pitcher in her service cart. She has drawn a red line on the ¼ cup mark of the measuring cup that serves as a pitcher. The red line provides a visual cue to the toddlers as they pour.

You decide." This is a guidance strategy called limited choice, discussed further in Chapter 13.

Toddler Meal Furnishings

Infants who can pull to sitting and standing and who are able to grasp objects on their own can gradually transition to sitting at a meal table with friends. In

Figure 12.2. Toddlers Participate in Meal

group care, a low table of sufficient size for a primary care group to sit together with their teacher can be placed on an easily washed surface to create the meal area. Depending on schedules, an infant room might have more than one meal table. The table should allow the adult seated with the infants at the table to reach across and assist an infant without having to stand up (Figure 12.2).

Cube chairs work well for infants (Figure 12.2). They are sufficiently low to allow infants to get in and out by themselves and to sit with their feet touching the floor. Older toddlers, used to sitting up at the table, enjoy low stools, benches, or child-size chairs. Proper chair height should allow the child's feet to touch the floor when seated (Cryer et al., 2004).

Toddlers enjoy taking an active role in the meal. Pushing serving carts from kitchen to the table area, distributing bibs, passing out and collecting empty serving dishes, each is an opportunity for toddlers to use emerging skills (Figure 12.3). After the meal, toddlers enjoy depositing bowls, cups, and utensils in separate receptacles, either on the meal table or near-

by. Such routines provide an experience in detecting differences and sorting. There may be other tasks as well in which toddlers can be involved, like pushing chairs under the table or wiping down the surface of the table with a clean damp cloth.

Toddlers enjoy being involved in all aspects of the meal, including hand washing. With up to 12 infants per room, a relaxing meal takes patience and a thoughtful plan. One option is to schedule the meal so that each primary care group washes hands and sits down for the meal in sequence, with a short lapse of time between groups. This reduces crowding around sinks, eliminates the need to rush, and keeps the noise level low.

Proper hand washing is a good defense against the spread of infections within group care. As a prelude to meals, clean-up following meals and messy activities, and a follow-up to diapering and toileting, hand washing is an invitation to toddlers to participate in a patterned, sequenced ritual that involves many emerging skills and concepts, including counting, sequencing, patterning, and causality. For example, the sequence

Figure 12.3. Pitching in at Mealtime

of steps involved in hand washing can be turned into a chant or a simple game.

A relaxed meal requires advance preparation. Eating and serving utensils as well as the food should be assembled and within reach of the teacher seated at each meal table. A serving cart or a tray, placed within reach of the teacher seated with the infants, ensures ready access to all the serving and cleaning items that will be needed before, during, and after the meal. When the meal table is located near the kitchen, a toddler can be assigned to take the empty pitcher or bowl to the kitchen to request a refill.

Toddlers enjoy participating in serving food and drink during the meal (Figure 12.2). They are eager to figure out how to use serving spoons, tongs, and pitchers. Each is a simple tool that takes time and practice to master. The following utensils make it easy to invite toddler participation during the meal:

- Low, wide bowls for eating, preferable to flat plates, because their gradual sides facilitate toddlers' picking up bits of food with a spoon or a fork
- Small forks and spoons of a size appropriate to toddlers' hands
- Low, wide serving bowls, noticeably different from individual bowls for eating, sized so that toddlers can easily see the contents and maneuver the serving spoon
- Short-handled serving spoons or simple serving tongs
- Absorbent cloth for sopping up spills
- Small, clear pitcher for serving beverage

Some children may not be ready to serve themselves or may not be used to serving themselves. Some families might discourage attempts to use serving utensils at home, so teachers need to be mindful of this difference, respect it, and avoid pressuring children to serve themselves. When children are reluctant to serve themselves, teachers may offer to serve them, while at the same time holding open the invitation for them to serve themselves.

One of the most interesting tools for toddlers is the pitcher. Toddlers have an ongoing interest in filling and emptying containers, a pursuit that prepares them to understand quantity and spatial relations, that is, how things fill and fit in space. Small serving pitchers and sturdy cups provide an opportunity for toddlers to explore how pitchers work and how liquid fits in and fills the space of a cup. Clear measuring cups are easily grasped by toddlers and serve well as a pitcher for pouring (see Figure 12.2). When using a clear pitcher, toddlers can watch the level of liquid change inside the pitcher, making it easier to learn to pour. This same principle applies to the selection of drinking cups, which should be clear or translucent and of a size easily grasped by a toddler.

Since they are not yet fully adept at serving and pouring, toddlers will spill or drop things, and they will move back and forth between using fingers or a utensil to eat. However, these are all opportunities for learning. Learning how to maneuver objects using the fingers is an emerging skill, leading to better coordination in using a spoon or fork. In time, toddlers figure out how a fork or a spoon keeps fingers from getting sticky or wet. Spills should be expected, with materials in place for clean-up. This includes an absorbent cloth on or near the table, readily avail-

able for soaking up spills. When a spill occurs, teachers can offer toddlers a chance to sop up the milk with a cloth. An absorbent cloth is preferable to a sponge, which suggests to the toddler squeezing, rather than sopping. Some teachers have in the serving cart a set of damp washcloths, each a different color, for wiping the face and hands of the toddlers before they leave the meal area.

Since toddlers must figure out which spoon to eat with and which spoon to serve with, it is not uncommon for them to get confused and attempt to eat from the serving spoon before putting it back in the serving bowl, but this becomes an opportunity to describe "big and little," or "your spoon," or "his, hers, and yours," which are also occasions for introducing new language and mealtime manners.

A toddler meal that is designed to support learning is rich in opportunities for toddlers to use emerging concepts and skills. The primary care teacher, seated with the toddlers at the table, supports their efforts to master new skills. Meals are also a time for conversation, so the primary care teacher narrates what the toddlers are doing, as they serve, pour, and eat, adding to the children's repertoire of words and phrases.

Safety and Sanitation During the Meal

In most infant centers, a kitchen and food preparation area is off limits to children. A half door or a half wall with a gate gives toddlers visual access to the area, while preventing them from entering. For safety reasons, kitchen equipment and kitchen counters should be beyond children's reach.

Safety precautions include keeping toddlers seated while they are eating. Because the muscles of the mouth are still maturing, toddlers have to work hard at positioning food in the mouth and controlling when to swallow. Doing so at the same time that they coordinate walking is risky. Giving clear direction to toddlers with respect to when the meal begins and when it ends, along with a clear statement that they may not eat or drink while walking around, reduces the risk of toddlers choking on food.

Sanitation is important in the kitchen and in the meal area. All surfaces should be cleaned and sanitized daily. This includes floors, which can harbor germs that get carried to the play area. Surfaces of meal tables and chairs should be sanitized before and after each use.

Reflection: Respectful Diapering

Listen to a diapering episode inspired by the respectful care philosophy of Magda Gerber (2002):

- Greet the child. "You are enjoying that basket, aren't you?"
- Say and demonstrate to the child what you are about to do. "You may not be ready, but I want to change your diaper. Come." (pause) "You have a toy in your hand. I will take it. (gentle tug on the toy to see whether the baby relinquishes it) "You're not ready to give it to me yet."
- Wait for the child's reaction. The baby looks up and smiles, but returns his gaze to the basket. "I will get things ready, and then I will be back, so you can play a minute more."
- Gesture and invite. "I'm ready to pick you up. I'll take the toy from you now." (pause, followed by gentle tug on the toy and baby relinquishing it) "Ok. Now you are ready. Come." The baby reaches, accepting the invitation.
- Describe what is about to happen. "We need to take your clothes off first. You can pull out your foot." (pause to let the baby kick his foot from the leg of the pants) "There! You did it! Thank you. Are you ready to help with the other side? Now, you can pull out the other foot."

How would you characterize the teacher's role? How would you characterize the baby's role? What evidence do you see of respect for what the baby has to offer? Does this baby reveal evidence of his emerging thinking?

DIAPERING AS INVITATION TO PARTICIPATE

Diapering provides another opportunity to invite infants to participate in the care and to use emerging skills and ideas. It is often overlooked when teachers think about planning curriculum, yet, as Gerber (2002) explains, infants are diapered "some six or seven thousand times" (p. 79). When we invite infants' participation in diapering and dressing, we take full advantage of these daily rituals as opportunities for conversation that promotes development of language, concepts, and skills.

To invite an infant to participate in the dressing routine, caregivers start by telling the baby what is about to happen. Next they ask for the infant's help, using both words and gestures, and then pause before continuing. By connecting word to action, they help the infant understand the meaning of words, to remember them, and to retrieve them as a way of anticipating what comes next. When taking off an infant's sock, for example, a caregiver might say, "And now it's time to take off your sock. I'll pull it halfway and you do the rest," followed by a pause, a tug on the end of the sock to pull it partially off, and another pause to allow the infant to pull it all the way off. By simplifying the task slightly, the caregiver supports the baby's success. In another example, putting on a shirt, the caregiver might offer the infant a chance to make a choice as to which arm to put in the sleeve first: "This sleeve first, or that sleeve?" pausing to see whether the infant responds with a gesture that indicates a choice.

Since conversation is central to the task of diapering, it is important to free the area of things that distract the baby from these conversations. Toys brought to the changing table or mobiles or mirrors hung above or to the side of the changing table risk distraction.

Diapering Area Furnishings

A diapering table or counter is best situated out of the flow of traffic and in a quiet area, in view of but set aside from the play area. It should be of comfortable height for those who use it, to avoid putting stress on the back. It also should consider babies' comfort, with respect to how they will use it. This will vary depending on the baby's age, but the most versatile changing table not only fits babies' size, but also accommodates how they move.

Infants who have begun to roll over or pull to standing often want to do so while being diapered, which may frustrate a caregiver focused on expediency. If seen from the baby's perspective, they are using their emerging motor skill to move into a position in which they feel balanced, in control, and ready to help out. Ideally, a raised diapering surface has raised sides sufficiently high to make rolling over and standing safe. The Pikler Institute uses a diapering table designed to take full advantage of babies' emerging motor skills. Figure 12.4 illustrates this design, a counter rimmed on three sides with rungs sufficiently high to allow infants to roll over and pull to standing during diapering. The higher sides invite infants to participate with a sense of balance and control.

Figure 12.4. Pikler Diapering Table

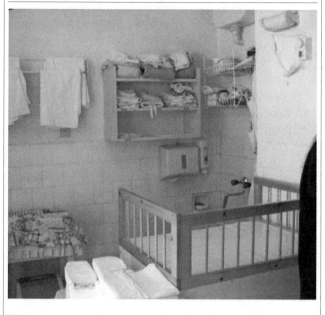

Figure 12.5. Stairs to Diapering Surface

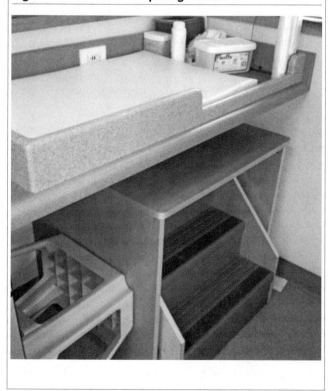

The diapering surface should be a washable pad, which for comfort may be covered with a paper liner. A paper liner, if used, should be disposed of after each use. Infants who have begun to climb stairs enjoy built-in stairs leading to a raised diapering surface (Figure 12.5). This minimizes the risk of back strain for the caregiver. Another option is to diaper toddlers

at floor level, with the toddler standing, using a rail or other object of support. The caregiver sits on a low stool adjacent to the toddler, in line with the toddler.

Diapering Area Safety and Sanitation

A storage area holding the supplies needed for diapering must be within reach of the changing table, so that the caregiver can keep at least one hand on the infant during diapering. When shallow shelves or counters are positioned to the side of the changing table, rather than above, babies can freely stand without risk of hitting an upper shelf. A covered receptacle for soiled diapers, with a foot-controlled lid, also should be within reach. If cloth diapers or cloth washcloths and towels are used, multiple covered receptacles are needed, one for soiled diapers and one for soiled linen. If soiled clothing is to be either sent home or laundered by the infant facility, it should be stored in an airtight disposable bag pending laundering. Items that should be stocked on a shelf adjacent to the diapering area, yet out of reach of children, include:

- Clean diapers
- Washcloths or paper towels for cleaning the infant's skin
- Towels for drying
- Disposable bags for used items and pen for marking
- Spray bottle with surface disinfectant solution and cloths for wiping surfaces

Figure 12.6 provides a comprehensive guide to diapering with respect and care.

NAPPING AS INVITATION TO PARTICIPATE

The room space for napping will vary depending on the layout of the facility. Some programs have separate napping rooms. Others have partitioned alcoves. The napping area should be quiet, separated from the play space and the other active areas of the room. It should be away from busy traffic paths and situated to maintain visual supervision. The younger the group of infants, the more varied the sleeping schedules, so for younger infants a separate space dedicated to napping works best. Older infants tend to sleep on similar schedules, so if the group consists primarily of older infants, the napping room can serve as a play space, when naptime is over.

Figure 12.6. Diapering with Respect and Care

- Make sure required supplies are within reach of the diaper-changing spot (changing mat, diapers, wiping cloths, paper towels, disposable gloves, covered garbage can, disinfectant in spray bottle).
- Wash hands. Put on disposable gloves, if necessary, that is, if stool is runny, has blood in it, or to protect an open cut.
- Tell child, with words and gestures, that you want to change her diaper.
- Pause before picking up the child, to give her time to anticipate what you are about to do.
- If the child is not yet able to pull to standing, place her on her back on the diapering surface. If she can pull to standing and the diapering surface allows, read her cues to determine whether she wants to stand, with support. If diapering surface is raised, never walk away and leave child unattended.
- At each step, describe what you are doing. Remove and set aside the child's clothes and soiled diaper.
- Moisten clean cloth with water and wipe anal area from front to back in one motion. Repeat with fresh cloth if necessary. Pay particular attention to cleaning within skin folds. Dry the child's skin.
- If using a disposable diaper and cloths, fold soiled wiping cloth inside soiled diaper and seal closed using tape strips of the diaper. Dispose in lined, covered garbage bin. If using a cloth diaper, deposit soiled diaper in a lined, covered diaper bin or, to be taken home, in an airtight bag. If child's clothes are soiled, place them in an airtight bag to be sent home.
- If using gloves, dispose of all soiled items prior to removing and disposing of the gloves.
- Wash the child's hands, using a clean cloth.
- Describe your actions as you diaper and dress the child, and allow her to help.
- Assist the child in returning to the play area.
- Immediately return to disinfect the diapering surface, sides, and sink handles.
- Wash your hands thoroughly.

Napping Furnishings

Every infant should have an assigned crib or mat for sleeping. Locating the crib or mat in the same spot each day provides a measure of predictability and security for the infant. The type of furnishings varies, depending on the age of the children served in the room. For babies not yet independently pulling to standing, cribs work well. Once infants master pulling to standing, they are safer if the bed is at floor level. Sleeping mats or low cots provide this security,

whereas cribs do not. The risk with cribs lies in the possibility that young infants are fairly top heavy, and the simple act of pulling to standing and hiking a leg up and over the side rails of a raised crib can result in a fall.

Cribs take floor space that otherwise might be used as activity space, so selection of napping furniture may be a function of facility size. Figure 12.7 illustrates two crib designs used in the infant centers in the city of Pistoia, Italy. The youngest infants sleep in round, low beds, designed like a nest, and the older infants sleep on low cots. For maximum ventilation, while infants are sleeping, the cribs and mats should be positioned so that there is ample air flow among them. The Infant/Toddler Environment Rating Scale suggests a distance of 3 feet (Cryer et al., 2004).

Napping Rituals

Primary care teachers get to know well each baby's way of communicating readiness for rest. Some babies get fussy; some slow down, yawn, and peer through drooping eyelids. Some become more active and irritable. Some babies expect to fall asleep in the arms of the caregiver, while others readily fall asleep on their own. Some babies are light sleepers and awake easily, while others sleep through noise. Some babies sleep with a familiar object from home. Some may want to play before falling asleep. Some babies are used to sleeping next to parents or siblings and may find it hard to adjust to individual cribs or mats. The experience of a baby at home influences sleeping preference and patterns in group care.

Whatever the pattern, the primary care teacher establishes a calm, predictable napping ritual, which over time creates the expectation in each child that falling asleep in this new environment is comfortable and secure. For the primary care teacher, this means moving through the same steps, in the same sequence, so that the baby can anticipate what comes next. This ritual may include the rhythmic sensations of a lullaby, a chant, a rocking motion, or a gentle, repetitive touch. Babies' need for sleep will vary, so a strict napping schedule is not appropriate in group care. Some infants take short, but more frequent, naps, while others take only one long nap. A baby's sleep pattern also may change from day to day.

Toddlers enjoy taking part in setting up the nap area and storing shoes or other items in preparation for a nap. Creating simple systems that involve them in recognizing where to store or find their things sup-

Figure 12.7. Pistoia Cribs and Cots

ports learning, calms the pace, and reduces anxiety that may accompany napping. For example, a row of low hooks on the wall near the napping area provides a place where toddlers find a cloth bag, tagged with the child's photo, an invitation for each toddler to store shoes and other clothing while napping.

Looking Back and Looking Forward

Infants delight in taking a participatory role in the daily care routines, especially those that involve them, like meals, diapering, and naps. Sharing food together, dressing, and preparing to nap provide opportunities for infants to use emerging skills and concepts. To plan learning opportunities within the routines of care, teachers observe, reflect, and interpret to discover what role the infant is ready to play, and they regularly modify the routines to create new contexts for infants' learning. Beyond the play spaces and the care routines lies a third context for teaching and learning, the conversatons and interactions woven throughout the day. Chapter 13 focuses on how adults use everyday conversations and interactions to guide infants as they build friendships and learn to negotiate conflicts.

Conversation and Guidance

[For newborns,] it is as if [they] walk on stage into a play whose enactment is already in progress—a play whose somewhat open plot determines what parts [they] may play and toward what . . . [they] may be heading. Others on stage already have a sense of what the play is about, enough of a sense to make negotiations with the newcomer possible. (Bruner, 1990, p. 34)

Infants look to those who provide their care in order to learn about the world they encounter, one rich in possibilities and replete with unknowns. Bruner compares the plight of an infant to walking out onto the stage of a play that is already underway. Infants are met by those already on the stage, those familiar with the play. As explored in Chapter 6, infants arrive exquisitely attuned to the minds of those they encounter. They detect feelings, they decipher intentions, and they use this information to exchange ideas with others. Chapter 6 described what scientists are learning about infants' sensitivity to the feelings of others; their natural desire to help others; and their ability to distinguish between behavior that helps from behavior that hinders. These talents showcase infants' social competence and provide a foundation for an important context for learning—making friends, keeping friends, and joining others in play.

Making friends begins in infancy, but the process of doing so is not always easy. It is not uncommon for toddlers to bite or hit others, to resist requests, or to erupt in tantrums. Playing with others brings delight and joy, but it also brings frustration and disappointment. Conflicts are messy for children and adults alike, yet conflicts are an important part of teaching and learning. In good times and in bad, caregivers guide infants in making friends and keeping friends. This chapter addresses how to incorporate such moments into the broad definition of curriculum.

Getting someone to engage in play, getting access to a toy that someone else has, or keeping someone

Reflection: Teacher as Guide to Infants' Social World

Consider how you might feel if you had just arrived in a country you had never visited before. The language spoken and the writing on the signs may be completely different from that to which you are accustomed. See yourself driving a car on a busy highway in this new place. You do not know how to read the road signs, nor do you know the rules of the road. You feel uncertain and tentative. You look around for someone who might serve as a guide, someone who knows the local language, customs, and rules for driving. This guide could alert you when you are about to do something wrong and might spare you a stiff fine for breaking a traffic law.

Compare this experience to the experience of a toddler who has his first encounters with peers or with unfamiliar caregivers. Does this toddler have to navigate a new social world? Just as you might appreciate the help of a local guide in your travels to a new country, is it possible that toddlers thrive when they have the support of a trusted adult who serves as a compassionate guide? How might toddlers feel if someone were to offer them clear directions when conflicts occur, instead of imposing a punishment? Will clear directions help them cope with their confusion, frustration, or sadness? What parallels can you see between guiding a toddler who ventures into a new social context and guiding a tourist who confronts a new land ?

from taking a toy that you have—these are all situations that infants encounter for the very first time as they begin to encounter peers. This requires that they learn to weather strong feelings and resolve conflicts with others. Negotiating strong feelings and conflicting desires is an important component of infants' learning and becomes a central focus of teaching. The section that follows explores what it means to help infants negotiate relations with others, in the context of play. Three strategies for doing so are explored—

Figure 13.1. Guidance Strategies and Related Contexts

Context for Difficult Behavior	Guidance Strategy
Child has done something unacceptable	Clear limits
Child refuses to comply with adult request	Limited choice
An overwhelming emotion	Acknowledgment

acknowledgment, clear limits, and limited choice. These strategies for negotiating conflicts with infants and young children build on infants' developing understanding of others' feelings, intentions, and ideas. They provide a framework for using conversation and narrative to guide children's behavior.

RESPECTFUL GUIDANCE

Consider the kind of assistance that a helpful guide might offer upon encountering a traveler lost and wandering. The guide first might empathize with the lost traveler and then inquire about the traveler's destination and plans for the journey. For infants, a trusted caregiver serves as guide to the social world, using clear, simple conversation to help them make sense of the limits of accepted behavior.

Acknowledge the Feeling or Intent

Biting or hitting others, grabbing toys away from others who are still using them, or using toys in ways that may damage them—these behaviors are not uncommon when the protagonists are toddlers. Other conflicts relate to compliance, when a child refuses to do as the adult requests. Figure 13.1 lists three common types of conflict encountered with toddlers.

Whatever the context, difficult and challenging behavior in infants and toddlers is always sparked by a feeling or intention that is real and can be recognized. By imagining the feelings, the desire, or the intention that led to the conflict (Fonagy, Gergely, Jurist, & Target, 2004), we acknowledge the experience as seen through the eyes of the child. Acknowledgment is a key component of conflict resolution. In a conflict situation, to acknowledge means to name or describe what it is the child appears to be feeling, wanting, or concerned with. A phrase of acknowledgment might be, "I know you are sad and crying, because you do not want your friend to leave," or, "When he drew on your paper, that made you angry." Like a considerate travel guide, the adult takes a moment to surmise the infant's feeling, intention, or desire that may have led to the conflict.

When a child is overcome with strong feelings, acknowledging those feelings is a way to help the child cope. At times, a conflict has no ready solution. Yet the child's feelings are real, a response to a disturbing situation. The child may cry incessantly, have a tantrum, or withdraw. Each is the child's way of coping with the disturbance, but it comes at a big emotional cost to the child, a cost that only intensifies when adults respond with threats or punishment. When a trusted adult verbally acknowledges the child's strong feelings, the child is reassured that his concerns have been heard, if not resolved.

When acknowledging a child's strong feelings, the aim is not to judge the appropriateness of the feelings with a statement like, "You're sad, but don't cry. That's nothing to cry about." Nor is the aim to resolve the situation that elicited the feelings, because this may be impossible, as is the case when a child cries relentlessly after watching his parent leave for work. The teacher might say to him, "I know you are sad and you want your Dad. You want your Dad to stay. He is going to work, but he will be back. You are missing him." By acknowledging his feelings, teachers show the child that his feelings are important and that his crying is understandable. It is also important that adults resist offering help or suggestions too quickly. In time, help or suggestions might be appropriate, but in the moment when children are experiencing intense feelings, they need to hear and feel a clear message that their emotions are heard and accepted by others as valid responses to the situation. Once calmed, children will be ready to accept help or suggestions.

Acknowledgment paves the way for conflict resolution, no matter what the age. When we acknowledge, we validate emotions as real, without giving value to accompanying misbehavior. A phrase of acknowledgment is like a bridge over which the infant and the adult can meet and resolve a difficult encounter together. It also serves as a bridge to reconnect children involved in a dispute.

Clear Limits: Convey the House Rules

Infants are innately curious and incessantly go in search of new experiences. They experiment and test to see what happens when they act on something or someone in a certain way. Each day brings new places and new objects to explore. However, each new encounter brings them face to face with expectations about how people and things should be treated or used. Infants do not come into the world knowing what behaviors their family or community regards as acceptable or unacceptable. They rely on those who care for them to tell them the limits of acceptable behavior, that is, what is acceptable and what is not.

Infants rely on adults for this important social knowledge. Magda Gerber (Lally, 2011a) describes this as learning the "house rules," her term for the limits of acceptable behavior in a particular context. House rules keep infants, others, and valued objects safe. Infants look to their caregivers for clear explanations of the house rules. Rules get confusing, because there might be one set of rules at home and another set of rules in another setting.

The best time to explain what is accepted behavior and what is not, is in the midst of a conflict (Gerber, 2002). Think about what happens when a crawler approaches another infant. With a look of curiosity, the crawler might tug on the other infant's hair, causing the infant to cry. The teacher who sees this encounter immediately goes near, soothes the hurt child and in the same moment states what is acceptable and what is not: "Gently, no pulling. It is not OK to pull Saul's hair. Pulling hair hurts." As she says this, she is softly touching each child's hair and saying, "Gently, gently. Not rough."

Using clear, simple phrases, adults introduce young infants to what they may do and what they may not do. With toddlers, whose language is more developed, an adult can be more descriptive, yet still clear and direct, when intervening in a conflict. The adult acknowledges the child's intent or desire, states clearly what the child may not do, states clearly what the child may do instead, and gives a brief reason why. Listen to a toddler teacher's intervention in a dispute between two toddlers, who both want the same toy.

Observation: Amelia lifts her arm as if to hit Carl, who holds tightly the handle of a wagon. I block Amelia's upraised arm and say to her, "Amelia, you may not hit people. I see you're angry, but you may not hit Carl. You really want the wagon, but Carl is still using the wagon. If you want the wagon, you can ask him, "Please, may I use the wagon?" I pause to see what happens. Amelia looks down and says nothing. I say to Carl, "Carl, Amelia wants to use the wagon, too, so when you

are through, please give it to Amelia." Amelia looks up and says in a low, emphatic voice, "My wagon, Carl."

Interpretation: Amelia wants the wagon. She is angry because Carl has it, and she sees Carl as the one keeping it from her. Her plan is to grab the wagon away from Carl, since he is the obstacle keeping her from the toy she wants. I can understand her anger and her plan, because she is just trying to find a way to get what she wants. So I acknowledge her anger but, in the same breath, I tell her that she may not hit others. My goal is to help her learn that hitting people is not OK, but I also want her to know what to do the next time she finds herself in this situation. So I give her a phrase to use to request the wagon.

In this vignette, the teacher acknowledged each child's feelings and intention. She saw that Amelia wanted to get the wagon, so she acknowledged her by saying, "I see you're angry. You really want the wagon." She acknowledged Carl's concern, as well: "Carl is still using the wagon." With these words, both Carl and Amelia feel heard and understood by the teacher, and both begin to see the teacher as an ally. Amelia interprets the teacher's furrowed brow and words as a cue to stop what she was doing. Seeing her trusted caregiver frown at her does not feel good and she feels rejected at first, but the teacher resolves this fear when she touches Amelia gently, smiles at her, and offers her an idea, "You can ask Carl, 'Please, may I use the wagon?'" The phrase is simple and easy for Amelia to repeat.

This vignette captures the essential components that lead to establishing clear limits and clear understanding of house rules. In no specific order, there are three components:

- Acknowledge the child's feelings, intention, goal, or desire.
- Describe what the child has done that is not acceptable.
- Explain why the behavior in unacceptable.
- Tell the child what he or she may do instead (an acceptable alternative) the next time this situation arises.

Something else quite subtle takes place as the adult intervenes in conflicts with children. When an adult reflects on a conflict to discern and acknowl-

Reflection: Saying What We Mean

Clearly stating what is allowed and what is not allowed clarifies the limits of acceptable behavior. When the limits of acceptable behavior are described in a clear statement of expectation, children make sense of them. When limits are phrased as a question, rather than a statement, children are easily confused. Compare how a toddler might hear and respond to each of these phrases. The first is a question and the second is a statement:

"Mary, please do not throw sand, ok?"
"Mary, please do not throw sand."

How do you think the toddler will respond to each request? Because young children are learning language for the very first time, they interpret what we say literally and are generally surprisingly compliant. As a result, is it possible that a toddler will hear the first phrase as an option, rather than as an expectation? How does phrasing the request as a question or as a statement change what the child hears and understands? Are children more likely to comply when the adult phrases a request as a statement rather than as a question?

edge what might be the child's intention, feeling, or concern, the adult's facial expression typically mirrors the child's feelings. We do this naturally and spontaneously, without awareness. In this example, Amelia saw her anger reflected in the teacher's face. Scientists call this marked mirroring (Fonagy et al., 2004). Humans make such "marked" versions of a look of emotion as a way to acknowledge and connect with one another in emotionally charged and potentially threatening social situations. With marked mirroring, the child knows immediately that the look on the adult's face is not the adult being angry. Instead, the child interprets this look as the adult being aware of the child's anger. In the exchange, Amelia does not think, "Wow! Now the teacher is angry with me!" Rather, the child interprets this expression to mean, "She understands my anger." Humans tend to use marked mirroring without even thinking. In this example, Amelia sees the teacher's marked expression as empathy, that is, "She knows how I feel."

With young infants, unacceptable behavior might take the form of a crawler pulling another baby's hair. The adult responds simply and clearly with an acknowledgement, "I know you want to touch him.

Touch gently, no pulling hair. Pulling hair hurts." With young infants, misbehavior is often a result of exploration and experimentation, fueled by the infant's natural curiosity. There is no malice or anger behind the misbehavior. The teacher's words are few but clear, as the infants' ability to comprehend speech is still limited. The teacher acknowledges the infant's intention, clearly tells her what it is that is not acceptable, and redirects her with words and gentle touches, modeling with her own hands what she wants the child to do instead. In addition, she gives a brief reason why.

With older infants, the misbehavior may still be simply curiosity and experimentation gone awry, but it also might be a result of anger or fear. It is up to the adult to observe and reflect on the context in order to discern the child's intention or goal. Adults may not always know precisely what feeling or intention led to the conflict, but, by observing and reflecting, they can make a fairly accurate guess.

Infants rely on adults to give them clear directions about expected behavior. From the infant's point of view, there is much room for confusion. Listen for the subtle differences in the meaning of words and phrases in the following:

- You may bite this plastic toy, but not that child's arm.
- You may push him on the bike, but you may not push him off the bike.
- You may ride the bike on the sidewalk, but you may not ride it in the street.
- You may throw this ball, but you may not throw the block.

Another source of confusion comes when we use vague language when making a request, for example, "Don't do that! You hurt him! I don't want to see you do that again." Is it possible that a toddler, trying to figure out what this means, will think, "Was it the biting she didn't like? Maybe she means that I'm not allowed to bite him, but that other children are okay to bite. Or maybe I'm not supposed to play with him at all." Sometimes misbehavior is simply a response to a child trying to figure out limits that are not clear.

When setting limits and redirecting children to acceptable options, a firm voice is important. Too often, teachers try hard to be nice and soften any direct statements with a lilting, singsong voice, a nonverbal cue that belies the seriousness of the teacher's statement. Teachers also attempt to soften the impact of

Reflection: Distraction or Redirection?

Sometimes teachers try to distract a child in order to stop misbehavior. With very young infants, distraction may work as a way to move them away from something that is overwhelming in order to help them calm down if they are upset or tired. However, distraction risks confusing rather than helping the child who has misbehaved. For example, a young crawler may bite the arm of another crawler who lies nearby. It might seem easiest for the teacher to simply move the biter to another area and distract the biter with a toy, saying, "Come over here with me, and we will read this book together." The teacher distracts the infant to another activity, but what is the lesson learned? Does this response help the infant figure out what is appropriate to bite and what is not? What has the infant learned with respect to acceptable ways to touch or connect with other infants? In contrast, what lessons are learned, if the following is what the infant hears? "You may not bite people. Biting hurts people. You can touch him gently, but do not bite him."

Figure 13.2. Why Infants Bite

- To gather information about the physical properties of people
- To explore the reactions of others and to make sense of people
- To massage sensitive gums, through the pressure of biting, when teeth are erupting
- To acquire needed sensory stimulation
- To relay a feeling or intention, that is, to express anger, frustration, fatigue, desire, or stress

their words by using "we" rather than "you," for example, "We don't hit others." A phrase initiated with "We don't" risks confusion as to whose behavior is being discussed. Very young children may be in the process of figuring out that "we" means something different from "you," so hearing, "We don't hit others," might suggest to them that the message is directed at *others*, not them. The point here is not to suggest that being nice is a fault, but that respectful, firm, clear, guiding words can still be kind.

Biting. Biting others is one of the most common transgressions encountered with infants. A toddler may bite to get a toy that is in the hands of another child. Indeed, in most instances, by biting, a child achieves his intended goal, because the child who is bitten will scream and often release the coveted toy. Eventually, toddlers acquire words and phrases that provide a more adaptive way to express their desires and intentions to others, but until then they are caught in a difficult period of transition.

Biting is clearly outside the limits of acceptable behavior, so respectful limit setting and redirection is an effective intervention. There are many reasons why infants bite (Figure 13.2), but an effective intervention follows the same pattern, while still acknowledging the specific context that triggered the bite. In response to a child who bites another, the adult ac-

knowledges the infant's concern, clearly states that biting people is not okay and that biting hurts people, and then gives the infant something to do, instead of biting, in order to satisfy her intention or feeling. This includes modeling acceptable behavior, like gently touching a child in the spot where he bit the other child, and using a phrase that the child can repeat in order to get what he wants, like, "Tell him you want the toy." For young infants, the intervention is short, simple, and clear. When adults respond with too many words, toddlers get lost in the onslaught of words.

In a few short sentences, an adult can make a clear, nonjudgmental point about biting. Listen for a phrase of acknowledgment, a clear limit, a redirection, and a reason why in the observation that follows:

Observation: The teacher sees toddler Anna, with furrowed brow, lean over and bite David on the arm. The teacher moves in between the two toddlers, gently touching the arm of each. The teacher says to Anna, "You may not bite people. I know you want the toy, but David is still using it. If you want the toy from David, say, 'I want the toy, please,' but you may not bite him. Biting hurts." The teacher turns to crying David and says sympathetically, "You got bitten. That hurt, didn't it?" The teacher remains close by, turns to look at Anna, and, after a short pause, says to her, "If you want the toy, tell David, 'I want the toy.' But I will not let you bite him."

Biters often require more than a single intervention. The biter, having heard the explanation of the limit and a redirection, may still seek to clarify what this really means. To do this, the biter might bite again in the same or a similar situation. For example, a biter might think, "Did the teacher mean just this child? Maybe it is acceptable for me to bite another child instead. I'll find out." When a toddler repeats the misbehavior, it may be that the toddler is just trying to clarify what is expected. When adults respond with clear limits and clear redirection, they support toddlers in learning the house rules.

Sharing. Another common toddler conflict involves sharing toys. Sharing is not new to toddlers, because they have been sharing time and attention with caregivers since birth. As newborns, they cling to the caregiver as an extension of themselves, and, by 9 months old, this sharing extends to objects, as infant and caregiver delight in sharing attention to a toy. Infants discover that these moments of shared joint attention keep the caregiver nearby. By around 1 year of age, infants initiate a back-and-forth exchange of joint attention, repeatedly handing an object to the caregiver and then taking it back, enjoying the power of social sharing (Rochat, 2009).

Crawlers delight in moving out into the surrounding world to explore the objects around them. Their encounters with other crawlers may result in two crawlers handling the same toy simultaneously, most often a gentle back-and-forth exchange, with the tugs escalating at times, but never to the point of being divisive. Such an encounter is simply shared joint attention, a moment spent exploring the actions of another, rather than a conflict over possession. When two crawlers tug on the same toy, the teacher observes to make sure they are safe, but there is no need to intervene. Each crawler experiences the pull of the other on the mutually held toy. The teacher's role is neither a protector of rights nor a negotiator of conflict, but instead a narrator of story. The crawlers might hear, "You both want that toy. Angelica wants it, and Tanisha wants it, too. You are both pulling on it." In this way, the teacher gives words to the actions of the crawlers as they experience the toy together.

With toddlers, however, conflicts over possession of toys are fraught with anger over rightful possession. They start to claim explicit possession as they invest more feelings in objects. The utterance, "Mine!" is one of the child's first expressive phrases and communicates clearly to others that "what I desire" is an extension of "me." Some version of the utterance "mine" appears across cultures around the second birthday (Rochat, 2009). At first glance, this sense of exclusivity may appear to make it hard for toddlers to learn what it means to share. However, toddlers' emerging sense of "mine" prepares them well for sharing, in that they have something of value to give away.

Reflection: Punishment Is Not a Solution

Many adults assume that the right response when a toddler misbehaves is to punish, chastise, or exclude. What does a child learn when hit, sent to a time-out chair, chastised, shamed, or humiliated? Because imitation is a potent learning strategy for infants, is it possible that the lesson learned is most likely this—when angry or facing conflict with someone, respond by hitting, harming, or rejecting them? What behaviors do we want infants to imitate, when feeling angry or in conflict with another person? What behaviors do we want to avoid having them imitate?

Sharing is being willing to give something to someone else. It happens gradually, as toddlers experiment with what it means to have and to give. In time, with many interactions with others, toddlers discover the social power of sharing. By giving something of value, that is, by relinquishing possession of a desired toy, they make friends happy and those friends stay nearby. By insisting on keeping something of value that someone else desires, they make friends sad, and friends go away. Toddlers' desire to make and keep friends is strong. Like all human beings, toddlers want to belong to the social group and to affiliate with friends. It is this drive that supports them in learning to share. Over the course of many disputes over toys, some more heated than others, toddlers figure out the social value of sharing, with respect to making and keeping friends.

Adults promote sharing by allowing a child to play with an object as long as the child wishes, that is, to retain control of it if another child tries to take it away. This at first may seem counter to the concept of sharing. However, children allowed to keep possession of a coveted toy are more inclined to give up the toy, but on their own terms. Having control over objects of value makes it possible for toddlers to surrender them to playmates when ready. In a sense, children maintain control over the object of value even as they give it away.

Sharing happens only when a child has been able to experience a sense of possession and then experience the social consequences of relinquishing possession to others. Genuine sharing does not come about by directives or coercive threats that sound like, "You need to share. Give it to him," or, "If you can't share your toys, I'm going to put them away, and neither of you will be able to use them." Genuine sharing develops over the course of many opportunities to give and receive.

When adults model sharing, they promote sharing, by helping children experience what it means to have and to give. Because imitation is a primary way infants acquire social behavior, modeling sharing is a potent strategy. Adults also promote sharing by helping toddlers construct understanding of what it means to wait. Waiting for another to give up a coveted toy can be hard for toddlers. When teachers give words to a waiting child's feelings, they acknowledge the waiting child's plight, but their words also guide the child who has the coveted toy. For example, a teacher might say to the child who has the toy, "Carl, Amelia wants to use the wagon, too. She will be waiting to use it when you are through."

For toddlers, a waiting list is a concrete way to experience what it means to wait. In this situation, the teacher might grab a clipboard and say to Amelia, "I'll start a waiting list. I'm writing at the top of the page, 'Waiting list for the wagon,' and I'm putting a number 1, and then I'm writing your name, Amelia, A, M, E, L, I, A." That means you will be the first one to use it when Carl is through playing with it. Would you like to use the pencil to write your name?" Often, when teachers invite such participation, the toddler will take the pencil and make a mark on the page. The teacher continues, "Do you want to hold onto the list, or shall we tape it over here on the wall? You decide."

In this situation, it is clear who rightfully possessed the toy. In other situations, the adult may be pulled into a conflict without knowing who had the toy first and who was trying to take it away. In this event, the adult takes on the role of conflict negotiator, acknowledging and helping the children solve the conflict, staying nearby to prevent physical harm, and describing what appears to be the conflict and the ideas and feelings involved. The teacher might say, "Looks like you both want the wagon." If one starts to grab it from the other, the teacher might say, "I will not let you pull it away, Amelia, but I will help you talk to Carl. Tell him what you want." In response, the toddler might say, "My wagon!" The teacher picks up on this, turns to Carl, and says, "Carl, did you hear Amelia? She wants to use the wagon. And so do you." Carl might insist, "No, my wagon!" The teacher turns to Amelia, "OK, so Carl says he wants to use the wagon, too. Did you hear Carl?" Resting a hand gently on the arm of each child, she continues, "You both want to use the wagon. That is a problem." Despite their moves to get the wagon, the teacher keeps a tight hold on the

> ### Reflection: Time-Out or Time-In?
>
> Many adults use time-out as a way to discipline a misbehaving child, essentially removing a disruptive or disobedient child from a conflict situation and isolating the child in a time-out spot designated for misbehaving children. The problem with time-out is that it humiliates and punishes children and isolates them from the context that they most need to learn how to manage (Katz & McClellan, 1997). Removing the child from the very situation that the child is trying to figure out defeats the goal of having the child learn how to resolve the situation. When we remove and isolate a child, we deny the child the opportunity to learn how to respond, with the adult's support, the next time the child is in this same situation. How might shadowing be used as a substitute for time-out? If the teacher shadows the child while the child remains in the conflict situation, what will the child learn? Could this be thought of as time-in, rather than time-out?

wagon, adding, "I'll hold it while you decide who will play with it."

They may both lose interest in talking and abandon the wagon, but they also might persist. Children often need encouragement to communicate in words what they want and what they feel. They also benefit from knowing that the caregiver trusts them to decide who will play with a disputed toy. A simple statement like, "We have a problem to solve. We will figure out together who gets to play with it," reveals this trust. Many times, in conflicts like the one between Carl and Amelia, if given the space and the time to come up with a solution, one of the children will do so. It might be something as simple as, "How about you sit here and I sit there?" or "I know! We can both use it!" When teachers see their role as ally, mentor, and coach to meaning-making infants and toddlers, they support them in building understanding of what it means to experience a desired object together and eventually to experience the social power inherent in the act of sharing.

When working with toddlers who repeatedly test a house rule, shadowing is a useful strategy. Shadowing means following a child who previously has transgressed a limit and observing closely to help him stay within the limits of acceptable behavior. To shadow, a teacher stays close by the child, comments on what is occurring, reminds the child what it is he can do to accomplish his goal, and models how the child might do so.

Frame a Limited Choice

A second context for guidance occurs when a child refuses to comply with a request made by an adult. Conflicts around compliance can be difficult contests of will for the adult and for the child. There are times, however, when things have to be done in a certain way, in a certain place, or at a certain time, so the adult needs the child to comply.

Most situations that require compliance offer a small, yet useful, window of opportunity in which the adult can involve the child in deciding the course of action. For example, a teacher may need all the children to be together inside, rather than some remaining in the yard. Leaving a child alone in the yard would not be an option, so if a child refuses to go inside, a conflict between teacher and child ensues. The strategy called limited choice helps children make sense of such mandates and involves them in deciding the course of action.

Limited choice builds on children's desire to do things and to make decisions on their own, a developing sense of autonomy. This guidance strategy respects children's desire for autonomy and turns a small degree of decision making over to children within clearly defined limits—limits that ensure that the task required by the adult gets accomplished. Limited choice is a win-win for child and adult. A limited choice has four parts.

1. Acknowledge the child's feeling, intention, or goal.
2. Clearly state to the child what you need him to do.
3. Clearly state the reason why you need the child to accommodate your request.
4. Offer the child two equally acceptable ways to accommodate the request.

With a limited choice, a child has the power to make the decision, yet within a limited range of options. Either option will satisfy the adult's request, so the adult can comfortably turn the decision over to the child.

Most toddlers, when given a limited choice, want to do things on their own, so they pick the option that ensures they can be independent of adult help. The key is to offer a choice that will get the child to do what is expected. In this example, the teacher offered two ways the child could choose to go inside. Another

---

Reflection: Limited Choice

Listen to how this teacher acknowledges the child's wish, states what the teacher needs the child to do and why, and offers two options to the child.

Observation #1

The teacher kneels near 2-year-old Mateo, who is filling bucket after bucket with sand in the sandbox. The teacher says to him, "I can see that you want to keep playing in the sandbox, but it is time to go inside. Either you may walk inside by yourself or you can hold my hand. Which do you want to do?" Mateo doesn't look up. The teacher waits silently. Mateo drops the bucket, shrugs, skirts around the teacher, and runs toward the door.

Success is not always so easy. A child may not respond to the options offered. It is important to persist with the limited choice to help the child see what it has to offer, in terms of control over the situation. It may be necessary to repeat the options several times. Listen to how this teacher persists with the limited choice, when the child balks at making a choice.

Observation #2

The teacher says, "I will count to five. If I get to five, and you still haven't decided, then I get to decide." The teacher counts, slowing down between four and five. On the count of five, the child still hasn't chosen an option, so the teacher extends his open palm as an invitation to walk indoors and says, "OK, you can hold my hand, and we'll walk together." Often at this point, the child's urge for independence overcomes him, and he heads indoors on his own.

---

might be, "Do you want to go in through this door or that door? You decide." The choice must relate directly to the expected behavior, or the strategy fails. For example, avoid saying, "You may go indoors and play with the blocks or the books," because the response might be, "I want to play with the blocks, but right now I'm still filling my bucket," and the child does not budge from the sandbox. It is also important not to transform a limited choice into a threat. This happens with a phrase like, "If you do not come inside now, you will not be able to read the story with us after lunch." Such "if–then" phrases are either threats or bribes and do little to help toddlers figure out the house rules. They only add confusion and anxiety to an already stressful situation.

Teachers who try limits and redirection or limited choice once or twice with a child and fail to see results immediately may grow impatient with the strategy and be tempted to discard it and look for another mode of discipline. However, testing what adults mean by a specific limit on behavior is a natural part of infants' learning about people. Children will test a limit we impose on them in order to clarify what we mean. When they test a limit by repeating a prohibited behavior, restate the limit and the redirection clearly, firmly, and concisely, telling the child what he may not do and what he may do instead to get his desires met. A consistent response, repeated as needed, is critical to the child's making sense of the limit. Expect repeat offenders, because it is part of infants' meaning-making process.

DIFFICULT BEHAVIOR: A CHILD SEEKING SAFETY

When a child shows a pattern of difficult behavior, it may be a sign that the child has experienced a traumatic event. Early life trauma, whether through abuse or accident, is not uncommon among infants. In the United States, it is the leading cause of death in the first 5 years of life (Lieberman, 2006). Children experience trauma when they are threatened with death, serious injury, or abandonment, or when they witness others in such a situation. A traumatized child may have viewed violence inflicted on the parent or may have been the victim himself of physical or emotional violence. Such children lose a sense of safety and protection that otherwise would be ensured by the trusted caregiver. Trauma also may come from a natural disaster like a hurricane or flood or from involvement in an accident, like a dog bite, car accident, or near drowning. The child is unable to control what is happening and is overwhelmed with fear, distress, anxiety, or horror.

Trauma can be damaging both physically and emotionally. Infants are capable of holding in memory the feelings and sensations of a traumatic event, even though they are not yet capable of remembering or recounting the event. These implicit memories of sights, sounds, feelings, and sensations are held within the child's brain and can be triggered by later life experiences. These later experiences may have nothing to do with the original trauma; however, a sensation similar to that experienced in the original moment of trauma may trigger the same sensation and feelings experienced during the trauma. For example, a loud sound, a person coming too near, or the look or the facial expression of someone—each might trigger implicit memories from a traumatic early life event. When this happens, the child may experience the same sense of threat and fear felt during the original traumatic experience (Perry, 2007; Siegel, 2012). The rush of feelings may make no sense to the child, nor does it make sense to the adult who is with the child. However, the sense of fear is real and the emotions triggered in the mind of the child are real. It is this fear or threat that may be the source of a child's defiance or aggression.

Children's traumatic stress often will display itself in anger, aggression, fear, disobedience, and inability to engage with others or with objects in play (Lieberman, 2006). A traumatized child may easily lose control, be fearful, disruptive, or excessively aggressive. The difficult behavior may be triggered when the child is most vulnerable—tired or stressed. A teacher may not be aware of the trauma, may not know the nature of the trauma, or may not clearly see the connection between the difficult behavior and what triggered it. The difficult behavior provoked by the traumatic memory can be extreme and disturbing for both child and teacher.

If teachers understand that the difficult behavior is the child's way of coping with overwhelming and intense feelings that remain long after the traumatic event, they are able to support the child in ways that help the child begin to heal the impact of the trauma. Lashing out at someone who comes too close, who attempts to take something away, who looks stern, or who talks in a loud voice—these are valid attempts to protect oneself in the face of fear or assault. Difficult behavior is very often a child's way of keeping safe, rather than simply willful disobedience.

How a child reacts in stressful situations is largely a function of how the stress response system of the brain organizes, prenatally and during infancy. A child whose early life experience was chaotic may have a stress response system that is highly reactive to threat, increasing the risk of defiant or aggressive behavior (Perry, 2006). Recall from Chapter 5 that circuits of neurons within the brain's stress response system can relay a signal of threat instantaneously. This stress response system bypasses the thinking brain, so a child who feels unsafe or threatened may not plan his actions, but, instead, simply may react to protect himself (Perry, 2007). If incoming information is deemed "bad," stress hormones flood the child's system. Some children may have a stress response

Research Highlight:
How Relationships Can Heal Trauma

Lieberman (2006) suggests that teachers of infants keep the following in mind as ways to help heal the impact of trauma:

- Give the child a sense of safety through predictable daily routines.
- Ensure stable relationships through primary care and continuity of care.
- Understand that aggression, noncompliance, and impulsivity often are triggered by situations that remind the child of a prior traumatic event or are the result of chronic stress or maltreatment.
- When the child is distressed when a trusted caregiver departs, make sure the caregiver says good-bye and reassure the child of the caregiver's return.
- Stay calm and avoid behaviors that will frighten an already traumatized child, including raising one's voice, using harsh language, reacting with anger, and isolation.
- Work collaboratively with family members on a course of action to reassure and support the child.
- Use play, exercise, body movement, dance, music, books, and other rhythmic activities to help the child regulate intense feelings that lead to hostile or aggressive behavior or withdrawal.

system that gets triggered easily, possibly due to prior experiences but possibly due to sensory-processing sensitivity. For a child whose stress response system is vulnerable, lashing out at others may be a protective move.

When dealing with outbursts of aggressive or hostile behavior, therefore, the immediate focus of intervention should be to help the child feel safe again. Children must feel safe before they can think and reason about their actions and the consequences of their actions. Perry (2006, 2007, 2008) suggests using patterned, repetitive behavior to calm a highly aggressive, fearful, or defiant child. This might include taking a walk, swinging back and forth on a swing, pounding rhythmically on a drum, or singing a rhythmic song or chant. Each provides a steady rhythm of movement rich in sensory input. Engaging children in such regulatory experiences calms them to a point of being able to think about and talk about what they did that was not acceptable and what they might do instead the next time they are in a similar situation.

Once the child calms and the thinking brain is engaged, teachers can offer suggestions for things a child might do to calm when threatened again. For example, "When you get mad, pretend you have a dandelion puff ball and blow the seeds away," or, "When someone makes you angry and you feel like hitting them, hit this pillow instead."

Looking Back and Looking Forward

Through the help of those who provide their care, infants and toddlers make sense of themselves in relation to others. Negotiating conflicts that emerge within episodes of play can be frustrating and overwhelming to infants and toddlers. They look to adults for support in handling the messiness of navigating conflicts with others. Through respectful guidance that includes acknowledgment, clear limits, and limited choice, adults support infants in using conversation and story to negotiate conflicts or to cope with overwhelming feelings. Through such strategies, adults introduce infants to the expectations for behavior that fit with the goals of their cultural group. They serve as a guide on the side, offering words and phrases for the toddlers to use in satisfying their needs, wants, and desires, but at the same time, helping them see and understand the needs, wants, and desires of others (Lally, 2011a). In this way, adults use conversation with infants to help them learn how to make friends and keep friends.

The next chapter revisits a question posed in the first chapter of this book, "How do we know they are learning?" This final chapter provides an opportunity to reflect on the many uses of documentation generated by observations of infants. Documentation as narrative will be explored as a tool to broaden awareness of the importance of the first 3 years and to transport the story of infants' learning beyond the walls of the infant program into the hands of those making decisions that impact the lives of infants and their families.

CHAPTER 14

Sharing Infants' Story of Learning

[Children] are autonomously capable of making meaning from their daily life experiences. . . . The central act of adults, therefore, is to activate, especially indirectly, the meaning-making competencies of children as a basis of all learning. They must try to capture the right moments, and then find the right approaches, for bringing together, into a fruitful dialogue, their meanings and interpretations with those children.
(Malaguzzi, 2012, p. 55)

> **Reflection: The Many Uses of Documentation**
>
> Review the material you have studied in this book. What have you learned about the many ways documentation can be used? Give an example of how it can be used in each of these contexts:
> - Curriculum planning
> - Assessment of infants' learning
> - Family engagement
> - Professional development of teachers
> - Program development
> - Advocacy for services that support young children and families

THE EXPRESSIONS ON A child's face, the child's gestures or actions, and their words—each adds to our understanding of a child's ideas, thoughts, and feelings, no matter how young the child. The many ways young children reveal to us their thinking inspired Loris Malaguzzi (2012; Edwards, Gandini, & Forman, 2012), the director of early childhood schools in Reggio Emilia, to describe young children as "having 100 languages and more" (Edwards et al., 2012, p. 3). This phrase has become synonymous with young children's amazing capacity to communicate, to represent, and to think and reason.

In the quote that introduces this chapter, Malaguzzi reminds us that infants are "capable of making meaning from their daily life experiences" and that teachers "activate, especially indirectly, the meaning-making competencies of children." When teachers observe children's play and document significant moments, they make visible the invisible—the thoughts, ideas, and concepts under construction in the mind of the child. Through play, children reveal their thinking, and through mindful observation, documentation, and dialogue about the documentation, teachers discover the next steps for what to do to engage them in going further in learning. Malaguzzi emphasizes that teachers "must try to capture the right moments, and then find the right approaches, for bringing together, into a fruitful dialogue, their meanings and interpretations."

In Chapter 4, you explored what it means to fruitfully engage in reflective dialogue around the documentation of infants' experiences, and in subsequent chapters you read examples of how teachers observe, document, and interpret the documentation, identifying emerging concepts and skills and generating ideas for what to offer next as contexts for learning. However, there is a broader application for this work. When shared with the community, documentation transports the story of infants' thinking beyond the early childhood setting and becomes a tool for guiding policies that shape services for children and families.

From a large body of scientific studies, from fields as diverse as developmental psychology, child development, neuroscience, pediatrics, and psychiatry, the evidence has accumulated, culminating in an undisputed conclusion—infants are more consciously aware, more attuned to others, and more instinctively analytical than ever imagined.

Periodically, as teachers review ongoing documentation, they discover significant moments that reveal how children think and learn. These moments have potential to inform others about infants' amazing capacity to learn. This final chapter invites you to select significant moments of children's experiences and document them in a way that tells the story of infant learning to a wider audience, beyond your own experience and outside the walls of the infant program.

DOCUMENTATION AS VISUAL NARRATIVE

A visual narrative uses photos and text to capture the story of children's learning (Giudici et al., 2001; Rubizzi, 2001). The first step in preparing a visual narrative is to carefully select the photos and notes that convey the story. Sift through the documentation in order to make a thoughtful selection. Doing so with others draws in multiple and clarifying perspectives and generates a reflective conversation. The following questions guide this process:

- What do you notice in the documentation?
- How are the infants revealing their thoughts and intentions?
- What photos and notes most clearly convey the story of infants' thinking in this moment of play or interaction?

A visual narrative is succinct and tells a clear story. It is not simply a collection of captioned photos nor is it the story of everything that happened in a curriculum project. It is a concise and compelling vignette that captures children in the act of making meaning (Figure 14.1).

A brief description introduces the context for the narrative. This may include the planning question that led to the documented event and brief interpretation of what took place. The text highlights what was exciting or particularly revealing within the children's play and invites the reader to reflect and interpret what the children might have been thinking.

A few photos, work samples, or quotes, carefully selected for the message they convey, provide the visual story. Key identifying information—the name of the program, the names and ages of the children involved in the event, and the date or time period of the documented event—establishes the context.

A visual narrative can be read by children, their families, and visitors. It can be posted near the entry to introduce visitors to the story of teaching and learning underway in the program. It can be distributed as a single sheet to invite the reader to appreciate the story of how infants learn. For families, it becomes the focal point for thinking with the teachers about the teaching and learning. When printed on sturdy paper, a visual narrative becomes a book that

Reflection: Formats for Visual Narrative

A visual narrative can take many different forms. It can be one sheet of paper, a short booklet, a small panel, a short media clip, or a document available through a website. The format should be inviting and easy to read. It should be designed with attention to ease of distribution and to minimizing cost. Ideas to consider include:

- **Use a standard format.** When created in standard print size, it can be easily reproduced and distributed. For example, a small panel, created using sections of lightweight display board, if cut to standard print size, can also be used to print paper copies for distribution.
- **Bind securely and attractively.** If prepared as a short booklet, bind with large binder rings or an attractive handmade binding.
- **Use a free-standing panel.** Several panels of display board can be taped together in fan-like fashion.
- **Use a hanging panel.** Several panels, to be read in succession, can be suspended on the wall, held by binder clips attached to a taut wire.

resides in the book and story play space and invites children to revisit their experiences. When mounted on the walls of the room or studied in reflective dialogue among teachers, a visual narrative becomes a point of reflection and professional development.

DOCUMENTATION AS TOOL FOR ADVOCACY

Many do not realize that science begins in moments when babies listen to the chirping of birds hidden in the branches of a tree, or that reading has its roots when a baby flips through the pages of a book, or that addition begins when babies pick up one block after another to fill a basket, or that babies are exquisitely attuned to others' behavior and language, or that the delicate art of negotiating conflicts begins in infancy. Documentation prepared as a visual narrative invites others to see how infants build knowledge that becomes the foundation for all later learning and achievement.

Early childhood education is an investment in individual children, but it is also an investment in society (Giudici, 2012). When prepared as a visual narrative, documentation provides authentic data for measuring quality in early childhood education

Figure 14.1. Visual Narrative: Caught in the Act of Learning

Severyn is 6 months old. Here you see him intent on examining, with eyes and fingers, a soap dish. He mouths it and turns it over as he stares at it. After a few minutes, he flings it to his right. In the second photo, to his left, there are two other soap dishes. One has a ribbed surface. The other, tucked below it, is identical to the one he first examined. He scans the toys in front of him and turning to his left, catches sight of this identical soap dish. He picks it up. He spends a few minutes mouthing it, peering at it, and fingering it. He turns to his right, looks down toward the spot where the first soap dish landed, and reaches to place one soap dish on top of the other. What do you think is going on in Severyn's mind?

What does Severyn reveal about his thinking? Here are some possibilities:

- He notices similarities and differences, selecting the two small white soap dishes with tiny holes and bumps, instead of the large white soap dish with ribs.
- He remembers the features of the first soap dish, returning to find it later.
- He appears to match two identical objects and, in doing so, he "makes two," the beginning of an important math skill.

In play with ordinary objects, infants build concepts of classification, spatial relations, causality, and number.

Reflection: Making the Message Clear

Format influences the effectiveness of a visual narrative. Consider how the following points enhance the readability of a visual narrative:

- Avoid slanting photos, as this interrupts the reader and distracts from a straightforward reading of the story.
- Crop photos to eliminate extraneous background, making better use of page space.
- Avoid crowding the photos. Leave space where the eye can rest. This keeps the reader engaged in the message.
- Be selective. Use only a few photos and samples that clearly convey the message.
- Avoid the temptation to use all photos available or every work sample collected. The intent is not to show each child's work. The intent is to relay a message about children's thinking and learning.
- Resist the temptation to add cute captions. Text should relay a clear message and, when placed near photos, should help the reader interpret children's thinking.
- Listen to what children say, record their words, and extract quotes that reveal their thinking.
- Keep the format simple. Decoration distracts the reader from seeing and hearing the children's thoughts and ideas.

Reflection: What Will You Take with You?

Reflect on what you will take from this book, and consider these questions as a measure of your learning:

- Do you know how to listen, watch for, and document what it is that engages infants?
- Do you know how to interpret what infants might be revealing within their play, that is, their thoughts and ideas?
- Do you have a vocabulary for naming the learning you see happening in moments of play and interaction?
- Do you know how to make that learning visible in order to share it with others?

transformative changes in educational policy (Cavallini, Filippini, Vecchi, & Trancossi, 2011; Filippini & Vecchi, 2005). Since every child is connected to a family and every family is connected to a community, documentation invites the broader community to listen to children's ways of knowing and to engage in thoughtful debate about policies related to early childhood education. Malaguzzi (2012) advises:

> Teachers must leave behind an isolated, silent mode of working that leaves no traces. Instead, they must discover ways to communicate and document the children's evolving experiences at school . . . and [help others] take a new and more inquisitive approach toward the whole school experience. (p. 46)

(Dahlberg, Moss, & Pence, 2013) and demonstrating the value of early childhood services, as an investment in society. Documentation can move the story of what children learn and how they learn beyond the walls of the program and into the hands of those who may know little about infants, their families, and the teachers who serve them. As such, documentation is a tool for civic engagement and a tool for advocating for effective services for children and families.

A visual narrative captures the story of infants' thinking in a way that can be shared with others. Rinaldi (2006b) describes documentation that gives rise to visual narrative as "visible listening." She explains, "If we believe that children possess their own theories, interpretations, and questions . . . then the most important verbs in educational practice are no longer 'to talk,' 'to explain' or 'to transmit'—but 'to listen'" (pp. 98–99). The teachers in the schools in Reggio Emilia have demonstrated to the world how listening, observing, and documenting can lead to

Looking Back and Looking Forward

In this book, you explored key research that demonstrates how infants learn and what infants learn, within each domain of development. You explored how to apply this research in practice, in respectfully caring for infants. Bruner (1990) suggests that for infants, it is as if they "walk on stage into a play whose enactment is already in progress—a play whose somewhat open plot determines what parts . . . [they] may play and toward what . . . [they] may be heading" (p. 34). Those who care for infants serve as guides to infants as they walk onto the stage of humanity. Rinaldi (2006a) reminds us that infants invite us to be their traveling companions "in this search for meaning" (p. 21), each moment a discovery, part of a larger web of investigating the world around them.

Afterword

Mary Jane Maguire-Fong writes about infants as active little beings who are struggling to understand the world around them and their relation to it. She writes about it beautifully and sensitively, as well as in an integrated and comprehensive form. The book is a tour de force. For me to add something to what she has written would be redundant, but that is all that I am left with, so redundant it will have to be.

She writes that infants are active makers of meaning. They do not simply receive meaning. She is absolutely right. When Bruner referred to all humans—infants and children included—as makers of meaning he chose the word 'makers' carefully. Those who 'make' things are not passive, but active creators of something new. Humans must (yes, must) make meaning about the world and themselves. To fail to do so is a psychic catastrophe. The infant bangs a block or a spoon and, as Piaget told us, the infant makes a sensori-motor meaning that both are the same—"bangable." The action is the meaning. A few short months later, for the same infant, one of these objects is for eating and the other is for building. The meaning made has changed; the actions have changed. The meaning the infant makes changes how the infant is in the world—how she makes sense of the world and of herself in it. Though difficult for adults to understand, because we are colonized by language, all infant meaning-making is done without language and without symbols, yet the meaning-making is powerful and continuous. It will only get more complex and coherent for the child as these yet-to-emerge meaning-making capacities develop.

Maguire-Fong explicates the developmental process, comprehensively, integrating information on brain, cognitive, behavioral, linguistic and social development. Yet critically, she goes beyond the wonders of the development of competencies to make tangible the foundational concept that normal development depends on the successful communication of meaning and that the typical way that meaning is made—the primary process for making meaning—is through active exchanges of information between children and the adults they are with. The process involves the bringing together of two (or more) meaning-making beings—the child and the adult—into a dyadic communicative process, a process that cannot exist in only one of them. And out of their dyadic engagement new meanings are co-created, which can be appropriated, as Vygotsky told us, by each of them into their own sense of themselves in the world. As a consequence, the child's and the adult's states of consciousness expand, but more so for the child, whose knowing is less coherent and complex than that of the adult.

And that is the whole point—to grow the child. Maguire-Fong makes it clear how to do it, in theory and in practice. She also makes it clear that the responsibility falls to us: to parents, to teachers, and to policy makers. To fail to do what Maguire-Fong tells us is to fail our children and to make their world meaningless—something totally senseless.

Ed Tronick
University Distinguished Professor
University of Massachusetts Boston
Research Associate
Harvard Medical School

References

Acredelo, L., & Goodwyn, S. (1996). *Baby signs: How to talk with your baby before your baby can talk.* Chicago, IL: Contemporary Books.

Adolph, K. E., & Berger, S. A. (2006). Motor development. In W. Damon & R. Lerner (Series Eds.) & D. Kuhn & R. S. Siegler (Vol. Eds.), *Handbook of child psychology: Vol. 2. Cognition, perception, and language* (6th ed., pp. 161–213). New York, NY: Wiley.

Ainsworth, M. D. S., Blehar, M. C., Waters, E., & Wall, S. (1978). *Patterns of attachment: A psychological study of the strange situation.* Hillsdale, NJ: Erlbaum.

Allen, J. G., Fonagy, P., & Bateman, A. W. (2008). *Mentalizing in clinical practice.* Washington, DC: American Psychiatric Publishing.

Als, H., Duffy, F. H., McAnulty, G. B., Rivkin, M. J. Vajapeyam, S., Mulkern, R. V., Warfield, S. K. , Huppi, P. S., Butler, S. C., Conneman, N., Fischer, C., & Eichenwald, E.C. (2004). Early experience alters brain function and structure. *Pediatrics, 113,* 846–857.

American Academy of Pediatrics. (2013). Injuries associated with infant walkers [Policy statement reaffirmed]. Pediatrics, 132, e281–e282, Retrieved from http://pediatrics.aappublications.org/content/132/1/e281.full

Baillargeon, R. (1994). How do infants learn about the physical world? *Current Directions in Psychological Science, 3,* 133–140.

Baillargeon, R., & DeVos, J. (1991). Object permanence in young infants: Further evidence. Child Development, 62, 1227–1246.

Barazzoni, R. (2000). *Brick by brick: The history of the XXV April municipal preschool in Villa Cella (RE).* Reggio Emilia, Italy: Municipality of Reggio Emilia.

Bayley, N. (1969). *Bayley scales of infant development* (1st ed.). New York, NY: Psychological Corporation.

Beebe, B., & Lachmann E. M. (1988). The contribution of mother–infant mutual influence to the origins of self- and object representations. *Psychoanalytic Psychology, 5,* 305–337.

Bell, S. M., & Ainsworth, M. S. (1972). Infant crying and maternal responsiveness. *Child Development, 43*(4), 1171–1190.

Bloom, L., Margulis, C., Tinker, E., & Fujita, N. (1996). Early conversations and word learning: Contributions from child and adult. *Child Development, 67,* 3154–3175.

Bove, C. (2001). Inserimento: A strategy for delicately beginning relationships and communications. In L. Gandini & C. Pope Edwards (Eds.), *Bambini: The Italian approach to infant/toddler care* (pp. 109–123). New York, NY: Teachers College Press.

Brazelton, T. B. (with Sparrow, J.). (2006). *Touchpoints, birth to 3: Your child's emotional and behavioral development.* Cambridge, MA: DeCapo Press.

Brazelton, T. B., & Sparrow, J. (2013). Foreword. In R. Lally, *For our babies: Ending the invisible neglect of America's infants* (p. xiv). New York, NY: Teachers College Press & San Francisco, CA: WestEd.

Bretherton, I. (1992). The origins of attachment theory: John Bowlby and Mary Ainsworth. *Developmental Psychology, 28,* 759–775.

Bruner, J. S. (1966). *Towards a theory of instruction.* Cambridge, MA: Belnap Press.

Bruner, J. S. (1975). The ontogenesis of speech acts. *Journal of Child Language, 2,* 1–19.

Bruner, J. (1990). *Acts of meaning.* Cambridge, MA: Harvard University Press.

Bruner, J. (2008). Culture and mind: Their fruitful incommensurability. *Ethos, 36,* 29–45.

Caldji, C., Diorio, J., Anisman, H., & Meaney, M. J. (2004, July 29). Maternal behavior regulates benzodiazepine/GABAA receptor subunit expression in brain regions associated with fear in BALB/c and C57BL/6 mice. *Neuropsychopharmacology, 7,* 1344–1352.

California Department of Education. (2006). *Infant/toddler learning and development program guidelines.* Sacramento, CA: Author.

California Department of Education. (2009). *California infant/toddler learning and development foundations.* Sacramento, CA: Author.

California Department of Education. (2010). *Infant–toddler caregiving: A guide to creating partnerships with families* (2nd ed.). Sacramento, CA: Author.

California Department of Education. (2012). *California infant/toddler curriculum framework.* Sacramento, CA: Author.

Cavallini, I., Filippini, T., Vecchi, V., & Trancossi, L. (2011). *The wonder of learning: The hundred languages of children.* Reggio Emilia, Italy: Reggio Children.

Centers for Disease Control and Prevention. (n.d.). Health effects of secondhand smoke [Fact sheet]. Retrieved from www.cdc.gov/tobacco/data_statistics/fact_sheets/secondhand_smoke/health_effects

Chess, S. (2011). Temperaments of infants and toddlers. In J. R. Lally (Ed.), *Infant–toddler caregiving: A guide to social-emotional growth and socialization* (2nd ed., pp. 3–12). Sacramento, CA: California Department of Education.

Clements, D. H. (2004). Major themes and recommendations. In D. H. Clements & J. Samara (Eds.), *Engaging young children in mathematics: Standards for early childhood educators* (pp. 7–77). Mahwah, NJ: Erlbaum.

Condon, W. S., & Sander, L. W. (1974). Synchrony demonstrated between movements of the neonate and adult speech. *Child Development, 45,* 456–462.

Committee for Economic Development. (2002). *Preschool for all: Investing in a productive and just society.* New York, NY: Author.

Committee on Integrating the Science of Early Childhood Development, Board on Children, Youth, and Families, & National Research Council (2000). *From neurons to neighborhoods: The science of early childhood development* (J. Shonkoff & D. Phillips, Eds.). Washington, DC: National Academy Press.

Copple, C., & Bredekamp, S. (Eds.). (2009). *Developmentally appropriate practice in early childhood programs.* Washington, DC: National Association for the Education of Young Children.

Cryer, D., Harms, T., & Riley, C. (2004). *All about the ITERS-R.* Lewisville, NC: Kaplan Early Learning.

Dahlberg, G., Moss, P., & Pence, A. (2013). *Beyond quality in early childhood education and care: Languages of evaluation.* New York, NY: Routledge.

David, M., & Appell, G. (2001). *Loczy: An unusual approach to mothering.* Budapest, Hungary: Pikler-Loczy Association for Young Children.

Davidson, A. (1979). Suggestions for language development. In M. Gerber (Ed.), *A manual for parents and professionals.* Los Angeles, CA: Resources for Infant Educarers.

De Bellis, M. D., Keshavan, M. S., Clark, D. B., Casey, B. J., Giedd, J. N., Boring, A. M., et al. (1999). Developmental traumatology, Part I: Brain development. *Biological Psychiatry, 45,* 1271–1284.

DeCasper, A. J., & Fifer, W. P. (1980). Of human bonding: Newborns prefer their mothers' voices. *Science, 208,* 1174–1176.

DeCasper, A. J., & Spence, M. J. (1986). Prenatal maternal speech influences newborns' perception of speech sounds. *Infant Behavior and Development, 9,* 133–150.

Derman-Sparks, L. (2013). Developing culturally responsive caregiving practices: Acknowledge, ask, and adapt. In E. Vermani & P. Mangione (Eds.), *A guide to culturally sensitive care* (2nd ed., pp. 68–94). Sacramento, CA: California Department of Education.

DiCorcia, J. D., & Tronick, E. (2011). Quotidian resilience: Exploring mechanisms that drive resilience from a perspective of everyday stress and coping. *Neuroscience and Biobehavioral Reviews, 35,* 1593–1602.

Edwards, C., Gandini, L., & Forman, G. (Eds.). (2012). *The hundred languages of children: The Reggio Emilia experience in transformation* (3rd ed.). Santa Barbara, CA: Praeger.

Eimas, P. D., Siqueland, E. R., Jusczk, P., & Vigorito, J. (1971, January 22). Speech perception in infants. *Science, 171,* 303–306.

Eliot, L. (1999). *What's going on in there? How the brain and mind develop in the first five years of life.* New York, NY: Bantam Books.

Farroni, T., Johnson, M. H., Menon, E., Zulian, L., Faraguna, D., & Csibra, G. (2005). Newborns' preference for face-relevant stimuli: Effects of contrast polarity. *Proceedings of the National Academy of Sciences, 102,* 17245–17250.

Farroni, T., Massaccesi, S., Pividori, D., & Johnson, M. H. (2004). Gaze following in newborns. *Infancy, 5,* 39–60.

Feldman, R., Magori-Cohen, R., Galili, G., Singer, M., & Louzoun, Y. (2011). Mother and infant coordinate heart rhythms through episodes of interaction synchrony. *Infant Behavior and Development, 34,* 569–577.

Fernald, A. (1985). Four-month-old infants prefer to listen to motherese. *Infant Behavior and Development, 8,* 181–195.

Fernald, A., Marchman, V. A., & Weisleder, A. (2013). SES differences in language processing skill and vocabulary are evident at 18 months. *Developmental Science, 16,* 234–248.

Field, T., Grizzle, N., Scafidi, F., Abrams, S., Richardson, S., Kuhn, C., et al. (1996). Massage therapy for infants of depressed mothers. *Infant Behavior and Development, 19,* 107–112.

Field, T. M., Woodson, R., Greenberg, R., & Cohen, C. (1982). Discrimination and imitation of facial expressions in newborns. *Science, 218,* 179–181.

Filippini, T., & Vecchi, V. (2005). *Hundred languages of children: Catalog of the exhibit.* Reggio Emilia, Italy: Reggio Children.

Fonagy, P., Gergely, G., Jurist, E., & Target, M. (2004). *Affect regulation, mentalization, and the development of self.* New York, NY: Other Press.

French, G. M., Nicholson, L., Skybo, T., Klein, E. G., Schwirian, P. M., Murray-Johnson, L., et al. (2012). An evaluation of mother-centered anticipatory guidance to reduce obesogenic infant feeding behaviors. *Pediatrics, 130*(3), e507–e517.

Gallese, V., Fadiga, L., Fogassi, L., & Rizzolatti, G. (1996). Action recognition in the prenatal cortex. *Brain, 119,* 593–609.

Gallistel, C. R., & Gelman, R. (1992). Preverbal and verbal counting and computation. *Cognition, 44,* 43–74.

Gandini, L. (2001). Reggio Emilia: Experiencing life in an infant–toddler center: Interview with Cristina Bondavalli. In L. Gandini & C. Pope Edwards (Eds.), *Bambini: The Italian approach to infant-toddler care* (pp. 55–66). New York, NY: Teachers College Press.

Gandini, L. (2012). Connecting through caring and learning spaces. In C. Edwards, L. Gandini, & G. Forman (Eds.), *The hundred languages of children: The Reggio Emilia experience in transformation* (3rd ed., pp. 317–341). Santa Barbara, CA: Praeger.

Garcia, E. E. (2005). *Teaching and learning in two languages: Bilingualism and schooling in the United States.* New York, NY: Teachers College Press.

Garcia-Sierra, A., Rivera-Gaxiola, M., Percaccio, C., Conboy, B. T., Romo, H., Klarman, L., et al. (2011). Bilingual language learning: An ERP study relating early brain responses to speech, language input, and later word production. *Journal of Phonetics, 39,* 546–557.

Gerber, M. (Ed). (1979). *The RIE manual: For parents and*

professionals. Los Angeles, CA: Resources for Infant Educarers.

Gerber, M. (2002). *Dear parent: Caring for infants with respect* (J. Weaver, Ed., 2nd ed.). Los Angeles, CA: Resources for Infant Educarers.

Gerber, M. (with Johnson, A.). (1998). *Your self-confident baby: How to encourage your child's natural abilities—from the very start.* New York, NY: Wiley.

Ghirardi, M. (Ed.). (2002). *Along the levee road.* Reggio Emilia, Italy: Reggio Children.

Giudici, C. (2012). Education as a strategic competence of the city. In Innovations in early education: The international Reggio Emilia exchange (Vol. 19, pp. 1–9). Roswell, GA: North American Reggio Emilia Alliance.

Giudici, C., Rinaldi, C., & Krechevsky, M. (Eds.). (2001). *Making learning visible: Children as individual and group learners.* Reggio Emilia, Italy: Reggio Children, President and Fellows of Harvard College, & Municipality of Reggio Emilia.

Golinkoff, R. M., & Hirsh-Pasek, K. (2000). *How babies talk: The magic and mystery of language in the first three years of life.* New York, NY: Penguin Group.

Gonzalez-Mena, J. (2007). *Diversity in early care and education: Honoring differences* (5th ed.). Columbus, OH: McGraw-Hill.

Gonzalez-Mena, J. (2013). Cultural sensitivity in caregiving routines: The essential activities of daily living. In A. Vermani & P. Mangione (Eds.), *A guide to culturally sensitive care* (2nd ed., pp. 56–66). Sacramento, CA: California Department of Education.

Gonzalez-Mena, J., & Eyer, D. W. (2012). *Infants, toddlers, and caregivers.* Columbus, OH: McGraw-Hill.

Goodsitt, J. V., Morgan, J. L., & Kuhl, P. K. (1993). Perceptual strategies in prelingual speech segmentation. *Journal of Child Language, 20,* 229–252.

Gopnik, A. (2009). *The philosophical baby: What children's minds tell us about truth, love, and the meaning of life.* New York, NY: Farrar, Straus & Giroux.

Gopnik, A., Meltzoff, A. N., & Kuhl, P. K. (1999). *The scientist in the crib: What early learning tells us about the mind.* New York, NY: HarperCollins.

Gould, P., & Sullivan, J. (1999). *The inclusive early childhood classroom.* Beltsville, MD: Gryphon House.

Greenspan, S. (with Lewis, N. B.). (1999). *Building healthy minds: The six experiences that create intelligence and emotional growth in babies and young children.* New York, NY: Da Capo.

Greenspan, S., & Wieder, S. (2006). *Engaging autism: Using the Floortime approach to help children relate, communicate, and think.* Cambridge, MA: Da Capo.

Gunnar, M. (1998). Quality of care and the buffering of stress physiology. *Newsletter of the Infant Mental Health Promotion Project, 21,* 1–4.

Gunnar, M., Brodersen, L., Nachmias, M., Buss, K., & Rigatuso, J. (1996). Stress reactivity and attachment security. *Developmental Psychobiology, 29*(3), 191–204.

Hamlin, J. K., & Wynn, K. (2012). Young infants prefer prosocial to antisocial others. *Cognitive Development, 26*(1), 30–39.

Hamlin, J. K., Wynn, K., & Bloom, P. (2010). Three-month-olds show a negativity bias in their social evaluations. *Developmental Science, 13,* 923–929.

Hamlin, J. K., Wynn, K., Bloom, P., & Mahajan, N. (2011). How infants and toddlers react to antisocial others. *Proceedings of the National Academy of Sciences, USA, 108,* 19931–19936.

Harden, B. J. (2012). Home-based early Head Start: Kitchen therapy. Retrieved from eclkc.ohs.acf.hhs.gov/hslc/tta-system/health/health-services-management/program-planning/health_art_00518_081205.html

Harrison, A. M. (2005). Herding the animals into the barn: A parent consultation model. *The Psychoanalytic Study of the Child, 60,* 128–153.

Hart, B., & Risley, T. R. (1995). *Meaningful differences in the everyday experiences of young American children.* Baltimore, MD: Brookes.

Hebb, D. O. (1949). *The organization of behavior: A neuropsychological theory.* New York, NY: Wiley.

Heckman, J. J., & Masterov, D. V. (2007, January). *The productivity argument for investing in young children.* Paper presented at the annual meeting of the Allied Social Sciences Association, Chicago, IL. Retrieved from jenni.uchicago.edu/human-inequality/papers/Heckman_final_all_wp_2007-03-22c_jsb.pdf

Helburn, S. W., Culkin, M. L., Morris, J. R., & Clifford, R. M. (Eds.). (1995). *Cost, quality and child outcomes in child care centers* (Tech. Rep.). Denver: University of Colorado Center for Research in Economic and Social Policy.

Hirsh-Pasek, K., & Golinkoff, R. M. (1991). Language comprehension: A new look at some old themes. In N. A. Krasnegor, D. M. Rumbaugh, R. L. Schiefelbusch, & M. Studdert-Kennedy (Eds.), *Biological and behavioral determinants of language development* (pp. 301–320). Hillsdale, NJ: Erlbaum.

Hirsh-Pasek, K., Golinkoff, R. M., Berk, L. E., & Singer, D. G. (2009). *A mandate for playful learning in preschool: Presenting the evidence.* New York, NY: Oxford University Press.

Huttenlocher, P. R. (1994). Synaptogenesis, synapse elimination, and neural plasticity in human cerebral cortex. In C. A. Nelson (Ed.), *Minnesota symposia on child psychology: Vol. 27. Threats to optimal development: Integrating biological, psychological, and social risk factors* (pp. 35–54). Hillsdale, NJ: Erlbaum.

Inhelder, B., & Piaget, J. (1964). *The early growth of logic in the child.* New York, NY: Harper & Row.

Ivanov, P. C., Ma, Q. D. Y., & Bartsch, R. P. (2009). Maternal–fetal heartbeat phase synchronization. *Proceedings of the National Academy of Sciences, USA, 106,* 13641–13642.

Johnson, S. C., Dweck, C. S., & Chen, F. S. (2007). Evidence for infants' internal working models of attachment. *Psychological Sciences, 18*(6), 501–502.

Jones, E., & Reynolds, G. (2011). *The play's the thing: Teachers' roles in children's play.* New York, NY: Teachers College Press.

Jusczyk, P. (2000). *The discovery of spoken language.* Cambridge, MA: MIT Press.

Kagen, J., & Snidman, N. (2004). *The long shadow of temperament.* Cambridge, MA: Harvard University Press.

Kálló, E., & Balog, G. (2005). *The origins of free play.* Budapest, Hungary: Pikler-Loczy Association for Young Children.

Kamii, C. (1990). *Achievement testing in the early grades: The games grown-ups play.* Washington, DC: National Association for the Education of Young Children.

Kamii, C., & DeVries, R. (1993). *Physical knowledge in preschool education: Implications of Piaget's theory.* New York, NY: Teachers College Press.

Kamii, C., Miyakawa, Y., & Kato, Y. (2004). The development of logico-mathematical knowledge in block-building activity at ages 1–4. *Journal of Research in Childhood Education, 19,* 44–57.

Kantrowitz, B., & Wingert, P. (1991, December 2). The ten best schools in the world and what we can learn from them. *Newsweek,* 50–59.

Katz, L. G., & McClellan, D. E. (1997). *Fostering children's social competence: The teacher's role.* Washington, DC: National Association for the Education of Young Children.

Kuhl, P. (2000). A new view of language acquisition. *Proceedings of the National Academy of Sciences, USA, 97,* 11850–11857.

Kuhl, P., & Rivera-Gaxiola, M. (2008). Neural substrates of language acquisition. *Annual Review of Neuroscience, 31,* 511–534.

Kuhl, P., Tsao, F.-M., & Liu, H.-M. (2003). Foreign-language experience in infancy: Effects of short-term exposure and social interaction in phonetic learning. *Proceedings of the National Academy of Sciences, USA, 100,* 9096–9101.

Lally, J. R. (2000). Infants have their own curriculum: A responsive approach to curriculum planning for infants and toddlers. *National Head Start Bulletin, 67,* 6–7.

Lally, J. R. (2001). Infant care in the United States and how the Italian experience can help. In L. Gandini & C. Pope Edwards (Eds.), *Bambini: The Italian approach to infant/toddler care* (pp. 15–22). New York, NY: Teachers College Press.

Lally, J. R. (2009, November). The science and psychology of infant–toddler care: How an understanding of early learning has transformed child care. *Zero to Three,* 47–53.

Lally, J. R. (2011a). Creating nurturing relationships with infants and toddlers. In J. R. Lally (Ed.), *Infant–toddler caregiving: A guide to social-emotional growth and socialization* (2nd ed., pp. 33–39). Sacramento, CA: California Department of Education.

Lally, J. R. (2011b). A developmental approach to the socialization, guidance, and discipline of infants and toddlers. In J. R. Lally (Ed.), *Infant–toddler caregiving: A guide to social-emotional growth and socialization* (2nd ed., pp. 51–70). Sacramento, CA: California Department of Education.

Lally, J. R. (2013). *For our babies: Ending the invisible neglect of America's infants.* New York, NY: Teachers College Press & San Francisco, CA: WestEd.

Lally, J. R. (Producer/Director), & Mangione, P. L. (Writer/Director). (2006). *New perspectives on infant/toddler learning, development, and care* [DVD, Disc 2, Chapter 4]. United States: California Department of Education.

Lally, J. R., Stewart, J., & Greenwald, D. (Eds.). (2009). *Infant–toddler caregiving: A guide to setting up environments* (2nd ed.). Sacramento, CA: California Department of Education.

Lambert, S. R., & Drack, A. V. (1996). Infantile cataracts. *Survey of Ophthalmology, 40*(6), 427–458.

Legerstee, M. (1997). Contingency effects of people and objects on subsequent cognitive functioning in three-month-old infants. *Social Development, 6,* 307–321.

Lerner, C. (2006). Reflective practice. In J. R. Lally, P. L. Mangione, & D. Greenwald (Eds.), *Concepts for care: 20 essays on infant/toddler development and learning* (pp. 91–94). San Francisco, CA: WestEd.

Levine, R. A., Dixon, S., Levine, S., Richman, A., Leiderman, P. H., Keefer, C. H., et al. (1994). *Child care and culture: Lessons from Africa.* New York, NY: Cambridge University Press.

Lewis, M., & Brooks-Gunn, J. (1979). *Social cognition and the acquisition of self.* New York, NY: Plenum Press.

Lieberman, A. (2006). Working with traumatized young children in child care and education settings. In J. R. Lally, P. L. Mangione, & D. Greenwald (Eds.), *Concepts for care: 20 essays on infant/toddler development and learning* (pp. 77–83). San Francisco, CA: WestEd.

Liu, D., Diorio, J., Tannenbaum, B., Caldji, C., Francis, D., Freedman, A., et al. (1997). Maternal care, hippocampal glucocorticoid receptors, and hypothalamic-pituitary-adrenal response to stress. *Science, 277,* 1659–1662.

Lombardi, J. (2003). *Time to care: Redesigning child care to promote education, support families, and build communities.* Philadelphia, PA: Temple University Press.

Louv, R. (2008). *Last child in the woods: Saving our children from nature-deficit disorder.* Chapel Hill, NC: Algonquin Books.

Maguire-Fong, M. J. (2006). Respectful teaching with infants and toddlers. In J. R. Lally, P. L. Mangione, & D. Greenwald (Eds.), *Concepts for care: 20 essays on infant/toddler development and learning* (pp. 117–122). San Francisco, CA: WestEd.

Mahler, M., Pine, F., & Bergman, A. (1975). *The psychological birth of the human infant.* New York, NY: Basic Books.

Malaguzzi, L. (1996). A story of fish with the children of silent movies. In S. Cipolla & E. Reverberi (Eds.), *The little ones of silent movies: Make-believe with children and fish at the infant–toddler center* (pp. 17–20). Reggio Emilia, Italy: Reggio Children.

Malaguzzi, L. (2012). History, ideas, and basic philosophy: An interview with Lella Gandini. In C. Pope Edwards, L. Gandini, & G. Forman (Eds.), *The hundred languages of children: The Reggio Emilia experience in transformation* (3rd ed., pp. 27–71). Santa Barbara, CA: Praeger.

Malloch, S. & Trevarthen, C. (2009). *Communicative musicality: Exploring the basis of human companionship.* Oxford, UK: Oxford University Press.

Mangione, P. (2011). Building a foundation for literacy in the first three years. In P. Mangione & D. Greenwald (Eds.), *A guide to language development and communication* (2nd ed., pp, 63–72). Sacramento, CA: California Department of Education.

Mangione, P. L., Lally, J. R., & Signer, S. (1993). *Essential connections: Ten keys to culturally sensitive child care, child care video magazine.* Sacramento, CA: California Department of Education.

McGowan, P., Sasaki, A., D'Alessio, A., Dymov, S., Labonte, B., Szyf, M., et al. (2009). Epigenetic regulation of the glucocorticoid receptor in human brain associates with childhood abuse. *Nature Neuroscience, 12,* 342–348.

Mead, M. N. (2008). Benefits of sunlight: A bright spot for human health. *Environmental Health Perspective, 116,* A160–A167.

Meltzoff, A. N. (2007). "Like me": A foundation for social cognition. *Developmental Science, 10,* 126–134.

Meltzoff, A. N., & Moore, M. K. (1977). Imitation of facial and manual gestures by human neonates. *Science, 198,* 75–78.

Meltzoff, A. N., & Moore, M. K. (1983). Newborn infants imitate adult facial gestures. *Child Development, 54,* 702–709.

Mendizza, M. (1994). Touch the future: Ashley Montagu, on being human. Retrieved from ttfuture.org/authors/ashleym

Moon, C., Lagercrantz, H., & Kuhl, P. (2013). Language experienced *in utero* affects vowel perception after birth. *Acta Paediatrica, 102,* 156–160.

Mullally, S. L., & Maguire, E. A. (2014). Learning to remember: The early ontogeny of episodic memory. *Developmental Cognitive Neuroscience, 9,* 12–29.

National Research Council. (2001). *Eager to learn: Educating our preschoolers. Committee on early childhood pedagogy.* (Barbara T. Bowman, M.Suzanne Donovan, and M.Susan Burns, eds.). Commission on Behavioral and Social Sciences and Education. Washington, DC: National Academy Press.

National Research Council & Institute of Medicine, Committee on Integrating the Science of Early Childhood Development, Board on Children, Youth, and Families (2000). *From neurons to neighborhoods: The science of early childhood development* (J. Shonkoff & D. Phillips, Eds.). Washington, DC: National Academy Press.

National Scientific Council on the Developing Child. (2007). The timing and quality of early experiences combine to shape brain architecture (Working paper #5). Retrieved from developingchild.harvard.edu/resources/reports_and_working_papers/working_papers/wp5/

Nazzi, T., Floccia, C., & Bertoncini, J. (1998). Discrimination of pitch contours by neonates. *Infant Behavior and Development, 21*(4), 779–784.

Nicholson, S. (1971). The theory of loose parts: How not to cheat children. *Landscape Architecture Quarterly, 62,* 30–34.

Nugent, J. K., Keefer, C. H., Minear, S., Johnson, L. C., & Blanchard, Y. (2007). *Understanding newborn behavior and early relationships: The newborn behavioral observations systems handbook.* Baltimore, MD: Brookes.

Olsen, T. (1961). *Tell me a riddle.* New York, NY: Delta/Seymour Lawrence.

Paley, V. G. (2011, November 2). *Who will save the kindergarten?* Paper presented at the annual conference of the National Association for the Education of Young Children, Orlando, FL. Retrieved from www.naeyc.org/content/who-will-save-kindergarten

Pascalis, O., de Schonen, S., Morton, J., Deruelle, C., & Fabre-Grenet, M. (1995). Mother's face recognition by neonates: A replication and an extension. *Infant Behavior and Development, 19,* 79–85.

Pawl, J. (1990). Infants in day care: Reflections on experiences, expectations and relationships. *Zero to Three, 10,* 1–28.

Pawl, J. (2003, November). Providing responsive care to infants. Paper presented at the WestEd Program for Infant/Toddler Care Special Seminars for California Community Colleges, Berkeley, CA.

Pawl, J. (2006). Being held in another's mind. In J. R. Lally, P. L. Mangione, & D. Greenwald (Eds.), *Concepts for care: 20 essays on infant/toddler development and learning* (pp. 71–75). San Francisco, CA: WestEd.

Pawl, J. (2011). Self-esteem, security, and social competence: Ten caregiving gifts. In J. R. Lally (Ed.), *Infant–toddler caregiving: A guide to social-emotional growth and socialization* (2nd ed., pp. 47–54). Sacramento, CA: California Department of Education.

Pawl, J., & St. John, M. (1998). *How you are is as important as what you do.* Washington, DC: Zero to Three.

Perry, B. D. (2002). The amazing human brain and human development. Retrieved from www.childtraumaacademy.com/index.html

Perry, B. D. (2004). *Maltreated children: Experience, brain development, and the next generation.* New York, NY: Norton.

Perry, B. D. (2006). Applying principles of neurodevelopment to clinical work with maltreated and traumatized children: The neurosequential model of therapeutics. In N. B. Webb (Ed.), *Working with traumatized youth in child welfare* (pp. 27–52). New York, NY: Guilford Press.

Perry, B. D. (2007). Stress, trauma, and post-traumatic stress disorders in children. Retrieved from childtrauma.org/cta-library/trauma-ptsd/

Perry, B. D. (2008). Child maltreatment: A neurodevelopmental perspective on the role of trauma and neglect in psychopathology. In T. Beauchaine & S. P. Hinshaw (Eds.), *Child and adolescent psychopathology* (pp. 93–129). Hoboken, NJ: Wiley.

Perry, B. D. (2009). Examining child maltreatment through a neurodevelopmental lens: Clinical applications of the neurosequential model of therapeutics. *Journal of Loss and Trauma, 14,* 240–255.

Perry, B. D. (2014a). Attachment: The first core strength. Retrieved from teacher.scholastic.com/professional/bruceperry/attachment.htm

Perry, B. D. (2014b). *Biological relativity: Time and the developing child.* Retrieved from teacher.scholastic.com/professional/bruceperry/biological_relativity.htm#author

Perry, B. D., & Marcellus, J. (2013). *The impact of abuse and neglect on the developing brain.* Retrieved from teacher.scholastic.com/professional/bruceperry/abuse_neglect.htm

Pikler, E. (1988). Give me time: The independent motor development of the infant up to free walking. *Pikler Institute training material* (pp. 31–43). Budapest, Hungary: Emmi Pikler International Public Foundation.

Pikler, E. (1994). Emmi Pikler, 1902–1984, Excerpts from "Peaceful babies—contented mothers." *Sensory Awareness Foundation Bulletin, 14,* 5–24.

Pikler, E. (2006). *Unfolding of infants' natural gross motor development.* Los Angeles, CA: Resources for Infant Educarers.

Porges, S. W. (2001). The polygaval theory: Phylogenetic substrates of a social nervous system. *International Journal of Psychophysiology, 42,* 123–146.

Porter, R. H., & Winberg, J. (1999). Unique salience of maternal breast odors for newborn infants. *Neuroscience Biobehavioral Review, 23,* 439–449.

Poulin-Dubois, D., Blaye, A., Coutya, J., & Bialystok, E. (2011). The effects of bilingualism on toddlers' executive functioning. *Journal of Experimental Child Psychology, 108,* 567–579.

Powell, B., Cooper, G., Hoffman, K., & Marvin, R. (2009). The circle of security. In C. Zeanah (Ed.), *Handbook of infant mental health* (3rd ed., pp. 450–467). New York, NY: Guilford Press.

Provence, S., Pawl, J., & Fenichel, J. (1992). *The zero to 3 child care anthology, 1984–1992.* Arlington, VA: Zero to Three.

Radke-Yarrow, M., & Zahn-Waxler, C. (1984). Roots, motives, and patterns in children's prosocial behavior. In E. Staub, D. Bar-Tal, J. Karylowski, & J. Reykowski (Eds.), *Development and maintenance of prosocial behavior* (pp. 81–99). New York, NY: Plenum Press.

Renfrew, M. J., Pokhrel, S., Quigley, M., McCormick, F., Fox-Rushby, J., Dodds, R., Duffy, S., Trueman, P., Williams, A. (2012). *Preventing disease and saving resources: The potential contribution of increasing breastfeeding rates in the UK.* unicef.org.uk/breastfeeding

Repacholi, B. M., & Gopnik, A. (1997). Early reasoning about desires: Evidence from 14- and 18-month-olds. *Developmental Psychology, 33,* 12–21.

Resendiz, M., Chen, Y., Ozturk, N. C., & Zhou, F. C. (2013). Epigenetic medicine and fetal alcohol spectrum disorders. *Epigenomics, 5*(1), 73–86.

Rigato, S., Menon, E., Johnson, M. H., Faraguna, D., & Farroni, T. (2011). Direct gaze may modulate face recognition in newborns. *Infant and Child Development, 20,* 20–34.

Rinaldi, C. (1994). Staff development in Reggio Emilia. In L. Katz & B. Cesarone (Eds.), Reflections on the Reggio Emilia approach (Perspectives from ERIC/EECE: A Monograph Series, No. 6, pp. 55–59). Urbana, IL: ERIC Clearinghouse on Elementary and Early Childhood Education.

Rinaldi, C. (2001). Documentation and assessment: What is the relationship? In C. Giudici, C. Rinaldi, & M. Krechevsky (Eds.), *Making learning visible: Children as individual and group learners* (pp. 78–89). Reggio Emilia, Italy: Reggio Children, President and Fellows of Harvard College, & Municipality of Reggio Emilia.

Rinaldi, C. (2006a). Creativity, shared meaning, and relationships. In J. R. Lally, P. L. Mangione, & D. Greenwald (Eds.), *Concepts for care: 20 essays on infant/toddler development and learning* (pp. 21–23). San Francisco, CA: WestEd.

Rinaldi, C. (2006b). *In dialogue with Reggio Emilia: Listening, researching, and learning.* New York, NY: Routledge.

Rochat, P. (2009). *Others in mind: Social origins of self-consciousness.* New York, NY: Cambridge University Press.

Rogoff, B. (1990). *Apprenticeship in thinking: Cognitive development in social context.* New York, NY: Oxford University Press.

Rogoff, B. (2003). *The cultural nature of human development.* New York, NY: Oxford University Press.

Rogoff, B. (with Gonzalez, C. P., Quiacain, C. C., & Quiacain, J. C.). (2011). *Developing destinies: A Mayan midwife and town.* New York, NY: Oxford University Press.

Rubizzi, L. (2001). Documenting the documenter. In C. Giudici, C. Rinaldi, & M. Krechevsky (Eds.), *Making learning visible: Children as individual and group learners* (pp. 94–115). Reggio Emilia, Italy: Reggio Children, President and Fellows of Harvard College, & Municipality of Reggio Emilia.

Santos, D. C., Gabbard, C., Goncalves, V. M. (2001). Motor development during the first year: A comparative study. *Journal of Genetic Psychology, 162,* 143–153.

Satter, E. (2000). *Child of mine: Feeding your child with love and good sense.* Boulder, CO: Bull Publishing.

Schore, A. N. (1994). *Affect regulation and the origin of the self: The Neurobiology of emotional development.* Hillsdale, NJ: Erlbaum.

Schore, A. N. (2002). Neurobiology of attachment and early personality organization. *Journal of Prenatal and Perinatal Psychology and Health, 16*(3), 249–263.

Siegel, D. (2012). *The developing mind: How relationships and the brain interact to shape who we are* (2nd ed.). New York, NY: Guilford Press.

Siegel, D., & Hartzell, M. (2003). *Parenting from the inside out: How a deeper self-understanding can help you raise children who thrive.* New York, NY: Penguin Group.

Singer, D. G., Golinkoff, R. M., & Hirsh-Pasek, K. (Eds.). (2006). *Play equals learning: How play motivates and enhances children's cognitive and social-emotional growth.* New York, NY: Oxford University Press.

Singer, D., & Revenson, T. (1978). *A Piaget primer: How a child thinks.* New York, NY: New American Library.

Slater, A., Riddell, P., Quinn, P. C., Pascalis, O., Lee, K., & Kelly, D. J. (2010). Visual perception. In J. G. Bremmer & T. D. Wachs (Eds.), *The Wiley–Blackwell handbook of infant development: Vol. 1, Basic research* (2nd ed., pp. 40–80). Oxford, UK: Wiley-Blackwell.

Smitsman, A. W., & Corbetta, D. (2010). Action in infancy—Perspectives, concepts, and challenges. In J. G. Bremmer & T. D. Wachs, (Eds.) *The Wiley–Blackwell handbook of infant development: Vol. 1, Basic research* (2nd ed., pp. 167–203). Oxford, UK: Wiley-Blackwell.

Sorce, J. F., Emde, R. N., Campos, J., & Klinnert, M. D. (1985). Maternal emotional signaling: Its effect on the visual cliff behavior of 1-year-olds. *Developmental Psychology, 21,* 195–200.

Spitz, R. A. (1949). The role of ecological factors in emotional development in infancy. *Child Development, 20*(3), 145–155.

Starkey, P., & Cooper, R. G. (1980). Perception of numbers by human infants. *Science, 210,* 1033–1035.

Starkey, P., Spelke, E. S., & Gelman, R. (1990). Numerical abstraction by human infants. *Cognition, 36,* 97–127.

Stern, D. (2000). *The interpersonal world of the infant: A view from psychoanalysis and developmental psychology.* New York, NY: Basic Books.

Stern, D. (2002). *The first relationship: Infant and mother.* Cambridge, MA: Harvard University Press.

Sumner, G., & Spietz, A. (1994). Caregiver/parent–child interaction feeding manual. Seattle: University of Washington, School of Nursing, NCAST-AVENUW.

Thelen, E., & Smith, L. B. (2006). Dynamic systems theories. In W. Damon (Series Ed.) & R. M. Lerner (Vol. Ed.), Handbook of child psychology: Vol. 1. Theoretical models of human development (6th ed., pp. 258–312). New York, NY: Wiley.

Thompson, R. A., Laible, D. J., & Ontai, L. L. (2003). Early understandings of emotion, morality, and self: Developing a working model. In R. Kail (Ed.), *Advances in child development and behavior* (Vol. 31, pp. 137–171). San Diego CA: Academic Press.

Thompson, R. A., & Newton, E. K. (2013). Baby altruists? Examining the complexity of prosocial motivation in young children. *Infancy, 18,* 120–133.

Tomasello, M. (2009). *Why we cooperate.* Cambridge, MA: MIT Press.

Torelli, L. (2006). Environments for infants and toddlers. In J. R. Lally, P. L. Mangione, & D. Greenwald (Eds.), *Concepts for care: 20 essays on infant/toddler development and learning* (pp. 85–88). San Francisco, CA: WestEd.

Trevarthen, C. (2005). First things first: Infants make good use of the sympathetic rhythm of imitation, without reason or language. *Journal of Child Psychotherapy, 31*(1), 91–113.

Trevarthen, C. (2011). What is it like to be a person who knows nothing? Defining the active intersubjective mind of the newborn human being. *Infant and Child Development, 20,* 119–135.

Tronick, E. (1989). Emotions and emotional communication in infants. *American Psychologist, 44*(2), 112–119.

Tronick, E. (2007). *The neurobehavioral and social-emotional development of infants and children.* New York, NY: Norton.

Tronick, E., & Beeghly, M. (2011). Infants' meaning-making and the development of mental health problems. *American Psychologist, 66,* 107–119.

U.S. Department of Labor. (2014). *Current population survey, Families with own children: Employment status of parents by age of youngest child and family type, 2012–2013 annual averages.* Available http://www.bls.gov/news.release/pdf/famee.pdf

VandenBerg, K., Browne, J., Perez, L., & Newstetter, A. (2009). *Getting to know your baby: Special start training program.* San Francisco: University of California, San Francisco, Department of Pediatrics, Division of Neonatology.

Vouloumanos, A., & Werker, J. F. (2007). Listening to language at birth: Evidence for a bias for speech in neonates. *Developmental Science, 10,* 159–164.

Vygotsky, L. S. (1986). *Thought and language.* Cambridge, MA: MIT Press.

Warneken, F., & Tomasello, M. (2007). Helping and cooperation at 14 months of age. *Infancy, 11*(3), 271–294.

Whitebrook, M., & Sakai, L. (2004). *By a thread: How child care centers hold on to teachers, how teachers build lasting careers.* Kalamazoo, MI: Upjohn Institute for Employment Research.

Whitehurst, G. J., & Lonigan, C. J. (1998). Child development and emergent literacy. *Child Development, 68,* 648–672.

Whitehurst, G. J., & Lonigan, C. J. (2002). Literacy development from prereaders to emergent readers. In S. Neuman & D. K. Dickinson (Eds.), Handbook of early literacy research (Vol. 1, pp. 11–29). New York, NY: Guilford Press.

Whitman, W. (2005). There was a child went forth. In D. S. Reynolds (Ed.), *Walt Whitman's leaves of grass* (p. 78). New York, NY: Oxford University Press. (Original work published 1855)

Wicker, B., Keysers, C., Plailly, J., Royet, J., Gallese, V., & Rizzolatti, G. (2003). Both of us disgusted in *my* insula: The common neural basis of seeing and feeling disgust. *Neuron, 40,* 655–664.

Widström, A. M., Ransjo-Arvidson, A. B., Christensson, K., Matthiesen, A. S., Winberg, J., & Uvnas-Moberg, K. (1987). Gastric suction in healthy newborn infants: Effects on circulation and developing feeding behavior. *Acta Paediatrica Scandinavica, 76,* 566–572.

Williamson, G. G., & Anzalone, M. E. (2001). *Sensory integration and self-regulation in infants and toddlers.* Washington, DC: Zero to Three.

Wynn, K. (1992). Addition and subtraction by human infants. *Nature, 358,* 749–750.

Xu, F., & Garcia, V. (2008). Intuitive statistics by 8-month-old infants. *Proceedings of the National Academy of Sciences, USA, 105,* 5012–5015.

Zigler, E. F., Finn-Stevenson, M., & Hill, N. W. (2003). *The first three years and beyond: Brain development and social policy.* New Haven, CT: Yale University Press.

Zigler, E. F., Singer, D. G., & Bishop-Josef, S. J. (2004). *Children's play: The roots of reading.* Washington, DC: Zero to Three.

Zimmerman, F. J., Christakis, D. A., & Meltzoff, A. N. (2007a). Association between media viewing and language development in children under age 2 years. *Journal of Pediatrics, 151,* 364–368.

Zimmerman, F. J., Christakis, D. A., & Meltzoff, A. N. (2007b). Television and DVD/video viewing in children younger than 2 years. *Archives of Pediatric & Adolescent Medicine, 161,* 473–479.

Index

About the Author

Mary Jane Maguire-Fong is professor of early childhood education at American River College in Sacramento, CA. She has been a preschool teacher, an infant center director, and administrator of early childhood programs serving families in the migrant farm worker community. Her work is inspired by the philosophy of teaching used in the birth to 5 programs in the city of Reggio Emilia, Italy. She serves as faculty for the Program for Infant/Toddler Care and holds an Infant–Parent Mental Health Certificate from the University of Massachusetts. She is a contributing author for the California Department of Education Infant/Toddler Curriculum Framework and the three volumes of the Preschool Curriculum Framework and authored a chapter in the WestEd publication *Concepts for Care: 20 Essays on Infant/Toddler Development and Learning*. Her college teaching includes courses specific to early childhood curriculum, infant-toddler and preschool learning cnvironments, practicum in early childhood settings, culture and diversity in early childhood education, children and families within the community, and administration and supervision of programs for young children. As department chair for early childhood education at American River College, she oversaw the development of a large early childhood teacher preparation program, including a practicum within a state-of-the-art college laboratory school for children birth through the school-age years. She sits on numerous policy committees and boards as an advocate for children and families. She has been a featured presenter for the Early Head Start National Resource Center and a webinar presenter for WestEd's *Schools Moving Up*. She has two children who have contributed generously to her understanding of how young children develop and learn.